Fractured Utopias
A Personal Odyssey with History

By Roger Burbach

FREEDOM VOICES

SAN FRANCISCO
2017

FREEDOM VOICES
P.O. Box 423115
San Francisco, CA 95142
www.freedomvoices.org
books@freedomvoices.org

Cover: Art Hazelwood and Jess Clarke © 2017 Freedom Voices.
Editing: Jess Clarke and Merula Furtado.
Some names and identifying details have been changed.

ISBN: 978-0-915117-29-1
Printed in the United States of America

TABLE OF CONTENTS

ORIGINS OF THE QUEST FOR UTOPIA

0. Prologue: Revolution, Love and the Longing for Utopia 7

1. Paradise Lost 11

2. Farm Boy, Prodigy of Nuns, Draft Dodgers, Bootleggers 24

3. Cuba's Revolution, Quandaries at Watertown High.....................37

4. Portrait of an Awkward Young Man as a Malcontent...................43

5. Mexico, the First Odyssey..50

6. Life in Cleveland's Ivory Tower...58

7. Paradoxes of a Peace Corps Volunteer..................................64

8. Gringo in the Andes...75

9. Nostalgia, Lovers and Idaho Potatoes....................................85

10. Joining the War At Home, 1968-69.......................................92

11. Cuba: Encountering a Spartan Utopia..................................100

12. Weathermen on a Sugar Boat, Nixon's War at Home 115

13. An Epiphany Begets a Utopian Vagabond..............................119

14. Levitating the Pentagon and Jail Time.................................123

UTOPIA FETTERED

15. The Long Trek Home from Paradise Lost................................128

16. Tribulations at Home and in Latin America 132

17. Rejoining a Dysfunctional Family...136

18. Agribusiness, Left Politics, New Lover..................................140

19. Imperial Decline and a Dysfunctional Left.............................147

20. Dole's Banana Republic Politics..154

21. Transitions: Amorous and Organizational 158

UTOPIA UNLEASHED

22 The Sandinista Insurgency, 1978.................................163

23 Transitions and the New Revolutionary Agenda 168

24 Life in the Big Apple..173

25 A Militant in the Sandinista Revolution 181

26 An Unsung Marriage in Toronto 188

27 Reagan Ascendancy, Clouds of War in Central America..........191

28. Killing Fields and Birth 196

29. Political Assassination in Managua...........................201

30. Contra War and the Nouveau International 207

31. Pope in Nicaragua–Specter of US Invasion....................215

32. Shared Utopia with International Solidarity Movement..........219

33. Soviet MiGs and Nicaraguan Democracy.......................226

34. Chile, the Dream..232

THE GLOBAL UNRAVELING OF UTOPIA

35. The Pact with a Dictator 239

36. Chile, Selling Out a Revolution..............................245

37. A Christian Woman, Marijuana Bust and War 250

38. Nirvana and the Woman of My Dreams......................259

39. Oceanic Crash: The End of Life as I Knew It................264

40. The Long Road Back and My Left Foot 268

41. Historic Utopia Torn Asunder..............................274

42. The Abyss 280

45. From Zapatismo to the Battle of Seattle 283

46. The Millennial Quest for Utopian Socialism 290

47. Mars and Utopian Existentialism 294

48. Epilogue: Utopia and the Grim Reaper....................296

ORIGINS OF THE QUEST FOR UTOPIA

0. Prologue
Revolution, Love and the Longing for Utopia

My quest for Utopia is embedded in my Catholic heritage. Like most Christian and Islamic religions, Catholicism is utopic, believing we will live in a perfect world in the afterlife. I spent eight years in grade school with the School Sisters of Notre Dame, then went to weekly religious classes while attending the only public high school in Watertown, Wisconsin. Next, I was involuntarily dispatched by my parents to St. Norbert College in De Pere, Wisconsin, the summer training camp of the Green Bay Packers. The "heathen" University of Wisconsin in Madison that I wanted to go to was verboten. But under the tutelage of the Norbertine priests, my parents' worst fears were realized: I became an atheist. I turned in St. Thomas Aquinas for Karl Marx. I was also moved by an early worldly-minded Catholic utopian, Thomas More, who King Henry VIII beheaded for not accepting royal infallibility in matters of church and state.

My utopian quest in the 1960s became bound up with revolutions. As a student of history, I was fascinated first by the French revolution, and then the Mexican and Bolshevik revolutions. Revolutions kicked open doors to new societies as oppressive rulers were overthrown and the frontiers of what is thinkable and plausible were dramatically extended. In *On Revolution*, the renowned political philosopher Hannah Arendt wrote, revolution is "inextricably bound up with the notion that the course of history suddenly begins anew, that an entirely new story, a story never known or told before, is about to unfold."

As destiny would have it, I came of age when the Cuban revolution, 90 miles from the shores of the US, galvanized the world's attention. At St. Norbert College in 1964, I realized that here was a socialist revolution that sought to end poverty and economic inequities. The revolution's influence extended far and wide. When I went to serve as a Peace Corps volunteer in an Andean village in Peru in 1966, I heard stories of Cuban-backed guerrillas fighting heroically in the nearby mountains, and Che Guevara was rumored to be leading a band of guerrillas in neighboring Bolivia.

I finally made it to Cuba in the summer of 1969 as part of a delegation of radical ex-Peace Corps volunteers. The revolutionary fervor was palpable as soon as we arrived. Although Che Guevara had died fighting in the jungles of Bolivia in October 1967, his dictum and thoughts on a new society were very much alive. On the road into Havana from the airport, billboards with Che's etched face proclaimed: "*Socialismo o Muerte*" (Socialism or Death) and "*Seamos realistas y hagamos lo imposible*" (Let us be realistic, do the impossible).

It was amazing, what the revolution had accomplished in a decade. Cuba had become the most egalitarian society in Latin America. A profound agrarian reform program had taken over the large landed estates; the factories and banks were under public ownership; and free education and medical care were available to everyone. It seemed as if a permanent revolution was occurring, not in as many countries as Leon Trotsky had called for, but in one country where the very nature of the human species was being debated.

For me, the burning question was whether a "new man and woman" could emerge in the midst of challenging revolutionary conditions. In his famous essay, "Man and Socialism", written in early 1965, Che Guevara argued: "In this period of the building of socialism we can see the new man and woman being born. The image is not yet completely finished—it never will be, since the process goes forward hand in hand with the development of new economic forms."

Che's utopian socialism was a living process in Cuba where the revolutionary government sought to forge a new person in a transformed political and social culture.

Che's thinking was boundless. He realized that revolutions are joined with emotions. In one of his most renowned statements he declared: "At the risk of seeming ridiculous, let me say that the true revolutionary is guided by a great feeling of love. It is impossible to think of a genuine revolutionary lacking this quality." In an earlier speech, "On Revolutionary Medicine," to militia units with medical trainees, Che grappled with the complexities of revolutionary love. He explained that it was insufficient to say one manifested love by simply going out and talking to and treating "the workers and the peasants." This is "practicing charity, and what we have to practice today is solidarity. We should not go to the people and say, 'Here we are!' …We should go instead with an inquiring mind and a humble spirit to learn at that great source of wisdom that is the people. Later, we will realize many times how mistaken we were in concepts that were so familiar, they became part of us and were an automatic part of our thinking. Often we need to change our concepts, not only the general concepts, the social or philosophical ones, but also sometimes our medical concepts."

It is the stranding together of revolution and the quest for a qualitatively different life that distinguished Che and has earned him a special place in the pantheon of revolutionary heroes. Che's revolutionary practice, his love for humanity, unwavering opposition to the forces of exploitation, courage, and selflessness, and his call for a new man and woman, make him an iconic figure whose words have echoed into the new millennium.

Che's words and example carried me on a journey to new revolutionary utopian quests. First in Chile, under the socialist democracy led by Salvador Allende which was struck down by General Augusto Pinochet's bombing of the Presidential Palace on September 11, 1973. And then in Nicaragua, where intent on helping to prevent "another Chile," I went to support the Sandinista Revolutionary government of a nation of 3 million people who resisted the onslaught of the US empire for over a decade.

My own quest for revolutionary Utopia, as well as Che's words on revolutionary love, left open the question of personal love—the deep romantic bond between two human beings. According to the accounts of Che's relationships with his two wives and four children, he was a loving father and husband, although he was often "absent." As my life unfolded, my loves and romances compelled me to realize that utopias are not only rational projects but also emotional experiences. They are made up of images, aspirations and anxieties, some of which are unconscious and escape, or resist rationalization.

Romantic love between two individuals is intrinsic to and shaped and affirmed by all societies. But whether or not it is part of the utopian longing is conditioned by the social order in which it exists. Building on the tradition of Karl Marx and Friedrich Engels, a little known Russian revolutionary and early feminist, Alexandra Kollontai, wrote about how love and the family are constrained and manipulated to serve the interests of capitalist society at large. Under capitalism, Kollontai contends that nearly all sexual relations and marriage are economic and property relations, "grounded in material and financial considerations, and economic dependence of the female sex on the family breadwinner—the husband."

This is an orthodox view, capturing the reality of early 20th century Europe. But it also helped make sense of my own upbringing in which my parents were trapped in a loveless marriage, driven to stay together out of economic necessity. Our family was primarily an economic unit, always struggling to make ends meet and to pay off the bankers at the end of the year to prevent foreclosure on our 160-acre farm.

Romantic love, because it runs so deep in the human psyche and predates capitalist society, can act as a subversive force, threatening the existent moral and legal order. True love is revolutionary in that it asserts the privilege of desire over social and economic interests. Consummated love not only celebrates the fusion of bodies and minds, it also opens up the possibility of envisioning a new world between two individuals. Love thus projects an aura of transgression, a "lightness of being," that both promises and demands a better world.

Passion and eroticism can be part of the longing for Utopia. The highest level of euphoria I have experienced is being caught up in a revolutionary milieu and sharing it intimately with another human being who is engaged in a similar quest. These passionate encounters can be part of, or lead to, a deeper romantic love, although I confess that in my case, I never settled on a single relationship, always searching for continual renovation and unique passionate encounters in the midst of revolutionary struggles.

Two utopian pillars, revolution and romance, have driven my life and shaped the narrative that follows. It ends in 1992, when my Utopias failed me and I faced an abyss.

I write these words almost a quarter century later, sitting in a wheel chair due to a spinal cord injury I suffered in 1992, hounded by multiple myeloma, an incurable blood cancer diagnosed in 2004, and shaking with Parkinson's disease.

Now constantly faced with the possibility of death, I find myself participating in personal Utopias comprised of interlinked circles of family and friends. One tends to think of old age as isolating people. But it doesn't have to be that way. In these latter years, I find myself more connected to myself, my once fractured family and our fractured but utopic world.

1. Paradise Lost

"*Viva, Chile, mierda*!" "Long live Chile, shit!" I heard someone yell outside my bedroom window in Santiago early on the morning of September 11, 1973. It was a Chilean vernacular phrase and I knew immediately what it meant: that a coup was taking place to overthrow President Salvador Allende. I roused Elizabeth, my companion sleeping next to me, and we turned on the radio to hear the final words of Allende as the radio transmitters were being silenced by the military:

"This is the last time I will address you... My words are not spoken in bitterness, but in disappointment... Foreign capital and imperialism united with the internal reactionary forces to create a climate so that the armed forces would break with tradition... there will be a moral judgment against those who betrayed the oath they took as soldiers of Chile... They have the strength; they can subjugate us, but they cannot halt social advances by either crime or force. History is ours and the people will make it."

After hearing his words Elizabeth decided she would go to stay with some friends nearby. I grabbed a revolver I had acquired a few months before and headed off to the Center for Socio-Economic Studies (CESO), a research center in Santiago where I worked. To get there I had to cut across town on foot, going by the presidential palace which was under siege. I took a circuitous route, swinging south of the palace, hoping to avoid the fighting.

To my surprise, I encountered a line of tanks backed up six blocks from the palace square, impeding my advance. So I veered even further south, only to hear yells of *"Alto!"* (Stop!) I looked up and saw a squad of soldiers stationed on top of a four story building with their guns pointed down at me. I froze not knowing what to do. Then I saw an elderly, working class couple a few yards in front of me who were heading in the same direction. The woman was sobbing. A soldier barked orders, telling them to put their hands above their heads, to walk another block south around the corner of the next street. I did likewise, encountering no more tanks or soldiers to the south as I continued on my trek to CESO.

At the research center I joined about two dozen of my colleagues. We had agreed previously that in case of a coup attempt we would assemble there and await orders from the government and the leftist political parties about how to participate in the resistance. We didn't expect to be involved in heavy fighting, but we thought we might help with logistical or communications support.

The office scene was chaotic as we tried to find out what was happening. The military on the radio issued a list of the 90 most wanted people, among them Teotonio dos Santos, a well-known Brazilian exile who was the director CESO. He became trapped in the building with the rest of us as the military issued a *toque de queda*, a curfew. For the next two days, anyone who ventured out on the streets could be shot.

By mid-afternoon we heard that Allende had died in the rubble of the presidential palace after it was bombed and assaulted by troops commanded by the military junta. Rumors circulated that Allende's recently deposed head of the army, Carlos Prats, was leading loyalist forces in the south. But these rumors proved to be false, and pockets of armed resistance around Santiago were quickly snuffed out. We posted sentries on a building next to the office to keep tabs on troop movements in a nearby army barracks.

We quickly realized there was little we could do if the army raided our office. In fact, the pistols that I and another person had would only get us in more trouble. So we buried them in a deep hole in the courtyard behind the building. Then we waited, hoping that something would stop the brutal military coup.

I had first entered CESO's iron grates in 1971, shortly after I arrived in Chile to research and write my doctoral dissertation. Like many young Americans, I was entranced with the experiment in democratic socialism that was taking place under Salvador Allende who was elected in 1970 as head of the Popular Unity coalition. This was a period unlike any other in my life—before or since. It felt like a political paradise as the people of Chile at the grassroots stood up and mobilized to make a better life for themselves and all the disadvantaged of the country. Authentic democracy was palpable as the popular classes took control of their food distribution systems and worked through unions and political organizations to take over factories, farms and mines where they historically labored to create the country's wealth.

On motorcycle trips up and down the country I'd seen spectacularly beautiful deserts, mountains, volcanoes, archipelagos, and one of the few surviving ancient redwood forests on the planet, outside of California. Stretching 2000 miles along the Pacific Ocean from north to south, Chile is an average of only 250 miles wide. To position Chile in relation to the United States, one needs to imagine a sliver of land that runs from Baja California, Mexico, up the entire US west coast to the Northwest Territories of Canada. Its unique geographic structure was set at the time of the conquest when the enormous Andean mountain range compelled the Spaniards to settle what would become Argentina from the Atlantic coast, while Chile had to be conquered by Spanish forces coming down the Pacific coast from the viceroyalty of Peru.

Chileans would tell me they come from the north, the center or the south, never from the east or the west since this sense of geographic place does not exist in the Chilean lexicon. The central valley, where the capital Santiago is located and most of the population lives, enjoys benign Mediterranean weather and rich soils. As the seasons are reversed with the northern hemisphere, Chile produces a cornucopia of fruits, vegetables and wines for the world market while the north is locked in winter.

The people who live in Chile are a rich blend of diverse racial origins. Many are mestizos, a mixture of Indian and European blood, though the Indian presence is much less prominent than in other Latin American societies like Peru and Bolivia. While upwards of a million of the fifteen million Chileans today consider themselves Mapuche Indians, many of the Chileans I have met, particularly in the central valley, like to lay claim to their Spanish origins, which they celebrate with *Dia de la Raza* on October 12 every year.

Others of European descent are also solidly represented in Chile. During the late nineteenth and early twentieth centuries, a large number of French, Italian and German immigrants arrived on Chile's shores, many establishing their own settlement colonies, some of which survive today. In this mix are a lesser number of English, Jewish, Arab, and Slavic immigrants, along with Gypsy communities, making Chile a unique and fascinating potpourri of peoples for such a small country.

I found the Chileans to be friendly and gracious. However, the upper class, which prefers to live in the Santiago suburbs of Providencia and Las Condes, can be obnoxious and conservative, even racist as they look down on the rest of society. The author Isabel Allende in her memoirs laments that many of the common people are insular and cantankerous. While there is some truth in this, I found in Chileans little of the arrogance that afflicts the "ugly American" to the north. And during my stay in Chile under the Popular Unity government, politics drew Chileans out of whatever insularity they possessed as they saw themselves as part of a much bigger world bent on revolutionary change.

President Allende's most powerful adversary proved to be the Hemispheric Colossus that lay more than 5,000 miles to the north—the United States. At the time of the Chilean elections in 1970, Henry Kissinger, then Nixon's National Security Adviser, declared: "I don't see why we need to stand idly by and watch a country go Communist due to the irresponsibility of its own people." As soon as Allende assumed office, the US engaged in covert activities and launched "the invisible blockade," hoping to destabilize the government. According to documents released years later, in 1971, the year I arrived there, the CIA spent $3.5 million on Chile. Right-wing terrorist groups like *Patria y Libertad* were funded, and the CIA was making almost daily contacts with the Chilean military.

It was evident in the daily newspaper coverage in 1971 that the domestic elites and business classes backed by the US had already closed ranks against Allende. To their horror, Chile was becoming a country in which the historical roles of the different social classes were being reversed. In the past, it had been the trade unions, the working poor and the leftist parties that had demonstrated against governments and gone out on picket lines. Now I saw the powerful decide to go on strike. Large commercial houses and shopkeepers closed their doors, making goods unavailable. The *latifundistas,* the large landowners, refused to plant their fields, creating food shortages. The owners of the means of transportation, mainly trucks and mini-buses, stopped their vehicles. To deal with the transport difficulties, I bought a bicycle that I peddled around the congested streets of Santiago, often beating the packed public buses to my destination.

Virtually every one of the thousand days that Allende's Popular Unity government remained in power was a day of high drama. It was an exciting period, one filled with social, cultural and political turbulence, unlike anything the country had experienced in its century and a half as a republic. It was a utopian endeavor to construct a new democratic socialist society. As Allende was fond of saying, it was a revolution with *"pan y vino"* "bread and wine," meaning that it drew on Chile's unique democratic legacy and its history of popular working class struggles dating back to the nineteenth century.

As promised, Allende nationalized the US copper corporations:

Anaconda, Kennecott and Cerro de Pasco. He expropriated eighty strategic companies, including ITT. There were educational reforms, and labor and health legislation—such as, the provision of one liter of milk for every child—all aimed at creating a more egalitarian, democratic and socialist society.

The right-wing and the business classes resorted to violence to overturn this experiment. Backed by the CIA, terrorist groups bombed and destroyed state railroads, power plants and key highways in order to create chaos and stop the country from functioning. In the midst of this struggle for control of Chile, Allende insisted, almost stubbornly, on maintaining the country's democratic institutions, even in the final months of his government when many of his supporters called on him to suspend parts of the constitution and purge the military of those officers conspiring to overthrow him.

The counter-revolutionary activities of the wealthy and well-to-do only infuriated the popular classes, generating even more support for Allende and the Popular Unity coalition. I witnessed a bitter struggle for control of the country's commerce and means of production. Workers, in the face of the transportation strike, went to their jobs on foot and organized worker brigades to keep products and essential commodities flowing to consumers and key industries. Peasants seized control of *latifundios* and workers took over scores of factories when the owners sabotaged or stopped production.

Soon after arriving in Santiago, hoping to do what little I could to support the revolutionary process through my doctoral research, I became a research associate at CESO. For my dissertation I had elected to study the relationship between the rising Chilean industrial bourgeoisie and multinational corporations during the course of the twentieth century. I began to meticulously enter historic and current data on the ties between the members of the bourgeoisie and foreign capital on the first computer-generated study at CESO. We believed that the distillation of this data would enable us to understand and expose the activities of the more treacherous sectors of the Chilean bourgeoisie.

I also joined the Frente de Informacion Norte-Americano (FIN), a group of North Americans resident in Chile who published periodic bulletins on US interventionist activities both within Chile and abroad. Through FIN I befriended Charlie Horman and other radical Americans who were part of the sixties generation that had gone to Chile. I remember playing pool with Charlie—who had been an amateur pool shark traveling around the US after his graduation from Harvard—after some of our meetings. Joining Charlie and other Americans, I demonstrated in front of the US embassy in Santiago against the Vietnam War.

In search of a place to live, one of my early stops in Santiago was the Peace Corps office. From 1966-68 I had served as a Peace Corps volunteer in the Peruvian highlands. Nostalgia and familiarity drove me to check out what was happening at my former organization of employment. There I met Valentina, the office executive secretary, an attractive Chilean with two kids and a German husband, Siegfried. She introduced me to a friend of hers, Jim Williams, who lived on a couple of hectares of land in an old gardener's house on the outskirts of Santiago. The place was idyllic, set behind the owner's mansion, with fruit trees, a vineyard and a big patio with an old stone barbecue pit. I became Jim's housemate.

There we held many a weekend fiesta with abundant wine, often a barbecued goat packed in from the countryside by a volunteer, and plenty of socializing with Chileans as well as foreigners from diverse countries. One of the more intriguing guests proved to be the Peace Corps director's wife, Rebecca, a close friend of Valentina's. I soon found out that Valentina had a liaison with Jim, and Rebecca would often accompany her to Jim's place, serving as a subterfuge. It wasn't long before Rebecca and I became more than good friends.

Rebecca's husband Ray, who I became convinced worked as a CIA informant, was quite often back in Washington, DC. Rebecca was younger than Ray, a damsel from Mississippi with soft blue eyes, dark blond hair and a slender figure. It soon became obvious that she was deeply alienated from her husband, in part because he had developed his sexual prowess in the brothels of the Dominican Republic where he had served as a Peace Corps volunteer shortly after the US invasion of that country in 1965. With such a resume, it wasn't difficult for me to imagine myself as something akin to a knight in shining armor bent on rescuing Rebecca from Ray's clutches.

On one of Ray's trips to Washington, Rebecca invited me to her house, a plush mansion with a pool and all the amenities imaginable. There we made love for the first time. It was magnificent, caressing her breasts, touching the silky light hair on her sex, and making love as Chilean folk music played in the background in the late spring of 1971.

Rebecca soon threw caution to the wind, driving with me to a beach house in the port town of Vina del Mar, often with Jim, Valentina and her kids. Valentina's husband, Siegfried, was still unaware of her on-again/off-again relationship with Jim. We'd spend hours on the beach, often swimming in the ocean, testing our endurance by swimming out to one of the large rock islands that dotted the Chilean coastline.

I almost drowned on one occasion when Jim, who was much stronger than I was, took off for a distant rock and I followed him. We made it there together, but Jim swam back ahead of me as I needed to catch my breath. When I set out, I found that I couldn't make it through the strong tow to the coastline. I began to swallow water as my strength faltered. After a struggle a couple of waves buoyed me from behind and I finally landed on the beach, where Rebecca waited to gather me in her arms.

I should have learned my lesson from this experience about the powers and dangers of the ocean, but my fascination with the sea only deepened over the years, eventually leading to a tragedy that put me in a wheelchair. The oceans, like the heavens and the stars, have always enchanted me—in large part because they are the closest I can ever come to seeing and experiencing infinity, a concept that has preoccupied my philosophic ruminations throughout my life.

After a couple of months, Rebecca's husband, on one of his trips back to Chile, became aware of what was going on. It may have been the CIA that informed him of our liaison. We now know that the agency was tailing many American dissidents. A virtual war was going on, not only among Chileans but also within the American community, as the radical contingent supported Allende and denounced the Nixon administration, while the multinational executives and the US embassy crowd turned the CIA on us, regarding us as traitors.

Ray confronted Rebecca with our affair. She didn't deny it. In fact, she said that she wanted to leave him. Ray, of course, was furious. Since I did not have a phone, he called Valentina and told her to get me to meet them in the middle of the night at a nearby plaza. I showed up at almost the same moment as Ray and Rebecca. He shoved her toward me, saying: "Get out! Go live with him."

At that time I was no longer living with Jim; we had both been evicted by the landowner, a reactionary who didn't like the gringos who supported Allende. I resided in a small apartment, hardly the place where Rebecca and I could live. So, that night at least, Ray's pronouncement was a non-starter. Rebecca was not about to collect her bags and move in with me. Moreover, I wasn't at all sure I wanted her to.

During the past year and a half, I had maintained an intense correspondence with a lover, Elizabeth Patelke, at Indiana University in Bloomington. I had met her at a softball game in the early spring of 1970 while I was a graduate student. I don't remember how well she played, but I do remember her cleavage, her voluptuous body and her dark brown eyes. She was shy and reticent, but I followed her home like a puppy dog and we wound up sleeping at her house the very first night. It was one of the more sensual relationships in my life.

Aside from the passion, we did not have a lot of common interests. She was pursuing a Master's degree in Slavic studies, was only marginally interested in politics, had never left the United States, and was deeply tied to her family in Lake Bluff, a suburb north of Chicago. I like to see my relationships as intellectual as well as romantic excursions. With her, I imagined that if we lived together I would learn Russian, adding to my repertoire of Spanish, French, Portuguese, and German. (The latter three, limited largely to reading comprehension as of 1970). It was an on-again/off-again relationship as we both, on occasion, veered off with other lovers. We were part of the counterculture generation, which at least in principle believed in open relationships, although the practice was often more difficult than what we preached. Heartaches and jealousies did not disappear. With Elizabeth, I remember these feelings drove me to go over to a house in the early morning to look at the window where I knew she was sleeping with another man, hoping she would not forsake me and that I would have another opportunity to experience her warmth and love.

When I went to Chile in 1971, I corresponded with her, as well as with another lover, Nancy, a more complicated woman whose profile was classic neurotic. She was brilliant but obsessed with the suffering of humanity, and we would go on for hours, if not days, discussing her angst about life. I was fascinated with Nancy. After the collapse of my relationship with Rebecca, I explored the possibility of either Nancy or Elizabeth coming to Chile. In spite of Nancy's more profound political concerns, including the devastation the US was unleashing on Latin America, it was Elizabeth who decided to come to Chile to be with me.

Elizabeth arrived in Santiago in February, 1972. I traveled with her to northern and southern Chile on a motor bike I had purchased a few months before. In June of that year she left but returned again in March, 1973. We were destined to live together through the fracturing of the Chilean paradise.

In March, Chile held parliamentary elections as dictated by the Chilean constitution. Both the opposition and the ruling coalition agreed that these elections would test the popularity of the government. To the surprise of many, Allende's coalition increased its percentage of votes and added to it seats in Congress. It was clear that the social and paramilitary insurrection of the elite was not working. They needed a bigger and more deadly assault on the government and it was right after the elections that many of the top military leaders decided to begin preparations for a coup d'etat.

To encourage the military to intervene, women from the upper-class neighborhoods of Santiago marched in front of military garrisons and threw grain and corn kernels, chanting "You are a bunch of chickens, you are not defending the honor of the women of Chile." Elizabeth and I lived just doors away from the residence of General Carlos Prats, the head of the Army who was loyal to Allende. In mid-August, we saw many of these upper-class women, this time led by the wives of conspiring military officers, demonstrating violently in front of the house. Days later Prats resigned and Augusto Pinochet became commander-in-chief of Chile's armed forces.

Two months before this, in June, 1973, a tank brigade rose up against the government and assaulted the presidential palace. Many supporters of the government immediately marched to the palace, including an American friend of mine, Frank Terrugi. In the ensuing melee, Frank was shot in the foot. While the wound was not serious, it was probably one of the reasons why he was fingered and executed when he was picked up after the coup in September.

Even in the waning days of the Popular Unity government, when the economy was in shambles and virtually everyone believed a confrontation was imminent, one still felt the popular impulse and drive of the people from below. I'll never forget the last major demonstration on September 4, 1973, when the Alameda, the main avenue in downtown Santiago, was packed with tens of thousands of marchers, all intent on passing by the presidential palace where Allende stood on a balcony waving to the crowd. This was no government-orchestrated demonstration in which people were trucked in from the barrios and countryside. These people came out of a deep sense of commitment, a belief that this was their government and that they would defend it to the end. I have a photo of this determined and euphoric demonstration hanging on the wall of my office to this day.

Exactly one week later the presidential palace was in flames. A coup led by General Augusto Pinochet brutally smashed the dreams of Chileans, as well as the hopes of many foreigners in Chile and abroad who for three years had watched in awe and solidarity as the Popular Unity government attempted to build a new socialism with a humane and democratic face.

When the *toque de queda* was lifted two days after the coup, I quickly abandoned the CESO office along with everyone else. Theotonio dos Santos, on the "most wanted" list, took exile with his wife at the Panamian embassy. I went to pick up Elizabeth at the house where she had been staying with friends and we returned to our apartment. We realized that we were in some danger, as we lived in a right wing residential area and many supporters of the coup were denouncing their foreign neighbors as "outside agitators" and "terrorists." We contacted Jim Williams and once again he extended his hospitality, inviting us to stay at his home in the center of Santiago. Given the diversity of the downtown area, it was much less dangerous, although on the first night there we witnessed a squad of policemen going into nearby apartments to confiscate "subversive" literature and books that they burned in a bonfire in the middle of the street.

Once housing was arranged, I had another serious problem to deal with—I had no passport. I had applied to become a Chilean resident earlier in the year and the migration office had retained my documents. Moreover, as part of the request for residency, Theotonio had written a letter on my behalf saying I was an employee of CESO.

It was with a great deal of anguish that I went to the migration office exactly a week after the coup. The office stood on the corner of the plaza next to the bombed-out presidential palace. I noted that there was a new head of the migration office, a gaunt, impeccably dressed man who looked like he could have been recruited from Franco's Spain. Fortunately, one of the older employees, a man named Fernando, was still there. I had often conversed with him, in part because of the rumpled suit he wore that accentuated, rather than hid, his working class background.

I went up to him and said, "Look, I've changed my mind, I don't want to be a Chilean resident anymore, I'd just like to get my passport and documents back."

He disappeared into the backroom and was gone for what seemed like an eternity. I kept looking over my shoulder, expecting a security officer to appear and haul me away. Fernando finally came back and proclaimed: "I can't give you back your passport."

I asked "Why not? What's wrong? I really need it."

He replied: "We approved your residency request several weeks ago and sent it over to the sub-secretary of the Ministry of the Interior for him to sign off on it. His office was in the presidential office, and as you can see by glancing across the street, we don't have much hope of getting your passport back."

I was shocked and relieved at the same time. Theotonio's letter was gone, and at least something of value to me had been sacrificed along with Salvador Allende. But now I had to go into the den of the enemy, the US embassy, to apply for a new passport.

The next day I went into the consulate office at the embassy and walked up to a desk officer who appeared to be Chilean-American. I immediately sensed that she was probably one of the most ill-disposed people to help out a young American who was up to no good in her country.

I told her about my destroyed passport and she, like Fernando, also went into the backroom. She reappeared rather quickly with a form for getting a replacement passport. I filled it out in front of her. I wrote down my old address where I lived before moving to Jim's place and checked the box saying I didn't have a phone there. I slid the completed form over to her and she said: "Put down your real address. We know you have a phone now." She was referring to Jim's place. Once again, I was shocked, but this time not relieved. The only way a lower level official at the embassy could have known so quickly about my vital living information was if the embassy (read CIA) had a fairly active and updated dossier on me.

Ray may have filled in part of that dossier. After I broke up with Rebecca, I saw her a few times but the meetings were awkward and we felt estranged from each other. Subsequently, she broke up with Ray and returned to the United States. I found out that Ray, working through the embassy, had tried to get the Chilean government to declare me persona non grata, to have me thrown out of the country. Of course, this request went nowhere at the time, given the tense relations between the Allende government and the United States.

The day after I went to the consulate, the Peace Corps called Jim and ordered him to throw me out because I was an "undesirable element who endangered the Peace Corps mission." Jim refused and resigned his position as a volunteer. Jim had had it, not only because of this intrusion into his life, but also because Chileans he had worked with were now imprisoned or "disappeared."

Within a week I got a new passport. The embassy obviously didn't care for me, to say the least, but there was no legitimate basis for the US government to deny me a passport. Also, the embassy already had its hands full with the relatives of Americans who were imprisoned or disappeared.

It was several days after the coup that Charlie Horman and Frank Terrugi were picked up. Frank was detained in the national stadium along with his roommate, David Hathaway, and thousands of others. They were apparently turned in by their landlady. Frank was soon separated from David, and no one ever saw him alive again. If I remember correctly, it was on September 22 that a government-controlled newspaper published an article that his bullet-riddled body was found on a street not far from the stadium.

Charlie was also picked up. As the movie *Missing* suggests, he was probably arrested and detained because he had found some damaging information on the US role in the coup in the port city of Valparaiso. His wife, Joyce, and then his father Edmund Horman, came to Chile to help search for him. His body was finally found in a Santiago cemetery in October.

I believe that the CIA approved the assassinations of Frank and Charlie. It seems to me that once any American was detained, the military officers in charge of handling them would contact the US embassy, i.e. the CIA. In the case of Frank, the bullet wound he had suffered back in June was probably incriminating, amplifying his dossier with the agency. They probably knew he had been active in the more militant wing of the Socialist party in the months leading up to the coup.

Charlie's inside knowledge of the coup combined with his history of working with the Frente de Informacion Norte-Americano undoubtedly were sufficient to put him on the CIA's "undesirable" list. As happened with Frank, the military officers in charge of Charlie consulted with the US embassy and received damaging information about his "subversive activities," which in effect gave the Chilean military the green light to get rid of him.

In hindsight, it was my good fortune not to be detained in any military round ups and prevented me from suffering a fate similar to Charlie's and Frank's. On one occasion, Jim, Elizabeth and I were walking on the streets when a half-dozen policemen stopped us and threw us against the wall with their machine guns pointed at us. They demanded to see our documents. Three American passports meant little to them and they were about to haul us away when Jim produced his Peace Corps carnet indicating that he was an employee of the US embassy. They let us go.

On another occasion, I was walking with Elizabeth in downtown Santiago into a small plaza when suddenly we noticed that a military operation was taking place and all the street exits from the plaza were closed off. By chance, I noticed an American friend, Mische, who was with her Chilean boyfriend, a high-level member of the Left Revolutionary Movement. Both were part of the underground resistance. I kept my eye on them as the soldiers began stopping and interrogating people. When they slipped into an unguarded alleyway, Elizabeth and I followed in their path, escaping the dragnet.

It quickly became clear that I could do little in Chile. Our friends in the resistance told sympathetic foreigners to leave, so that we could be of more help abroad doing solidarity work and informing the world of the atrocities of Pinochet and the military junta.

Elizabeth and I decided to leave by bus via the Andean border with Argentina, believing that the security checks there would be less intensive than if we tried flying out of Santiago. On October 9, 1973 we reached the last Chilean outpost, high in the Andean mountains. The migration officials checked our bags scrupulously. I, of course, had gotten rid of anything that would incriminate me, but they found a comic book in my luggage published by a left wing press and confiscated it.

As I looked back at Chile from the Argentine side of the border, I swore to myself that I would return soon. I ardently believed Allende's last words, "Sooner rather than later the great avenues will be open again, through which will pass a free man, constructing a better society."

The international community and the Chilean people with their long democratic history would not tolerate for long such an odious military regime. I thought Chile would be different from the other countries in Latin America that were taken over by their militaries. How wrong I was. It would be eleven years before I set foot in Chile again, and another six years after that before General Augusto Pinochet was forced to surrender power.

2. Farm Boy, Prodigy of Nuns, Draft Dodgers, Bootleggers

A change is gonna come...
-Sam Cooke

After crossing the Chilean border, Elizabeth and I checked into a hostel in the picturesque Andean city of Mendoza, known for its vineyards and great wines. At a cafe next door, we consumed a bottle of red wine along with a plate of Argentine beef and salad, then dropped into bed completely exhausted. We arose to a crisp spring morning and took a day-long bus trip to Buenos Aires where we stayed at a friend's flat who had also fled from Chile several weeks before. After a couple of days' rest, we caught a string of buses to Sao Paulo, and finally Brasilia in the Cerrado, the vast dry tropical savanna region of Brazil. There we counted our depleted monetary resources and decided that Elizabeth would be able to fly to Miami and then take a train to her parents' home near Chicago.

I only had enough money left to catch a cheap flight to Panama. Landing in Panama on a warm tropical day, I started hitchhiking up the Pan American highway, intent on making it to California in a week. The first night in Panama I camped out on a beach, next to a small hamlet. A nearby café carried the World Series game on the radio. It was the year the New York Mets won the Series.

As the waves lapped back and forth on the sand, I looked up at the brightly shining stars. It was an existential moment. I felt at one with the vast universe in spite of all that had happened in Chile. Now twenty-nine years old, I slept on the narrow isthmus of land that had served as a crossroads between North and South America for indigenous peoples starting 10,000 years ago.

Since leaving St. Norbert College in Wisconsin eight years before, I had journeyed far and wide around the Americas and traveled to Western European cities. The words of Jean-Paul Sartre from his book *Nausea*, one of the canonical works of existentialism, spoke to my own odyssey: "I have crossed the seas, I have left cities behind me, and I have followed the source of rivers towards their source or plunged into forests, always making for other cities. I have had women, I have fought with men; and I could never turn back any more than a record can spin in reverse."

Lying on the beach, my mind drifted back to my origins. I had grown up in rural America, my first home being a small farming community in northeastern Nebraska near the banks of the Missouri River. I was born at dawn on June 18, 1944, when the eyes of the world were riveted on the beaches of Normandy, France where the Allied forces had landed twelve days before to begin their final assault on Nazi Germany. A rare "war baby," my father was not at Normandy or any other World War II battle front because President Franklin D. Roosevelt had decreed that farmers were needed at home to produce food for the Allied war effort.

Twenty years before, my grandfather, Mathais, had fallen off a barn roof, suffering a multiple fractured leg. Destitute, as were many farm families in the early 1920s due to the collapse of farm prices in the aftermath of World War I, Mathais Burbach somehow managed to get admitted to the Mayo Clinic in Minnesota, reportedly the best medical center in the Midwest, where he became a victim of "modern medicine." While the doctors were operating on his leg he suffered a blood clot that went to his brain and killed him.

For my father, Hubert, just eight years old at the time, his dad's funeral was a macabre experience. A wake at a funeral parlor was out of the question because of the cost, so the services were held at home.

"The night before the funeral," my father told me, "I crept into the room where my father's body was laid. There he was, half naked on a table with half-dollar coins in his eyes to keep them from opening.] I fled from the room horrified." My father, like many of the men of his time in the rural Midwest, was not given to introspection, and I have never been able to discern just what sort of psychological scars the experience of my grandfather's early death left on him. It may, however, explain the sense of fatalism that permeated his life. He felt the world was against him, that life dished out hardships and tragedies, and he cautioned his children to expect the same. Years later, in the 1980s, when I was taking frequent trips to war-torn Nicaragua, my father said to me, "Stay home, your young son needs you alive; not a dead father sent home in a box."

After the death of my grandfather, my grandmother Frances Burbach, with ten children to raise, managed a 240-acre farm in Bow Valley, Nebraska. She ran that farm, and the family, with a determined hand. She was the epitome of a stark, blunt, disciplined German woman. I don't remember her ever smiling or joking. The high point of her day came when she had the one bottle of beer she allotted herself, saying, "It's good for your health." I may get my serious bent from her, but the ironic sense of humor certainly doesn't come from Grandma Frances.

My grandmother spoke only German to her six sons and four daughters and my father didn't learn English until he went to grade school. There was no family car, only horses that were used to work the fields. Years later, when I complained to my father about the 50-minute bus trip I had to take to attend school, he would counter, "I had to walk two miles to get to school every morning."

My dad was only able to finish the eighth grade, as all hands were needed on the farm, particularly those of the boys to work in the fields. He never talked about his lack of education but he did speak out about feeling trapped in farming, often wishing he had been able to move to the big city to seek his fortune in life. All my uncles and aunts on the Burbach side of the family became farmers or farm wives. Only in his mid-fifties did my dad become the first to abandon farming by getting a job in a factory in Milwaukee. To this day, the Bow Valley farm remains in family hands with my Uncle Roman and his sons running it. When I visit the members of the Burbach clan who still inhabit northeastern Nebraska, I feel like time has stood still, that I am witnessing another period in history.

My earlier ancestors did not lead such steadfast lives. I come from a long line of German peasants on the make who migrated across oceans and continents, occasionally working as merchants and often skirting the law in their quest for a better life. My great-great grandfather, Jacob Burbach, married Gertrude Marx in 1837. Over a dozen years later they left Cologne, Prussia for the United States and settled in Milwaukee, Wisconsin with six children. They were fleeing the revolutionary upheavals of 1848 that shook much of Europe, particularly the German principalities and France.

My attention has riveted on Gertrude Marx ever since I found her in the family tree. Marx is often a Jewish name and the great Karl Marx hailed from Trier, a town in the Rhineland, not far from Cologne. Gertrude was born in 1814, four years before Karl. The official records indicate that she was a practicing Christian, dying with the last rites administered to her by a Catholic priest from St. Matthais Parish in Milwaukee, Wisconsin. But as history tells us, it was quite common for Jews to convert to Christianity, given the staunch anti-Semitism that afflicted Europe, as well as the United States. Even in the case of Karl Marx, all his uncles were rabbis, but his father abandoned the Judaic religion and formally became a (non-practicing) Christian so he could be a lawyer in Prussia. The patriarchal nature of Prussian society also meant that Jacob Burbach would very likely have insisted that his 23-year-old bride abandon any Judaic religious beliefs she might have held.

It is very doubtful that Gertrude was related to Karl, given that she appears to have come from poor rural stock while Karl came from a line of professional and urban folk. It is probable, however, that Jacob and Gertrude comprised part of the broad socialist upheaval that Karl Marx helped inspire in the mid and late nineteenth century. (He wrote the *Communist Manifesto* in 1848 with Friedrich Engels.) The German immigrants who went to Milwaukee endowed the city with a rich socialist legacy, often dominating the city's politics and electing Socialist mayors, right up until the end of the 1950s. Moreover, after the 1848 European upheavals, a number of radical Germans fled to the southeastern corner of Wisconsin, not far from Milwaukee, and became known as "Latin farmers." Highly educated in their homeland, they had learned Latin in school and would occasionally use Latin words or phrases as they tilled the land and greeted their neighbors.

My father once told me, "your great-great Grandfather Jacob worked as a milkman, selling bottled milk from house to house in Milwaukee in a horse-drawn cart along with his sons." One of the sons, Werner, moved to Nebraska to live with a brother of Gertrude's, eventually buying his own farm. And it was one of Werner's son's, Mathais Burbach, who married Frances in 1903. With no place for him on his parent's farm, Mathais worked as a carpenter in Harrington, a small community in northeastern Nebraska, while his 19-year-old bride labored as a milkmaid until they saved up enough money to buy what is now the family farm in Bow Valley.

My mother, born Rita Albrecht, grew up on a farm about 20 miles from Bow Valley in a community called Menomonie. The oldest of ten children, her parents were perhaps even poorer than my Dad's family. As an infant, her first words were German but as she told me, "When the United States entered World War I, anti-German sentiment forced my family to stop speaking German at home." I suspect that my fraternal family's strong family ties to the German communities in Milwaukee and Nebraska enabled the Burbachs to continue speaking German, while the Albrechts were more vulnerable and insecure as more recent homesteaders in Nebraska. Neither Grandpa Ted Albrecht nor the woman he married, Josephine Tramp, ever spoke a word of German around me. In Contrast, Grandma Frances Burbach would speak German with my Dad until the day she died in 1968. To enforce the speaking of German at home, my father said that when he was a young boy, "Your grandmother would strike me on my hands with a ruler if I spoke English."

On my mother's side of the family I can boast of a rich legacy of draft-dodgers and bootleggers. The Albrechts and the Tramps fled from Germany in the 1860's, '70s and '80s, when Chancellor Otto von Bismarck, at the behest of the German Kaiser, waged war in central Europe to unify the German principalities into a common nation. To many a young peasant, the distant farm lands in America looked much more appealing than fighting and dying for the new German state. One of my great grandfathers fought in the Austro-Prussian War in 1866 and after that fled to the United States, tired of warfare.

Another of my great grandfathers, Franz Albrecht, was inducted into the Kaiser's Navy and jumped ship around 1880 in Rio de Janeiro, Brazil. From there he headed to the United States where he joined his wife Elizabeth and their two sons who had come over from Germany. In Nebraska, they homesteaded a piece of land with a stream running through it. To the lament of succeeding generations of Albrechts, they soon traded their farm for the land of a sheep herder on an adjacent homestead who wanted the creek to water his sheep. Along with the herder's waterless and more barren piece of land, Franz and Elizabeth got $16 and a muzzle loading shotgun.

Fearful that Germany would come after Franz for desertion, the lands were registered in Elizabeth's name. In 1893, Franz finally became a US citizen, swearing in his citizenship papers, "to renounce forever all allegiance to any foreign Prince... particularly to the Emperor of Germany." Ten years later, finally feeling secure in his new homeland, and reflecting the patriarchal nature of society, he had his wife sign the farm over to him. It was this farm that his youngest song, my grandfather Ted Albrecht, lived and worked on until he formally purchased it in 1922. My mother was born on the farm in 1915, one year after the 28-year-old Ted married 18-year-old Josephine Tramp.

To make ends meet on their barren lands, my mother's parents resorted to making bootleg whiskey during the Prohibition era. One day in the mid-1920s, Federal Marshals raided their farm and axed their liquor still into pieces. My mother recounts: "I was terribly embarrassed as news of the raid spread throughout the community and my school friends found out about it." Somehow her parents managed to avoid spending time in jail, perhaps because the local magistrate sympathized with an impoverished family with ten kids to feed.

The youngest of my mother's brothers, Floyd, took over the Albrecht farm in the mid-1950s, never making much off the land but somehow persevering until he died in 2008. When I was ten to twelve years old, and my parents had moved away from the area, I would often come to visit him on his farm, helping him out in the fields and with the chores in the barn. It was more fun to hang around with a young uncle than to be at home doing the routine farm work for my father. I would occasionally go hunting on the farm with Grandpa Ted who taught me how to use a shotgun (not the old family muzzle loading musket!) to shoot at the jack rabbits that hopped across the fields. I never managed to hit anything, one time almost knocking my shoulder off as the gun kicked back at me. I'm not sure if my failure as a hunter simply reflected my lack of hunting skills or my latent anti-war tendencies.

Uncle Floyd taught me some of the more interesting vices of life. Continuing the family home brewing tradition, he one day said, "Come on Roger, I want to show you something." He took me to his mulberry fermenting vat in a small shed set a 100 yards back from the farmhouse. There, he gave me the end of a hose inserted into a huge wooden barrel and said, "try this." I sipped a sweet-tasting wine and soon became a frequent visitor to the shed, always sucking the juice straight out of the hose. One evening, I showed up drunk at the dinner table. Uncle Floyd laughed his ass off as I fell off my chair. I felt so embarrassed I stopped sipping wine, at least until my teenage years.

On Grandma Frances Burbach's farm, the understanding was that when each of the sons married, they would spend the first year or two on the farm, earning half the annual harvest. After that they had to make their own way in the world. Thus, when I was about a year old, my parents moved to Wisconsin, following in the footsteps of a brother who had migrated there several years before. We became sharecroppers as my parents had no money to make a down payment for a farm.

My early memories on the different farms we moved to virtually every year or so are fairly pleasant. I trailed around after my father in the fields and enjoyed being with him in the barn while he milked the cows. Once a year, we would load the family into the car (I remember most vividly a 1953 Pontiac) and drive back to Nebraska to visit my grandparents and cousins, including Uncle Floyd.

These trips enabled me to begin taking up the wholesome family tradition of dealing in illicit activities. In Nebraska, firecrackers could be openly purchased while in Wisconsin they were illegal. Assisted by my father, I would load up the trunk of the Pontiac in Nebraska with bundles of fireworks. A pack of two-dozen firecrackers cost 16 cents. I would sell them to my friends in Wisconsin for $1 a pack. I justified this extravagant markup by the fact that the firecrackers constituted my only source of spending money as I earned no allowance from working on the farm.

The wanderlust bug that has shaped my entire life bit me at an early age. One bright summer day, when I was five years old, I walked off into a big cornfield with my dog, intent on finding out what was at the other end of the field. When my father came in from the barn for supper, he said to my mom, "Where's Rog?"

My mom responded, "I thought he was with you." They launched a search for me, even calling in the landlord to help. Finally, as it was getting dark, they spotted the upright tail of my big St. Bernard just barely visible above the corn tassels as he followed me through the cornrows. When they caught up with me, I was still walking away, determined to reach the other end of the field.

The year I entered grade school, my parents finally managed to buy a farm of their own near Watertown, Wisconsin. As chance would have it, this was one of the main communities where the Latin Farmers from Germany had settled in the 1850s. Carl Schurz, who had fought in the 1848 European revolutions and would go on to become an abolitionist and a prominent figure in Abraham Lincoln's Republican party, resided in Watertown for a few years in the 1850s with his wife Margarethe Meyer Schurz. Margarethe founded the first kindergarten in the United States in 1856 in Watertown, which is now an historical monument called the Octagon house.

I never went to kindergarten as I was too old when I arrived in Watertown. I was sent off to attend the local Catholic grade school, St. Henry's, taught by the School Sisters of Notre Dame. From then on, my pleasant childhood turned into one of alienation and frustration. As Isabel Allende notes in her memoirs on growing up in Chile, "a happy childhood is a myth." My unhappiness stemmed in large part from the harsh discipline and the neuroses instilled by the Catholic religion.

In school I did enjoy learning to read and write. But I quickly became bored and disillusioned with the nuns and the religious routine at St. Henry's. Every day, rain or shine, my brothers and sisters and I got up at 6:30 to catch the school bus. After a 50 minute ride, we spent another 45 minutes listening to a priest chant in Latin as he performed a high mass.

Those of us who fasted and took communion, finally ate breakfast as our first act in the classroom. We then had our first class of the day—an hour of religious instruction. A good deal of moralizing was interjected into the subsequent classes, be it art, history or even math. For me, it would have been a relief if the nuns had limited their religious interventions to teaching "Creationism" in a designated science class, as demanded by some of today's evangelicals. The word evolution was never mentioned in grade school so the nuns did not have to reconcile the biblical creation of the world in six days with what they taught us in science class.

I can thank my mother for my advances in learning in grade school. Both of my parents have always struck me as quite intelligent, in spite of their impoverished upbringings. But it was my mother who had the good fortune to complete high school and attend a year of college, mainly because she didn't have to work in the fields on her parents' farm. This qualified her to become a teacher at a nearby rural school, remaining there until she married my father at the age of 27.

At home she helped us with our homework and provided tutoring, believing that education was the route for her children to escape from our disadvantaged life. A fervent Catholic like the grade school nuns—she had one sister who joined the Maryknoll order and another who became an Ursuline nun—her tutoring was laced with Catholic precepts. She even told me on occasion, "I hope my first-born will become a priest." But at least her concern for my education, whether or not I became a member of the clergy, meant I had time to indulge my reading interests at home. Sometimes my mother would even lobby my dad so I could skip some of my farm chores to do my homework and more reading. This served as an incentive to be even more studious, anything to avoid the endless drudgery of work on the farm.

To escape the boredom in the classroom I began reading books on my lap beneath my desk as the nuns droned on. Edgar Rice Burroughs' Tarzan was one of my favorites, not only because it is a fascinating story but also because I became sexually aroused when Tarzan had his more intimate encounters with Jane. One of my teachers, Sr. Columbine, a short squat gregarious nun, finally caught on to my secret reading sessions and pounced on me. She confiscated the Tarzan book, and as I sat there red-faced, she held it up in front of the class saying, "What inappropriate, disgusting reading for a young Catholic boy." I think Tarzan rose to the top of the grade school reading list as several of my classmates asked me how they could get a hold of the banned book.

While growing up, I had as little to do with my six younger siblings as possible. I was the oldest and it was only years later, after I left the farm, that I would come to appreciate my brothers and sisters and begin to seek them out and interact with them more closely. On hindsight, I think it was largely the differences in age that made me so distant from them. My nearest sibling, Marie, was four years younger. (My mother had three miscarriages after me; the family joke being that it took her a while to get over the shock of seeing her first born.) I had few activities in common with my sister, other than the frequent fights and arguments that took place between us. When Del Rey, the youngest member of the family was born, I was already a sophomore in high school and had little interest in yet another infant at home. Moreover, it was an embarrassment as none of my friends in school had parents who were still begetting children.

As with most families in rural America, sex was a taboo subject. My early knowledge of sexual relations was gleaned from a big green-covered hardback book on marriage and procreation that I discovered at the bottom of a black chest, buried under blankets and articles of clothing. It contained nude pictures of women in different stages of pregnancy and showed the male penis and testicles that produced the seed for fertilizing the woman. But it illustrated nothing about the act of sexual intercourse itself. For years, I wondered if the man consciously penetrated the woman, or if the sperm simply flowed to the woman from the man while they were asleep. Such a ludicrous idea probably stemmed in part from the virgin birth of Jesus that the nuns propounded in grade school.

I was about 14 years old, fixing cattle fences with my father one day when he said to me, "Rog, do you know how babies are made?"

I responded, "I'm not really sure."

Then he said, "You know what the bull does to the cow in order to make calves, don't you?" I replied yes, and then he said, "The man gets an erection like the bull and puts his seed in the woman. Have you ever gotten an erection?"

I replied, "No," even though at that very moment I had one of the biggest hard-ons ever as my father was telling me about sex.

Years later, when I had sexual relations, it was difficult for me to separate sex from the thought of impregnating the woman I was with. I am certain it was because I had learned on the farm that sex was always associated with fertilizing the female.

Running parallel to this obsession with conception was the tremendous fear I had of getting a woman pregnant because of the traumas I experienced at home as each new child came along in our household. Given the constant arguments and bickering between my parents and our difficult economic circumstances, the last thing I wanted to do was to get married and assume all the responsibilities that having children entailed. I did not overcome this fear until I was 37. But over the years before then I had great sex arising from the tension of wanting to impregnate a woman while at the same time fearing a pregnancy.

I was a sinful child, or so I thought at the time. Because of my impure thoughts, my lies (however petty), the disobedience of my parents' commands, and even the occasional theft of a Captain Marvel comic book from the local news store, I became pretty much convinced at a young age that I would end up burning in hell. Although we did not read Dante's *Inferno* in class, his description of souls cast into the different levels of hell for their various sins reflected the religious discourse at school and led me to think I would go straight to hell when I died. I, of course, wanted to go to heaven, but even that seemed somewhat vaporous, a place in the distant sky where someone floated around aimlessly. A troubled Utopia became embedded in my mind; a Utopia of blissful meaninglessness in a paradise gained only if one managed to avoid the dark side of Utopia, the infinite Inferno.

A very Germanic Catholicism was taught at St. Henry's, one containing few of the soft edges of the Catholicism I later experienced in Latin America. No mercy was shown to non-Catholics; the followers of Martin Luther were condemned to hell for breaking with the Pope. We were told not to play with the kids at the nearby Lutheran and Protestant schools, even on the school bus, because they were heretics. It was as if the religious wars of seventeenth century Europe were still being waged in the schools of Watertown, Wisconsin.

The reality of daily living trumped religious ideology when it came to the Borchardts, our neighbors on the farm across the road. They were a Lutheran family with five children, and I became good friends with their eldest son, Glenn, who was two years older than me. We have remained lifelong friends. He and I both left the farm, went on to university to earn doctoral degrees, and even lived together for several years in California. I remember getting into fights with Glenn's younger brother, Lyle, sometimes over religion. But Glenn never cared much about church preaching, being more interested in his own projects. Early on, he displayed a methodical, almost scientific approach in his hobbies and endeavors, be they searching for old Indian arrowheads in the fields, raising a calf to show at the county fair, trapping and hunting, or taxidermy. I tried to mimic him, but at that stage in my life I didn't seem to have the perseverance to succeed like he did in earning money from his exploits. The illicit trade in firecrackers was more appealing and easier for me to make a quick buck.

Due to the constant reminders in school and at church that hell awaited me, thoughts of my own death and mortality obsessed me. I became a rural version of Woody Allen with a growing neurosis about death. My life-long insomnia is related to a deep-seated anxiety over my ever-approaching demise. Early on, I endlessly pondered the ideas of eternity and infinity, trying to understand what it meant that heaven or hell would go on forever.

My neurotic obsession with death was in part reinforced by the terror that nuclear weapons held after the Soviet Union got the hydrogen bomb. We heard about the US tests in the Nevada desert and the Pacific islands which produced tremendous shock waves, eliminating all signs of life in their immediate path. One of our neighbors, Gilbert Buedler, started circulating obscure news and magazine articles that claimed the nuclear tests produced Strontium 90 that got into our cows' milk and produced deformed babies. We laughed at him, thinking it was a crackpot idea. Years later, we realized he was one of the most perceptive farmers around.

There were also religious paradoxes I began to mull over. Why should a pagan baby born in Africa be stuck in limbo for an eternity if I failed to donate $5 to save his or her soul? This raised other questions about how the act of pagan salvation actually occurred: Did the $5 wind up in Africa in return for the pagan baby's parents agreeing to a baptism, or did the local priest squirrel away the money and merely say a prayer to rescue the lost soul?

My ruminations about eternity and the heavens led to an interest in the cosmos around me, especially to a deep curiosity about the planets, the stars, and the universe. The grade school project that earned me the greatest praise was a speech I gave on the properties of the nine planets, their moons, and their orbits around the sun. When I sat down after a ten minute oration, Sr. Columbine came up, caressed my face, and said "You are an outstanding student." It was my minute of fame in grade school. This early "success" and curiosity about the heavens turned me into a lifelong amateur cosmologist of sorts. I am, to this day, a particularly avid reader of hard science fiction, like that of Arthur C. Clarke or Kim Stanley Robinson. I never cared for science fiction writers who create complete fantasy worlds or attribute special telepathic powers to future human beings.

To the extent that I developed progressive ideas during my childhood, they came from my home life, particularly my father, who in spite of a limited education, was very much interested in politics and the larger world beyond the farm. He always had the radio on in the barn, especially when the hourly news came on. He detested the incumbent president,

Dwight Eisenhower, and his Secretary of Agriculture, Edgar Taft Benson, who cut farm support prices in the name of the "free market," stripping away the benefits the small family farmer had won in the 1930s during Franklin Roosevelt's New Deal.

In 1954, we almost lost our farm as we failed to make the $1000 annual mortgage payment. My father took up a mid-night shift in the local factory. In the winter months, when my mother's garden provided no fresh produce, our diet consisted largely of red kidney beans baked with frankfurters. Because of the hard work and meager earnings of our farm, my father always told me, "Whatever you do when you grow up, you don't want to be a farmer."

In the mid-1950s, he became an organizer for the National Farmers Organization (NFO), a militant organization in the Midwest that called for collective bargaining. Drawing support from the United Auto Workers, the NFO asserted that farmers, like factory workers, should engage in collective bargaining with the corporations that bought and processed our milk. If the corporations would not agree to a fair price, the farmers should organize picket lines around the milk processing plants and go on strike, i.e. withhold production by dumping their milk if necessary.

My father spent long hours recruiting neighbors and attending regional meetings of the NFO. In his stump talk with other farmers, he would rattle off figures demonstrating that we received only pennies on the dollar at the supermarket price for a gallon of milk while the corporations and their executives grew rich with the profits.

I don't remember the exact year we got our TV in the mid-1950s, but I do remember my father constructing a homemade TV antenna with several thin wires strung across two bowed strips of wood that he hoisted atop our roof on an aluminum pole. The evening and nightly TV news programs were among his favorites. He would often fall asleep in front of the TV news and weather reports, weary from a long day's work. In 1956, I recall watching the Democratic National Convention with him as Adlai Stevenson was selected once again for an ill-fated run against Dwight Eisenhower.

I remember nothing of the anti-Communist McCarthy hearings. We probably did not have a TV when they took place. Or perhaps, I do not recall the hearings because the witch-hunt and the blacklists had little relevance for our rural communities. There were not many Communists in the rural Midwest to be called before McCarthy's committee, particularly in his home state of Wisconsin.

Even though I come from a lineage of socialists and populists, anti-

Communism was deeply ingrained in my family's worldview. One of the early TV programs I watched was Herbert Philbrick's "I Led Three Lives," the lives being those of a citizen, a communist, and an FBI informant. Philbrick was relentless in his pursuit of agents of the Communist party, most of whom were portrayed as sinister and mentally unbalanced people.

One of my mother's favorite programs was Bishop Fulton J. Sheen's "Life is Worth Living." While Sheen was a staunch defender of the Catholic faith and an anti-Communist, his program was surprisingly ecumenical and even had a certain cerebral flair. On occasion, he would quote from Shakespeare and discuss the Judaic origins of the Ten Commandments. Perhaps aware of how boys like me suffered under the tutelage of nuns, Sheen encouraged other Bishops to allow the nuns in their fold to watch "Life is Worth Living" as many religious orders were forbidden to watch TV in the 1950s. He was, in effect, a precursor of Pope John XXIII and Vatican II as the religious sectarianism I experienced in school was noticeably absent on Bishop Sheen's program.

3. Cuba's Revolution, Quandaries at Watertown High

"Redemption looks to the small fissure in the ongoing catastrophe."
–Walter Benjamin, Central Park

On January 1, 1959, as I fed hay to the cows in their stanchions in the barn, I heard over the radio that dictator Fulgencio Batista had fled Cuba, ceding control of the country to a band of bearded guerrillas led by Fidel Castro. A cold harsh day in Wisconsin—the cow platters turned into frozen rocks—and this historic moment on the faraway Caribbean Island would shape the trajectory of my life.

Four months earlier I had entered Watertown High School as a freshman. I felt lucky that my parents did not have the money to send me to yet another Catholic school, the elite Sacred Heart Academy in Watertown. It was a relief to escape from the parochialism of St. Henry's. I would no longer have to relive the religious wars of seventeenth century Europe.

But I soon found out that I had transferred from a religious milieu to a world where the awkwardness of my teenage years was compounded by social discrimination. The sons and daughters of the merchant and business families dominated the social life of the school; the children of farmers were viewed as second-class citizens. My socialization at school was further complicated by transportation difficulties. If I participated in sports or other social activities, I had to miss the 3:30 school bus and my parents had to pick me up two hours later—just when the chores needed to be done.

The high school teachers, while secular, were only a cut above the grade school nuns. I remember little about them; they are all now gray, fading images. There is one exception, Robert French, my social studies instructor. A misfit who dressed in a rumpled suit and drove the only Volvo in town, he used the class lectern to denounce the mores of conformism that gripped our community and the world at large. I took his class in 1960. John F. Kennedy was running for president and lambasted Richard Nixon for the alleged "missile gap" with the Soviet Union. In the midst of the campaign, *US News & World Report* ran a special issue on the number of Americans and Soviet citizens who would die in a nuclear conflagration. Mr. French held up the magazine in front of the class, denouncing the lunacy of US leaders stockpiling nuclear weapons and coldly calculating what percentage of humanity would be wiped out. "How could there be any victors with such human devastation and suffering?" he demanded.

Mr. French was asked to find another teaching post after a few years at Watertown High. Some of the students, including me, signed a petition on his behalf, but it was to no avail. He drove his Volvo to Madison where an early whiff of the rebellious '60s proved more accommodating to his worldly views.

I was socially frustrated throughout high school, attending none of the proms, feeling lucky if I made it to a football game and the dance afterward. In my Junior year, I developed a mad crush on Dolores Higgins, a striking redhead with blue eyes. She came from the countryside but managed to break the school's social barriers by being elected class president. One of our class's brightest students, she usually got straight A's. I made it a point to run into her in the school's hallways, but I was terribly self-conscious and never knew what to say. Somehow I managed to capture her attention and we dated during our senior year.

While my fellow male classmates were boasting about their sexual prowess, I was too embarrassed to even make out with Dolores. One night when I drove her home, we parked, I dithered, awkwardly putting my arm around her. Finally she said, "You can kiss me." No sparks flew as I planted a kiss on her lips. The sexual repression of my Catholicism and my concern with impure thoughts made it impossible for me to kiss her passionately, let alone have sex with her.

In high school, I opted to take the most advanced math classes I could get into—algebra, geometry, trigonometry, and calculus—believing that this was the foundation for becoming an astronomer, or getting into another field of science. This was the Sputnik era, the country had been shocked by the Soviet Union's launching of a basketball-sized satellite into orbit in October, 1957. A year later, when I became a freshman, even the teachers at Watertown High School were talking about how to encourage their students to become scientists so we could "catch the Russians."

However, I soon gravitated to politics and international issues related to the Soviet Union and the Cold War. No political science courses were offered, but I found myself taken by political history. After the Cuban Revolution, I convinced my world history teacher to allow me to do my term paper on the French Revolution and Napoleon, given that the events in Cuba were not considered history.

My high school years from 1958 to 1962 bridged two very different decades. The Eisenhower years and the drab fifties depicted by "the corporate men in the gray flannel suits," gave way to the Kennedy years with the awakening civil rights movement in the South and the new president saying, "Ask not what your country can do for you—ask what you can do for your country."

The presidential election of 1960 became grist for discussion in the social studies classes and even in the high school hallways. Wisconsin was the scene of a hard fought primary campaign for the Democratic nomination between Hubert Humphrey and John F. Kennedy. Though my father was an avid Humphrey supporter because of his years as a populist Senator in next door Minnesota, Kennedy captured the student imagination at Watertown High. I leaned towards Kennedy, also influenced by the coincidence that one of my best friends in high school was named Clyde Kennedy who ardently campaigned for him. (Clyde would later go on to be an arch-conservative, supporting Ronald Reagan and George W. Bush.)

I found myself in a peculiar social niche in high school. My farm boy status and social awkwardness were compensated for by what others noted as my perceptiveness and pensiveness. In the senior yearbook, *The Orbit*, the words "One who thinks before he acts" were appended beneath my photo. Yet, I was not tagged a geek as I did only moderately well in math and science classes.

My peculiar status played itself out at the Winter Ball, a high school dance held every December at the Elks Club. Playing on my social awkwardness with girls, my friends at the Winter Ball decided, as a prank, to launch a campaign to elect me king of the ball. I won, hands down. This meant I had to do a coronation dance with the elected queen, Wendy Quirk, a sophomore. I didn't even know how to dance properly, but Wendy was nice, telling me, "Just put your arm around me and follow my steps." I was so embarrassed. The next day my picture appeared in the Watertown Daily Times. My mother saw it, of course, and said "Roger, how nice, you must be proud of yourself." I didn't have the nerve to explain to her that it was only a prank played on me by my friends.

Somehow, despite its being banned in many schools, I stumbled across a copy of J. D. Salinger's *Catcher in the Rye*. It spoke to my sentiments of isolation and alienation as a high school student, but I had difficulty relating to the main character, Holden Caulfield, who attended a prep school and grew up in New York City. I thought he was a jerk ,wearing his red hunting cap around, using it as an entree to philosophize about the migratory patterns of ducks. I felt I was one up on him as a real huntsman.

In high school, I often went hunting with Glenn Borchardt and Jim Schmitt, a classmate who lived on a farm a couple of miles away. One Sunday, at about 5 a.m., we took off to nearby Mud Lake. As usual, I didn't manage to shoot anything, and I don't remember my friends having any better luck. At about 9:30, I told them I had to get home to go with my parents to the obligatory Sunday mass at 11:00. Glenn and Jim demurred, saying, "Let's stay a bit longer." As time marched on, I became increasingly nervous but they refused to leave, chuckling, "Oh come on Roger, church isn't that important." They finally got me home at about 11:30, well after my parents had left.

I was terrified as I waited for them to return. When they arrived, my father marched up to my bedroom where I was holed up, took away my shotgun and tore up my hunting license. I was taken aback by his severity, since my mother was usually the disciplinarian, especially concerning religious matters. Years later, when I queried my father about it, he replied, "Your mother made me do it." Deepening the conspiracy even further, when I later recounted this story to Jim, he said, "Roger, it was no accident you got home late. We wanted to get you in trouble."

Baseball was the only high school sport I tried out for but I was cut from the Watertown High Goslings fairly early in spring training, partly because it was difficult to make all the practices and partly because I wasn't that good a player. But with the local neighborhood farm kids, including Glenn and Jim, we managed to put together our own team in the summer. We practiced in the village of Richwood, three miles from my home, a community known mainly for its two taverns and a makeshift baseball diamond where cattle often grazed. Our manager was Paul Plasil, a wiry enjoyable man who chain-smoked and didn't know that much about baseball. But his enthusiasm for the game was contagious and we didn't mind at all that his son, Joe, was usually the starting pitcher. Our victories were few and far between as we played against much better summer teams from communities as far as 40 miles away.

The summer of my senior year, we had zero victories and twelve defeats as we went up against the team from Watertown in the last game of the season. They were 11 and 1 and needed to win to remain tied for first place with the team from Beaver Dam. To our amazement, we beat them in the 9th inning. It may have helped that they weren't aware of the locations of all the cow hoof holes in the outfield grass that they tripped over. The victory was even sweeter than if we had won the league championship. We had knocked the Watertown "dandies" out of first place. We celebrated wildly on the only street of Richwood.

The closest I came to losing my virginity was with Kathleen Becker in the hay mow of our barn one evening in the summer of my senior year. My parents had taken off for Nebraska on their annual trip, leaving me home alone to do the chores. I didn't mind, as it gave me the liberty of organizing a big party with my friends. On Friday morning, we drove to Milwaukee in a friend's car, found a liquor store that would sell us beer, and filled the trunk with about ten cases. We took them to the farm and threw the bottles in the cow watering tank to cool off. The next day, about 15 friends came over, girls as well as boys, and we proceeded to get royally drunk.

Towards evening, Kathleen, whom I knew had a crush on me ever since grade school, lured me into the hay mow. We proceeded to kiss passionately; I touched her breasts, got a rather nice erection, and sensed she was willing to "go all the way." But my Catholic morality stopped me. I simply couldn't have sex with someone I didn't love or envision having a serious relationship with. Eventually, someone found us in the hay mow and my opportunity to throw away my virginity disappeared. It would be another three long years before I would finally "do it."

Life at home became increasingly unhappy and conflicted, even more so than life at Watertown High. My parents bickered and quarreled incessantly, they were not happy with their lives. My dad was increasingly absent. In addition to being on the road as an NFO organizer, he frequently went to meetings of the Volunteer Fireman's Association, invariably held at one of the two local taverns in Richwood that fronted each other.

Frequently, he would leave in the late afternoon. I would get home from school about 4:30 and begin the chores, rounding up the cows grazing in the fields, and feeding them a grain concentrate as they stood in their stanchions waiting to be milked. Normally, my father would be doing other tasks in or around the barn, and then we would proceed to milk the cows in our herd with milking machines. But as his fireman meetings became more frequent, he would often show up late, hoping that I would start the milking routine alone. His arrivals became later and later, until finally I went on strike and refused to start milking until he showed up. He became upset with me, insisting that I was capable of starting and finishing the milking. But I was steadfast, claiming incompetence and an inability to deal with all the evening chores alone. Then he turned to my Mom, insisting that she could help me with the milking or perhaps send one of my sisters to the barn.

My mom absolutely refused. Going back to the time of their marriage, she had made it clear that there would be a strict division of labor with her husband. She would attend to all the household tasks, put three meals on the table every day, tend to the family garden, and take care of the needs of her children. This division of labor also extended to the sons and daughters as they grew older. The girls would help out in the house, while the boys assisted their father in the fields and the barn. A corollary of this arrangement was that the boys expected to be served and taken care of in the house. We did not wash dishes or do any laundry, a gender separation that was deeply resented by my sisters.

The upshot of this familial labor structure was that the nine members of the family were locked into conflict and resentment. There was little or no space for love, affection or the enjoyment of simple experiences together. Everything was contested, self-interest was the norm. Egotism stood unchecked, and I confess that as the oldest son I did nothing to overcome this appalling situation, indeed I exacerbated it. I would be sullen at family meals, refuse to do any tasks or chores that were not strictly required, and use my "eldest son" status to impose on my siblings. One time, I slapped my brother Joel around when he refused to feed the heifers in the feed lot as I had ordered.

Surprisingly, the patriarchal structure of my family did not engender deeply sexist attitudes on my part. I think it had to do with my mother's intelligence and strength. Even before I reached my teenage years I remember thinking that there was no reason why she or my sisters should not be considered the equals of any male. Reflecting this view, I tried to act as a mentor to my younger sister Ann as she struggled through her own experiences at school and home. But I was psychologically scarred by my years on the family farm, and carried these scars with me into my adult life. I was never violent, but my self-centeredness caused me to look at any relationship in terms of what was in it for me. It has taken me years to overcome this, even as I later sought to become a "new man" under the influence of San Francisco's "flower power" and Che Guevara's call for "revolutionary love."

4. Portrait of an Awkward Young Man as a Malcontent

Who is more eager to change things than the man who is most discontented with his present position? Who is more reckless about creating disorder than the man who knows he has nothing to lose and thinks he may have something to gain? ...So I reflect on the wonderfully wise and sacred institutions of the Utopians, who are so well governed with so few laws. –Thomas More, Utopia

When it came time for college, my mother, the 'minister of education' in the family, decreed that I had to go to a Catholic school. The "heathen" University of Wisconsin that Glenn Borchardt and many of my friends attended was out of the question. This left me with two options: Marquette University in Milwaukee, which was too expensive, and St. Norbert College in northern Wisconsin, about five miles outside of Green Bay.

It was a beautiful fall day in 1962 when my parents dropped me off at the freshman dormitory on the St. Norbert College campus of eleven hundred students. It may have been a Catholic school, but I was delighted to finally have my liberty. I had no chores, only the complete freedom to study and take the courses I elected. I buried my nose in the books, took extra courses each semester, and graduated in three years.

I started out with an interest in math or history as majors, but C's in calculus and trigonometry convinced me that my future lay in studying history. Father Robert Cornell, the chairman of the history department became my mentor. I remember at the end of the first semester, Cornell called me into his office and said: "Roger, I don't understand why you are doing so well, your test scores from high school are only mediocre." I had come into my own in college.

Active in Democratic Party politics, Cornell encouraged me to enter the largely dormant Young Democrats on campus. In my sophomore year I became president of the chapter, mainly by default, as nobody else wanted the position. There wasn't too much interest in politics on campus at the start of the 1960s. Our membership numbered around a dozen students.

At St. Norbert's I quickly grew to detest one of the requirements—the Reserve Officers Training Corps (ROTC) program—a two-year course designed to produce junior officers for the army. I loathed the classes and the discipline, particularly the officer-instructors barking orders at us as we marched around campus every Tuesday morning with empty M-16s on our shoulders. During the winter of my sophomore year I gathered together a group of like-minded students in my dormitory room and we made a large banner of Mickey Mouse with the letters R.O.T.C. scrawled around it. Then we took the banner out to the flagpole in the middle of the night and strung it up. I hiked up the pole, tying off the rope at the very top so it could not be easily retrieved. The next morning, as we as-sembled in front of the pole for our weekly military drill, I could hardly contain my laughter as the cadets stood around staring at the Mickey Mouse banner. One of the army officers finally shimmed up the poll to untie the rope as a student pushed on his butt. An investigation was launched to find the culprits but our secret cell was never uncovered. It was my first escapade into "guerrilla" politics.

In a philosophy course I finally read Thomas More's *Utopia*, the first book to ever develop the concept. I had heard about More in grade school, where he was lauded by the nuns as a Catholic martyr who was beheaded for supporting the Pope rather than giving in to Henry VIII's proclamation of infallibility and decrees to the subjects of his realm to accept his divorce and remarriage. Of course, we weren't told that the Pope had granted divorces to other royal families, or that much of the wrangling between Pope Clement VII and Henry took place over who would control the monastic lands and ecclesiastical tributes of England. Written ten years before More's death, *Utopia* is the tale of an idyllic non-Christian commonwealth in which religious tolerance is practiced.

During the first semester of my sophomore year I began planning my first foray beyond the Midwest, a hitchhiking excursion to Dallas, Texas over Thanksgiving vacation with a classmate, Skip Collins. As fate would have it, we scheduled our departure just days after John F. Kennedy was assassinated in Dallas on November 22. We went in spite of admonitions from our parents and stayed with family friends of Skip and with my aunt who was an Ursuline nun in Dallas. We went to the spot of the assassination and for the first time in my life, I felt like I had made a rendezvous with history; an awesome sensation that I have savored each time I found—or put—myself on the cusp of history-in-the-making.

Most people in Dallas were obsessed with the assassination and in deep mourning. But Skip's family friends, a married couple with two young children, were Republicans with little sympathy for the Kennedys. One night, they took us to a Playboy Club for dinner and dancing. I had to borrow an oversized suit from the husband and felt totally out of place. At one point, I put my hand in the coat pocket and found that I had been provided with a couple of condoms. I was totally shocked, thinking at first that he must have accidentally left them there, but then realizing they might have been meant for me. I couldn't even work up enough courage to buy a drink for one of the Playboy Bunnies at the bar, let alone ask her for a dance or think of having sex with her.

On the way back from Texas we hitchhiked through the staunchly segregated border town of Texarkana. The civil rights movement was beginning to mobilize around voting rights for blacks in the south but I hadn't been involved. It was early morning when we were dropped off there, and we asked a white night watchman who was getting off duty where we could find a place to sleep. He hostilely declared: "We don't have any room in this town for transients." He could tell that we were northern students and possible civil rights sympathizers. So we got out of town fast.

St. Norbert's was largely quiescent in the early 1960's, but on other campuses a growing social awareness was taking hold. In nearby Michigan, the newly founded Students for a Democratic Society (SDS) released the Port Huron Statement in 1962, the year I entered college. Calling for the construction of a new, truly "participatory democracy," the statement proclaimed: "While two-thirds of mankind suffers under-nourishment, our own upper classes revel amidst superfluous abundance... Although mankind desperately needs revolutionary leadership, America rests in national stalemate, its goals ambiguous and tradition-bound instead of informed and clear, its democratic system apathetic and manipulated rather than 'of, by, and for the people'." SDS chapters soon took root on most of the major campuses across the US.

Then in 1964, the free speech movement erupted at the University of California, Berkeley. Mario Savio, in a speech that shook university communities across the United States, denounced the "autocracy" that ran the university as a machine spewing out "raw materials" to be used up. "There is a time when the operation of the machine becomes so odious, makes you so sick at heart, that you can't take part! You can't even passively take part! And you've got to put your bodies upon the gears and upon the wheels… upon the levers, upon all the apparatus, and you've got to make it stop!" proclaimed Savio.

I was only dimly aware of these declarations, but as Bob Dylan's lyrics noted, "the times, they are a-changin." This rang true even at St. Norbert College. The death of John F. Kennedy had shaken our Catholic campus, and then the 1964 presidential campaign caused a noticeable uptick in political interest as arch-conservative Barry Goldwater ran against Lyndon Johnson. That year, I got funding from the Democratic Party in Green Bay to put out a newspaper on campus in which I published my first article, deriding the militaristic agenda of Goldwater while lauding Johnson's social programs, particularly his war on poverty and his civil rights program.

In the Wisconsin Democratic primary in 1964, Alabama Governor George Wallace ran for president on a state's rights agenda and the continuation of segregation in the southern states. I heard Wallace was campaigning in northern Wisconsin and called his field office. To my surprise, I wound up talking to Wallace himself and asked him to speak at St. Norbert College. He agreed.

Not about to give him an uncontested platform, I talked to Tom Holton, the only black student on campus who was vice-president of the Young Democrats. I suggested that I resign as president, and he would then take over my position, thus being the one to introduce Wallace. Tom, however, felt uncomfortable with the idea, perhaps thinking it was a shallow way of playing the race card.

I curtly introduced Wallace when he showed up and he rapidly stumbled through his speech, sensing that the audience was not very hospitable. When he finished, Holton stood up and asked, "Why doesn't your attending entourage from Alabama have any people of color?" Wallace lamely responded: "I have the support of many Negroes in Alabama."

The auditorium where Wallace spoke was overflowing, largely out of curiosity, although many were hostile to him and showed their opposition by not applauding. The Associated Press wire service picked up the event for national newspapers, reporting that Wallace received a "cool reception." It ran a photo of a picket sign saying "Wall-Ass," perhaps the most suggestive poster to ever appear at a public event at St. Norbert's.

When Wallace walked off the stage, he gave me an icy stare, probably wondering if this was really the seemingly nice white boy he had talked to over the phone.

At about this time I began to imagine I might have a political career, even hallucinating that I could become president someday. In the regional Democratic Party, Father Cornell was intent on rebuilding the Democratic chapter, hoping to move out the "elders" and replace them with a coalition of labor leaders, young professionals and small business interests. Several days before the caucus to elect new leadership, Cornell realized he didn't have enough votes for his slate to win. So he called on me to turn out the students. Our dozen enlisted members could not swing the election, so we announced we were setting up a keg of beer and free food at the hall in Green Bay where the election was to be held. We tripled our membership overnight and the reform ticket won control of the party. After I left St Norbert's, Cornell went on to run for Congress and in 1969, he became the second Catholic priest to serve in the House of Representatives.

For my part I soon became largely disillusioned with party politics. Although I enjoyed the idea of politics, I couldn't stomach the fact that in order to win you had to stuff the ballot box by turning out voters with a keg of beer donated by the local liquor merchant. As the Port Huron statement proclaimed, the existent order in America appeared "apathetic," even at the local reform level in northern Wisconsin.

I had become an idealist, I was searching for a new world that went beyond the one we knew and experienced. Along with fellow students, I began to read Karl Marx, Herbert Marcuse, Eric Fromm, C. Wright Mills, and other radical intellectuals. As a history major, I became particularly enamored with William Appleman Williams, a radical historian at the University of Wisconsin. His seminal work, the *Tragedy of American Diplomacy*, depicted US policies on behalf of business interests dating back to the War of 1898.

I began to meet with a floating group of about six to ten radical students every Friday night over a fish fry at the local bar. There we would discuss Marx, the revolution in Cuba, atheism, the conflict in Vietnam, and just about everything that was taboo in the classroom. We soon became known around campus as the "Malcontents." An equally appropriate title might have been the "misfits." About half of the gang was of Irish descent and supported the Northern Ireland independence movement. Two members were star basketball players, one a closet gay and the other an alcoholic. One woman was a brilliant math major who went on to Harvard law school and became the Chief Justice of the Supreme Court of Colorado. We even had a maverick Republican in our ranks.

Even though I was a founding member of the Malcontents, I continued to go to Mass every Sunday. Still obsessed with all of my sins going back to grade school, I believed the fires of hell awaited me if I abandoned my faith. Then at one of our fish fry seminars, a fellow Malcontent and close friend, Mike Roe, turned to me and said, "How can you talk about Marx and still go to Mass?" The following Sunday, a cold winter day in February, I turned off my alarm clock at 8 AM and went back to sleep. Marx and a warm bed had won out over the fear of the fires of hell. Even though I hadn't attended the University of Wisconsin, I had nonetheless become the heathen my mother feared. I had rejected Dante's Inferno and I began to take up Karl Marx's more contemporary version of More's Utopia.

As I had diligently buried my nose in the books and spent no time on dating or romance, I realized by the end of my second year that I had accumulated enough credits to graduate in three years if I attended summer school. To help support myself, I worked in the kitchen, serving the Green Bay Packers who held their summer training camp at St Norbert's. These were the years of fame for the Packers with Vince Lombardi as coach, Bart Starr as quarterback, Paul Horning as halfback, and Willie Davis as defensive lineman. I met them all in the serving room, and even waited on them for a special dinner with their wives and friends at the closing of summer camp. "Golden Boy" Horning struck me as particularly cocky and obnoxious, while Star and Davis seemed to be sort of half way decent guys.

One day, when I was working the breakfast shift for the Packers, I took a break and heaped my plate with food from the serving trays. At that moment, Lombardi was passing through the line, saw me eating and queried, "Is he eating Packer eggs and bacon?" The kitchen manager replied in the affirmative, acknowledging that I had broken the rule that none of the premium food brought in by the Packers for their meals was to be eaten by the kitchen staff. For my act of indiscretion, I was demoted to washing dishes in the basement.

I was stunned by Lombardi paying such attention to detail as to note who was eating what food. Years later, I heard that Lombardi's own wife and son found him intolerable, in part because of the maniacal attention he paid to detail. It probably explained why he coached the Packers to greatness but it also meant he was unbearable in his human relations. A few years later, I shuddered when I heard President Nixon say that if he had had his druthers, he would have picked Vince Lombardi as his vice president in the 1972 elections. The real world of politics, as we know, made Nixon turn once again to Spiro Agnew.

In my last year at St. Norbert's, the college hired its first Latin American history professor, Robert Padden. This proved pivotal for my future studies and career because until then only US and European history were taught at St. Norbert's. Latin America opened up to me a whole new arena of political and intellectual ferment. I subsequently applied to graduate school in Latin American history and received two doctoral fellowships, one for the Catholic University of the Americas and the other for Western Reserve University in Cleveland, Ohio. I chose the latter, having had my fill of Catholic schools.

I was just short of twenty-one years old when my parents attended my St. Norbert graduation ceremonies in early June 1965. The astronaut John Glenn was the commencement speaker. I thought Glenn's address on the greatness of America and our destiny to be the first on the moon was rubbish. On the trip back to the farm I had a heated argument with my parents, particularly my mother, over John Glenn, religion, politics, and just about everything else in life. Fortunately, I only stayed home for a week that summer. In mid-June, I said good bye, hitchhiked to Laredo, Texas, and from there took a bus to Mexico City. My odyssey with Latin America and the world at large had begun.

5. Mexico, the First Odyssey

Self-discovery is above all the realization that we are alone: it is the opening of an impalpable, transparent wall–that of our consciousness–between the world and ourselves.
–Octavio Paz, Labyrinth of Solitude

A scrawny, 21-year-old kid when I crossed the US border into Mexico, I rented a cheap hotel room in Nuevo Laredo. The next day I went to the local plaza for lunch, and then sat on a park bench. An innocent-looking young woman soon came up and sat down next to me. I took the initiative, saying "Ola, como te llamas?" wanting to practice my Spanish as well as being interested in meeting a Mexican woman for the first time. She responded, "Cristina." We hung out for a few hours and then had dinner. I must say it was a very limited conversation. She was shy, spoke no English, and I quickly realized just how inadequate my college Spanish was.

At dusk I went back to the hotel, picked up my bags and headed off to the transit terminal to catch an overnight Pullman bus to Mexico City. As the night set in, I passed through the Sierra Madre mountains and then Monterrey, a flourishing commercial and industrial city. Looking out the window at the dark sky and the lights of the city below, I was filled with awe and pleasure. I had put the insular life of rural Wisconsin behind me and embarked on a journey to explore the world.

Given its proximity to the United States, Mexico was the logical first stop. I had borrowed against the fellowship stipend I would receive at graduate school in the fall to spend the summer learning Spanish and studying the culture and history of Mexico at the University of the Americas. I was part of the new generation of "Latin Americanists" being trained at US universities to understand why the United States had "lost Cuba" and how to stop the spread of guerrilla movements and leftist influence throughout the hemisphere. But I was also part of the generation of the sixties that began to critique the US role in the world, realizing that the poverty and social discontent that afflicted much of the third world were bound up in a global system of exploitation.

In Mexico City I soon found a "pension," a boarding house just two blocks from the flower market on the southeastern corner of the 850-hectare Chapultepec Forest, a splendid park with museums, small lakes, a castle, and extensive wooded areas. The first major metropolis I had ever known, Mexico City immediately captivated me with its bustling activity, its historic architecture, and its rich cultural spectacle. A city of about 7 million, it was not yet the humongous, polluted city it would become a decade later, reaching 20 million inhabitants by the mid-1980s.

The mid 60s were still considered part of the "Golden Age" for Mexico City, an era extending from 1945 to 1970. Not yet overwhelmed by modernity, the city contained the old along with the new. I would often take the bus from the corner of Chapultepec up the Paseo de la Reforma, a Parisian-style boulevard lined with gardens, trees and heroic statuary interspaced with new glass and steel skyscrapers. Arriving near the Zocalo, the main plaza of the city from whence the Aztecs had ruled before the Spanish conquest, I would disembark to admire many of the old churches and palaces that fronted on the plaza. Indian vendors in traditional dress sold tacos, fresh grilled corn-on-the-cob and many other appealing foods that I hesitated to eat because of "Montezuma's Revenge," the diarrhea that afflicted me even when I avoided the outdoor food stands. Close to the Zocalo were arcades and an open air market that sold everything from shoes and Del Monte canned goods to merchandise that appealed to tourists, including jewelry, postcards and traditionally designed rugs.

As a first-time foreign traveler south of the border with an emergent social and political awareness, my primary imperative was to try to understand the culture and society around me. I had read *The Ugly American* and was determined not to display my gringo heritage any more than I had to. But I admit to being pretty ignorant when I arrived in Mexico City. Before I left Wisconsin, I bought a pair of shorts that I put on for the first time when I took a stroll into Chapultepec Park. I was greeted by jeers, whistling and cries of "*maricon*," homosexual. I hurried back to the pension, took off my shorts, and to this day I have never purchased another pair of shorts.

I attended the University of the Americas in Puebla, over an hour's bus ride from where I resided by Chapultepec Park. My knowledge of Spanish was rudimentary, so except for intensive Spanish, my other classes were in English. My "pension" was at a three-story house owned by Senora Rosario who lived there with her 10-year-old son. I paid $100 per month for a room and a couple of meals a day. I loved the hot hand-made tortillas that Senora Rosario served at each meal. For breakfast we had tortillas with eggs and great-tasting beans (much better than the "pork 'n beans" my mother had made at home). Later in the day it was usually beef, pork or chicken served with rice and beans and more tortillas. We had very little salad or fruit but that was actually a blessing for a gringo with a digestive tract not adapted to the local bacteria.

When I came to Mexico in 1965, guerrilla conflicts backed by Cuba were raging across Latin America and I had come to believe that they represented the future hope of the continent. This belief in revolution was the Utopia that would drive my studies, my travels and my work in Latin America over the coming decades.

Given this political starting point, I had a strong interest in the revolution that began in 1910 in Mexico, the first modern revolution on the continent. The *ancien regime* of Porfirio Diaz was overthrown in 1911, and after a decade of conflict, it led to the founding of a new government and a constitution that incorporated many of the revolutionary ideals that the people had fought for, particularly land reform. The revolutionary reforms reached their apogee with the government of Lazaro Cardenas from 1934-40, which stood up to US oil interests and deepened the process of agrarian reform. This land reform and similar efforts by leftist governments in Bolivia and Guatemala in the early 1950s were precursors to the far more radical process of agrarian reform that took hold in Cuba.

Under Cardenas, Mexico developed a system that would become known as state capitalism. The Mexican federal government, often in opposition to the greedy local economic elites and even multinationals, would take over strategic sectors of the economy, expropriating many large haciendas and seizing the holdings of the Standard Oil Company. But Cardenas left the fundamentals of capitalism in place, allowing the market, the profit motive and the private accumulation of wealth to serve as the motor force of the economy.

This distinguished the Mexican revolution from the profound transformations that took place in the Cuban revolution. Many of us in the "Sixties generation," alienated by consumerism and the stifling US political system, saw the Cuban experiment as a decisive break with the evils foisted on the first and third worlds by capitalism, particularly by US imperialism.

In Mexico, at the end of World War II, a new generation of politicians took over from the old revolutionary guard, enabling a business class to consolidate, which played down the reforms and turned Mexico City into the economic locomotive of the country's capitalist development. Manufacturing plants began to ring the city and a veneer of prosperity took hold as a new middle class emerged. Peasants and rural workers from the countryside flooded into the city, searching for meager paying jobs, and taking up residence in the marginal areas of the city. Oscar Lewis' *The Children of Sanchez*, about a community of rural immigrants in Mexico City, gave me an insight into the living conditions among the poor, a view that I took in firsthand when I went to Tepito, a barrio north of the Zocalo where the Sanchez family lived.

In Tepito, I struck up a conversation with a man sitting in front of his adobe hut. He invited me in for a coffee and to meet his wife and three of his four children who lived in three rooms with a dirt floor. We had a simple conversation, given my Spanish, but I fully understood his wife when she exclaimed, "My husband and I find whatever work we can. Our hope is that our children, by going to school, will have more opportunities and a better life."

President Diaz Ordaz (1964-70), who had assumed the presidency the year before I arrived in Mexico, stood at the apex of a political system ruled by the Institutional Revolutionary party, the PRI. Residing at Los Pinos, an opulent estate next to Chapultepec Park, the president would wine and dine the different groups that shared in the trappings of power while issuing orders and bestowing favors through the political machine that he ran.

In theory, the PRI was set up in 1929 to maintain the revolutionary ideals by representing the interests of the workers, the peasants and the middle class. In practice, the party sat atop a political pyramid of power with the president anointing his successor every six years. A caste of politicians at the top enriched themselves, forming an uneasy but lucrative relationship with the new bourgeoisie. Trade unions were a formal part of the PRI-dominated system but the workers were rarely permitted to go on strike and the leaders were often just as corrupt as the government bureaucrats. Sometimes they even held prominent posts in the government. I met one worker in Mexico City in a cantina, a bar, who told me after a couple of beers: "We have a trade union controlled by labor bosses that does nothing for us. We can't strike for higher wages. Whenever a worker becomes insubordinate, complaining about the working conditions or calling for higher wages, he is fired and his union will not defend him."

I looked for any signs that the ideals of the Mexican revolution were still alive, but found none. However, surface appearances, especially for a young American in a new milieu, can prove deceptive. Three short years later, students rose up against the government just before the 1968 Olympics scheduled to be held in Mexico. They called for democracy and an end to the corrupt political system. They were brutally repressed in a massacre on October 2, 1968 in the Plaza de las Tres Culturas in the Tlatelolco section of Mexico City. Mexican politics would never be the same.

Solely in its foreign relations did Mexico maintain a revolutionary façade. Rejecting US pressures, it was the only country in Latin America that refused to sever diplomatic ties with socialist Cuba. Mexico adhered to the principle of non-intervention, primarily due to the long history of US intervention and territorial seizures in Mexico, arguing that no nation, however powerful, had the right to dictate what kind of government Cuba or any other country in the Americas could choose.

One day I went to the Cuban embassy in Mexico City. At the huge gate of the embassy I pushed the speaker button. A brusque attendant asked me over the intercom what I wanted and in my broken Spanish I tried to explain that I would like to speak to someone about the Cuban revolution and to discuss the possibility of visiting Cuba. I was told: "*Vayase!* Go away, no one is interested in talking to you." Rebuffed, it took me another four years to acquire a political précis that would earn me a visa to fly from Mexico City to Havana, Cuba.

In the summer of 1965, Senora Rosario's pension rather than the Cuban embassy proved to be the site where I enhanced my understanding of the real world. A couple of weeks after I arrived, a 30-year-old man from Ghana, Adinorty "Ed" Publampu, appeared at the pension. Very gregarious and personable, he had driven from Los Angeles, where he currently lived, to Mexico City to study social psychology under Eric Fromm, the radical social critic and psychoanalyst who blended the thought of Marx and Freud. Ed, as he was called, had left Ghana as a young man and signed up for the US army, becoming a paratrooper. In one of his jumps, he severely injured his back, was discharged, and received a disability pension from the army. He used this income, plus GI education monies, to study social psychology at the University of California, Los Angeles. Ed provided me with a piece of advice that has guided my travels ever since: "You can't focus on just what your ultimate destination is. A road trip is an experience in itself. It is to be taken in and enjoyed, it is part of life."

I had read some of Eric Fromm's writings at St. Norbert College and was impressed to meet someone who studied under him. When Ed returned to the pension in the evenings, we would talk about his sessions with Fromm. I managed to meet Fromm once, but did little more than shake his hand. Ed himself was a walking history book, recounting stories from the anti-colonial revolution in Ghana and describing the nationalistic, anti-imperialist policies of Ghana's first president, Kwane Nkrumah.

Towards the end of July, a young couple from southern California, Mary Helen and Tom Williams, came to spend a couple of weeks at Senora Rosario's place. About a half-year earlier they had returned to the United States from Cuzco, Peru where they had served in the Peace Corps for over two years as grade school teachers. An interesting, attractive couple, I took up with them, eagerly listening to their stories about what it was like to be in the Peace Corps. As members of one of the earlier contingents to go to Peru they had served under Peace Corps Country Director, Frank Mankowitz, a colorful personality from Hollywood who would go on to become a key advisor to Robert F. Kennedy, serving as his press secretary at the time of his assassination in June 1968.

I liked Tom a lot, but I soon developed a closer rapport with Mary Helen who was five years older than me. She, more than Tom, was willing to talk about life in the highlands of Peru: from the isolation that she felt as a foreigner surrounded by an indigenous culture, to the occasional joys that she experienced as people opened up and invited her to their fiestas and into their homes.

Mary Helen was easy to get along with and struck me as "the girl next door" with her brown hair, bright blue eyes and cheery personality. We began to go out more and more together, exploring the sights of Mexico City. The Anthropology Museum, opened the year before with large displays of the different Indian civilizations that had once dominated Mexico Valley and Mesoamerica, became one of our favorite haunts.

Then one day, she told me, "Tom will be leaving tomorrow for California and I'll be staying around for a few more days." We went out more frequently and on her last evening, we went to the Ballet Folklorico at the Bellas Artes Theater. It was a stunning event. I was awed by the dances and performances representing the different regions and cultures of Mexico.

Afterward, we went back to the pension and talked. Mary Helen became very sad and tears came to her eyes. I asked "What's wrong?" and slowly her story poured out. "Our marriage is breaking up. I'm pretty certain Tom is seeing a Mexican woman." I put my arm around her and we embraced and kissed as we sat on the corner of her bed. I had never slept with a woman, and from what I could gather, Mary Helen's only relationship had been with Tom. Neither of us felt the compulsion to go any further that night.

The next day, she flew back to Long Beach, California to sort things out at her parents' house. She invited me to come visit her. As fate would have it, Ed was driving back to Los Angeles in late August, about the time I had to return to the United States. I had always dreamed of visiting California, and I could hardly believe my luck. I had fallen for a girl from the Golden State.

The trip back with Ed was something else. We headed for Guadalajara, and then to a route along the Pacific coast. Ed had a very different sense of travel and life than I did. I believed travel was a question of getting from your starting point to your destination as quickly as possible. Don't waste any time. In part, this was bound up with my Catholic-instilled belief that life was limited, that we only had so much time to accomplish our goals in life before we faced eternity or the void. Ed's approach was the polar opposite. He was in no hurry to get back to Los Angeles. We stopped at local markets, fishing villages, or perhaps just to try out a local restaurant, any place that Ed found interesting on the road of life. Seeing my impatience, he told me more than once in different words: "You have to take it easy, look at all the wonders around us. We'll have plenty of time in Los Angeles."

I thought I would go berserk from impatience, but I was learning. One night, as we were getting closer to the border, we traveled through a series of mountain passes in the rain and thunder. The road was slick and we passed old dilapidated buses on hair pin turns that I thought would push us off the cliff into the canyons below. I had never been so terrified in my life, but Ed just kept on driving and chuckling as he told me stories of similar roads he had driven on in other parts of the world. Somehow we made it through the storm and a day or so later we arrived at his home in the San Fernando Valley where he lived with his American girlfriend.

I called Mary Helen as soon as I arrived. She came to Ed's place where we spent the night together in the same bed, kissing passionately while I laid on top of her. We were semi-naked, topless, and for the first time in my life, a woman wrapped her legs around me. I was surprised, not really knowing how people made love, but of course, I found it pleasurable, especially on my first warm summer night in California. The next day, she invited me to the cottage she had just rented in Seal Beach, a short block from the ocean. We slept together again, but went no further than the night before.

We became even closer as we took long walks out on the often fogged-in pier of Seal Beach. One day, we went to her parents' house that fronted one of the canals of Long Beach and I met her younger brother who was into Bob Dylan's music. I had listened to a couple of Dylan's early albums at college, but this was the first time I really began to get into his poetic songs and lyrics that spoke to the alienation of the Sixties generation. I developed a lifelong enchantment with Dylan's music.

At my suggestion, Mary Helen drove up the California coast to the Bay Area in her MG convertible. There I hooked up with my old high school friend, Jim Schmitt, who lived in Alameda and was bent on making his fortune in the construction industry. I became enamored with the Bay Area, especially driving over all the bridges that spanned the Bay. We visited Sproul Plaza at the University of California Berkeley where the year before Mario Savio had shaken the university and the world by setting off the Free Speech Movement. We then went to Sausalito, where a friend of Mary Helen's lived on a houseboat. All in all, I found the Bay Area spectacular, a worldly paradise where I determined I would live someday.

After that we returned to Seal Beach. On the last night before I headed off for graduate school in Cleveland, we made love for the first time. She allowed me to slip down her underpants, and I touched her sex with my member. It was incredibly warm. I'll never forget the heat of her sex at that moment as I slipped into her. I felt transformed. It was an intense sensation that I knew I'd never forget as long as I lived.

The next day we drove to Las Vegas and spent the night there, making love many times. I never wanted to stop experiencing the warmth of her sex. In the morning, we sadly parted ways as she dropped me off on Interstate Highway 15 and I began to hitchhike across the desert, on my way back to the Midwest and graduate school. It had been an amazing summer odyssey. Like the desert sands, my whole life seemed to shimmer in front of me.

6. Life in Cleveland's Ivory Tower

"Do stuff. Be clenched, curious. Not waiting for inspiration's shove or society's kiss on your forehead. Pay attention. It's all about paying attention. Attention is vitality. It connects you with others. It makes you eager. Stay eager."
–Susan Sontag, Vassar College Commencement Speech, 2003

On March 8, 1965 President Johnson dispatched 3,500 Marines to South Vietnam, marking the start of the US ground war. By the end of the year almost 200,000 soldiers were fighting in the biggest land war since the Korean conflict. Ho Chi Minh, the leader of North Vietnam said, if the Americans "want to make war for 20 years then we shall make war for 20 years."

As I returned from my trip to Mexico, the gathering war in Vietnam hung like an ominous cloud over the country. I had been looking forward to graduate school at Western Reserve University in Cleveland. The challenge of seminars, higher level studies and mingling with like-minded students all seemed appealing. But after a few months I became disillusioned with the university and the city. Cleveland had none of the charm or cosmopolitan flair of Mexico City. Located on the eastern side of the city, the university was a classic ivory tower, part of a larger academic complex that included the Case Institute of Technology. (Case would merge with Western Reserve in 1967 to become Case Western Reserve University.) To the west of the university lay the predominantly poor African-American part of the city, to the southeast Shaker Heights, one of the richest suburbs in America. A mile or so to the north was Lake Erie, the most polluted of the Great Lakes. A few years before I arrived, fires had ignited on the water due to the heavy oils and refuse that floated on the surface.

After Sputnik was launched by the Soviet Union in 1957, Congress not only invested in science but also began funding language and regional studies programs at universities around the country, hoping to create an intelligentsia of "international experts" to meet the perceived threat of Communism. After the triumph of the Cuban revolution and the spread of guerrilla movements, even more money was allocated to Latin American studies and I received a National Defense Education Act (NDEA) Fellowship for my doctoral studies at Western Reserve University.

I was certainly aware of the origins of my funding but my consciousness, nourished by the emergent left in the United States, had already advanced to the point where I had no qualms about taking funds from questionable sources as long as I was clear about my own objectives. This was the first time, but not the last, that I would procure money from governmental sources in order to broaden my experiences and foster a critical understanding of the US role in the world at large.

The Latin American studies program at Western Reserve was staffed by one Latin American history professor, Robert Randall, my advisor. The only other professor who could be considered a Latin Americanist was a lecturer on Mesoamerican archeology. The first semester, I took a course in colonial Latin American history from Randall and a seminar to help me prepare for writing my master's thesis. In addition, I had two elective courses—classical Greek history and the diplomatic history of Europe from 1919 to 1939. The last class, an evening seminar, was particularly excruciating as I had an elderly woman professor who usually caused most of the class to nod off about half way through the two-hour session.

My romance with Mary Helen continued. Those were the days of expensive telephone rates, so we both wound up with hefty phone bills each month. We got together three times during the year, twice I flew to California and once she came to Cleveland. Of course, we found the days at her pad in Seal Beach more enjoyable. Her visit to Cleveland in the middle of winter was a largely dreary one. The main highlights I remember were attending a performance of the Cleveland Symphony orchestra with her and trying deep fried frog legs for the first time at a restaurant.

Mary Helen, five years older than me, was more a girl of the fifties than the sixties. She wanted a traditional relationship, and did not really accept the idea of "free love" that was fast becoming the norm among the generation of the sixties. "Darling" with Julie Christie, was one of her favorite movies because Christie looked for love "in all the wrong places" and wound up alone and alienated at the end of the movie. But in spite of these differences and problems, Mary Helen and I were very much in love and couldn't imagine our lives without each other.

Mary Helen was very concerned about getting pregnant. In addition to using birth control I also practiced withdrawal before I came. Perhaps it was frustrating, but it also taught me how to control my desires, and this was important in all my subsequent relationships. I am forever indebted to her for sensitizing me to understanding what is going on in a woman's head as well as her body.

I came to realize early on in our relationship that Mary Helen had a neurosis about sex. After making love she would often spend a long time in the bathroom with the faucet running. I found out that she was frantically scrubbing her hands, trying to wipe off the invisible stains she felt were there because of what she had done. We talked about it, but there was no real resolution. I even wrote a letter about it to my amateur psychologist friend, Adintorty "Ed" Publampu. It was an embarrassing mistake on my part as Ed went over to her house one evening when she was alone and tried to talk to her in very intimate terms about having sex, allegedly to find a "cure" for her. Mary Helen called me and said: "Roger, how could you do this to me, it was very upsetting." I said, "I'm really sorry, I made a terrible mistake." I learned to respect the privacy of my conversations with women who would confide in me; particularly I leaned not to talk to other men about them.

Politically in Cleveland, I hooked up with the local SDS chapter and became involved in its tutorial outreach program to the Black community. I was assigned to work with a fifth grader, Michael, who lived with his mother in a fairly nice house, certainly not the stereotype of an impoverished African-American home. His mother and mine had a lot in common, as both recognized the importance of education for their children to move up in life. I worked with Michael on math, reading and spelling, and we would take in extracurricular events, such as a French comedy by Molière (that I probably got more out of than Michael).

Religion, philosophy and my own mortality remained obsessions for me. I occasionally attended the Unitarian Church. Having a very liberal creed, it required no belief in the divinity of Christ and you could even get away without believing in God. For me, it was a transition, as I needed something to do on the Sabbath after twenty years of a habitual Sunday mass. The preacher at the Unitarian church often gave a good talk on politics or an important social issue facing Cleveland or the world. Someone later told me that it is not at all uncommon for ex-Catholics to make a stopover at the Unitarian church on their way to a new system of beliefs. My sister Ann, about a decade later, also went from Catholicism to the Unitarian Church, later developing her own spiritualist view of the world that Contrasted with my atheism.

The war in Vietnam moved onto center stage in US politics. "Search and destroy" missions began as US troops under General William Westmoreland attempted to root out the Vietcong guerillas in the countryside. Secretary of Defense Robert McNamara began admitting that US casualties would reach a thousand per month. In response, the anti-war movement gathered momentum across the United States, and I participated in my first anti-war demonstration in Cleveland in October 1965.

Draft conscription was stepped up to meet the ever-increasing demand for troops and by early 1966, the country was increasingly polarized by the war. Senator William Fulbright held nationally televised hearings, and Senator Wayne Morse, a harsh critic of the war, tried to repeal the Bay of Tonkin resolution that had first authorized US military action in Vietnam. Senator Robert F. Kennedy publicly broke with Lyndon Johnson over the bombing of North Vietnam.

By the spring of 1966, I was fed up with Case Western and the city of Cleveland. My courses provided no inspiration and the war in Vietnam pulled my mind in other directions, including the apprehension that my draft board in Watertown, Wisconsin would cancel my student deferment. I swore I would never be inducted into the military, and thanks in part to Mary Helen, I opted to sign up for the Peace Corps. Aside from giving me a new deferment, it would enable me to get out of academia and into a "real world" experience. While the Peace Corps was in some ways just one more US government program designed to fight communism, it still had some of the allure and idealism of the Kennedy years.

In my application I wrote that I wanted to be a Peace Corps Volunteer in Chile. The country's politics, its strong leftist parties, militant trade unions, and democratic tradition had captivated my attention. But, alas, I was assigned to Peru, quite an irony given that Mary Helen had served as a volunteer in the same country.

After being accepted, I wrote to Senator Gaylord Nelson of Wisconsin and Senator Robert F. Kennedy, asking them if they could possibly find a way for me to use the three remaining years of my fellowship when I returned from the Peace Corps. Nelson wrote back saying his office could find no loophole that would allow me to tap into the fellowship later on.

Kennedy wrote a very different response that caught me by surprise.

He said that anyone who truly wanted to serve his country and help other people abroad "should not expect to maintain their privileges." I, of course, don't know if Kennedy himself drafted the letter, but the idealism that was manifest in it was striking. I became an ardent Kennedy supporter for the presidency even though Senator Eugene McCarthy was the first anti-war presidential candidate. Kennedy struck me as having a martyr's complex after his brother's assassination. He was on a mission to profoundly shake the world and if necessary, give up his own life in the process. To this day, I believe that Robert F Kennedy's assassination in June 1968 deprived the United States of one of its greatest and most volatile leaders.

Peace Corps training was to start in the fall of 1966, so I was off to Mexico City for the summer again, this time to gather research data for my Master's thesis. Making one of the more absurd decisions in my life, I decided to do my thesis on Mexico City's municipal government under the Spaniards in the sixteenth century. I had become somewhat of a historical purist, believing that in order to understand a nation's politics and culture one had to study its very origins. The only pleasant aspect of researching this obscure topic was that all the records of the "*cabildo*," the municipal government of Mexico City, were located in the archives of the Anthropology Museum in Chapultepec Park. It was refreshing to walk every morning through the park to the Museum that was barely two years old and to take my seat in an ornate room with all the research facilities one could wish for. If I needed a break, I would wonder through the Museum itself, going to the open-air restaurant or viewing the different displays of the pre-conquest Indian civilizations.

Mary Helen came to Mexico City with me and, not wanting to awaken the ghost of her past relationship with her now ex-husband Tom, we stayed at a different pension in the same neighborhood. John Patterson, a member of the Malcontents at St. Norbert College, came to stay at my new pension, intent on learning Spanish. Being a tall handsome former basketball player from St. Norbert's, it seemed like all the girls who wandered by the pension wanted to jump his bones. He soon became frightened by all the female attention and was also overwhelmed by culture shock in Mexico City. He fled back to Wisconsin after a couple of weeks. Years later, I found out that he was gay, and tragically, he died of AIDS in the 1980s.

Mark Braford, my roommate at Western Reserve also came down with his girlfriend, Susan. One evening, Mark, Susan and Mary Helen came stomping through Chapultepec park in the middle of a rain storm to pick me up at the end of a long day at the museum. They laughed at my over-zealous habits of spending ten-hour days in the archives, as I often turned down their invitations to go out on the town. I was still imbued with the Anglo-Saxon work ethic, believing that one had to focus single mindedly to be a "success" in life. My two years as a Peace Corps volunteer living in an Andean village would soften some of the rigid edges of this American gringo. But even with my compulsion to overwork, I had great fun that summer. Mary Helen and I had a very romantic week in Acapulco. Although overrun by tourists, we enjoyed the beaches, the simple cottage we had, and the cuisine.

7. Paradoxes of a Peace Corps Volunteer

"Warfare is a means and not an end. Warfare is a tool of revolutionaries. The important thing is the revolution! The important thing is the revolutionary cause, revolutionary ideas, revolutionary objectives, revolutionary sentiments, revolutionary virtues!"
—Fidel Castro, Speech at Che Guevara's memorial service, 1967

Along with 30 other Peace Corps volunteers, I stood in the plaza of Ayacucho, Peru as rain clouds gathered in the Andean sky on a Saturday morning in early February, 1967. We were receiving the keys to the city from the mayor. Nearby, a group of university militants began to assemble and chant, Yanqui, Go Home" and *"Yanquis, fuera de Vietnam."* Minutes later, we dispersed as the demonstrators began pelting us with pebbles and rotting oranges. Manuel Rubén Abimael Guzmán, the future leader of the Maoist Shining Path guerrillas and a professor at the local university, numbered among the protest organizers.

I had arrived in Ayacucho the day before, after an eight-hour bus trip from the Mantaro Valley where I worked as a Peace Corps volunteer. I had come to the old colonial city to participate in a month-long Peace Corps training course on cooperatives. These were conflictive times in the Andes, not just in Ayacucho, but also in Bolivia to the south where Che Guevara was fighting with a band of guerrillas.

My two years in the Peace Corps were riddled with paradoxes. While formally working for the US government, I sympathized with the anti-

American demonstrators in Ayacucho and supported the revolutionary movements epitomized by Che Guevara. I had been thrust into a quandary faced by many leftists in the 1960s—how to engage in public service while opposing the US empire.

The Peace Corps at its inception seemed to represent the best progressive tradition in the United States, having a spirit of humanitarian internationalism marked by a concern for the downtrodden and exploited of the world. Tapping into the emerging idealism on US campuses, John F. Kennedy, as a presidential candidate, first broached the idea of the Peace Corps in October 1960 with students at the University of Michigan, Ann Arbor. Once in office, Kennedy moved quickly to set up the Peace Corps and told an early gathering of the organization's new staff, "The Peace Corps, it seems to me, gives us the opportunity to emphasize a very different part of our American character… and that is the idealistic sense of purpose."

I entered the Peace Corps at its zenith in 1966. To meet the ever-increasing demand for volunteers abroad, the Peace Corps' ranks surged from 10,000 in 1964 to 15,000 in 1966 serving in 55 countries. At home, the Peace Corps' allure grew with more than 42,000 Americans applying each year from 1964 to 1966, double the number that submitted applications during its first full year of existence in 1962.

The Vietnam War in 1966 led to increasingly vehement protests and questions over the direction of US foreign policy. But when I joined the Peace Corps, many in the United States still saw the Peace Corps as an international counterpart to the progressive struggle at home. Martin Luther King's march on Washington in August 1963, the Freedom Summer in Mississippi in 1964, and the passage of the Civil Rights Acts of 1964 and 1965—these all nourished the idealism that compelled many of us to enter the Peace Corps.

To be sure, signs of discontent with US policy among volunteers were already appearing as I signed up. In Chile in 1965, volunteers drafted a letter opposing the Vietnam War. And in the Dominican Republic during the US invasion in 1965, Peace Corps volunteers assisted wounded Dominicans who resisted the intervention and then wrote a letter of protest that was waylaid by the Peace Corps staff. On joining the Corps, I saw myself as part of this dissident movement and intended to manifest my opposition to the war in Vietnam and US foreign policy whenever the opportunity presented itself.

For me, joining the Peace Corps was an existential act, a rebellion against a traditional career while searching for meaningful work with those who did not have the same advantages that I did to rise above my underprivileged background. This was after all the 1960s, when many of us dreamed that a new world was possible, one in which we could live out our ideals in our life's work.

In November 1966, I left New York City for Peru with 20 other Peace Corps volunteers. We departed from the JFK airport just before sunset and the next morning we flew over the spectacular snow-capped Andean mountains before touching down in Lima. As I disembarked, I eagerly looked forward to my life in a strange new land. But I also felt a sense of loss as I abandoned my friends and family. To a 22-year-old, two years seemed an eternity, far different from my summer jaunts to Mexico City.

It was amazing to arrive in Lima with its colonial edifices and church-es set among modern office buildings, and with "*barriadas*," or impov-erished communities, ringing the outskirts of the capital city. But I had little time to explore the city. We were put up in a small two-star hotel for three days to receive our assignments and our in-country orientation along with $100 to help us settle into our communities. One member of our group promptly took his hundred dollar bill and spent it at a brothel in Callao, Lima's main port known for its red light district. I guess it was his way of "settling in."

I was assigned to the community of Matahuasi to help set up a dairy cooperative. Matahuasi is in the Mantaro Valley, over 10,000 feet above sea level—a seven-hour drive by car into the central highlands. It had a population of about 2,500. Considered a bread basket for Lima, the Mantaro Valley produced staple foods and vegetables, particularly pota-toes, the tuber crop that pre-colonial Peru gave to the world.

My training for this assignment was a joke. In September 1966, the volunteers in my group reported to a camp on a small lake just outside of Kansas City, Missouri. The University of Missouri had a contract to train volunteers for Peru, but as I quickly found out, the university had no prior experience in Latin American affairs or in training volunteers, except for a group that had inaugurated the camp two months earlier and left for Peru just as we arrived.

Most prior training programs for Peru had been run out of Puerto Rico or Cornell University in Ithaca, New York. The latter had a strong Latin American Studies program with a focus on Peru, but precisely be-cause of the onslaught of new volunteers in the mid-1960s, these training sites were overloaded, and for some reason that I could never discern, the University of Missouri won the contract for the new Peace Corps train-ing program. We did have intensive language training classes every day for two months, and informative discussions about Peruvian culture and politics with two former volunteers who had served in Peru. But that was about it in terms of serious preparation for our work abroad.

Bernie Kleinman, a pleasant but somewhat eccentric professor of psychology from the University of Missouri, was a key figure in our program. He was designated to weed out the volunteers who did not have the psychological profile deemed necessary to make the transition to living in a foreign country. Kleinman himself had no experience in Latin America.

His other assignment was to teach us how to engage the "native" peoples. I remember he had some half-baked idea that he tried to explain on the black board on which he drew two circles, one representing the volunteer, and the other the "local" who we were to interact with. The goal of the volunteer was to engage the local, listen to his or her feedback, and if the volunteer was successful, the two circles would intersect. The more the circles intersected, the more successful the volunteer.

Mary Helen, who had been a volunteer in Peru, came to Kansas City during the last week of October, providing me with more insights into the country than the entire two month training program. After our summer together in Mexico, Mary Helen had returned to Long Beach to work as a substitute teacher so we would have more flexibility in seeing each other as I entered the Peace Corps. At the camp, we joked about Kleinman's lectures on how to get along with the natives. We also got a chuckle over how the volunteers had to demonstrate their physical preparedness for Peru by remaining afloat in the camp's artificial lake for an hour. One story that probably did more to help me prepare for Peru than all of Bernie's lectures was Mary Helen's recounting of her dinner with a local Quechua Indian leader. As the guest of honor, she got an eyeball in her beef soup. A good Peace Corps volunteer, she pretended to be pleased with her special serving, but she quickly found a pretext to head for the toilet and disposed of the eyeball tucked in her handbag.

In spite of the fact that we both wanted different things out of the relationship, Mary Helen and I agreed in Kansas City that she would come to Peru in June 1967 after the school year ended. She wanted to get married at some point in the near future, but I just couldn't see myself committing to a permanent relationship with anyone at that point in my life. I probably should have broken up with her, but I couldn't bear the thought of never seeing her again. She was my first love, and I truly enjoyed her sparkling and cheerful personality. In Peru, we believed we could sort things out.

Aside from the surreal and dysfunctional training program in Missouri, there was a certain logic behind the Peace Corps decision to send volunteers to the highlands of Peru to live in peasant communities. At Cornell University, a group of anthropologists had been studying Peru's Andean indigenous cultures since the late 1940s. In the mid-1950s, they bought a hacienda in the community of Vicos, where many of the Indians had worked as 20th century serfs. A 1962 CBS documentary narrated by Walter Cronkite showed how the Vicos hacienda, under the supervision of Cornell anthropologists, had been turned over to the peasants who now tilled their own lands and organized their own communal governing councils.

When the Peace Corps first began to arrive in Peru, Cornell University signed a three-year contract to evaluate the performance of the volunteers who worked in Vicos and other highland communities. Only after I left the Peace Corps did I discover this study, which among other things, described how three volunteers working at the university in Ayacucho had been driven out by militant students in 1963, four years before I arrived in the city as part of the Peace Corps cooperative training program.

To get to the Mantaro Valley, the Peace Corps gave me a train ticket from Lima to Huancayo, the commercial hub of the valley. I boarded the train at eight in the morning and after about five hours, we reached Ticlio Pass, 15,700 feet above sea level, and the highest point traversed by any train in the world. I felt light-headed as I gazed out the train window at the magnificent snow-capped peaks surrounding the pass. It was astounding. I was literally and figuratively on top of the world.

I felt slightly faint due to lack of oxygen at the high altitude, but I was better off than Scott, another volunteer who was on the train with me. He came down with "*soroche*," or mountain sickness with a severe migraine and nausea. I later found out that one of the best remedies for soroche is an indigenous tea brewed with the leaves of the coca plant. But Scott had to content himself with a more conventional remedy: The train carried an oxygen tank on board and his symptoms began to disappear once he inhaled deeply through a facemask attached to the tank.

After Ticlio Pass we descended into the bleak mining town of La Oroya at 12,000 ft. Poor Indian vendors approached the train trying to sell us their wares and prepared foodstuffs. Scott and his wife got off there to take an hour-long bus ride to Cerro de Pasco, another mining community where they would live. The town bore the name of the giant foreign corporation that owned the mines, as well as the surrounding haciendas.

The agricultural and grazing lands of the area had been ruined when a mining smelter began operating in La Oroya in 1922, belching out deadly fumes and dumping contaminated filings in the streams and rivers. The Cerro de Pasco Corporation then bought up the polluted lands, curtailed some of the more harmful emissions and introduced large flocks of sheep and cattle to graze the hills, now tended by some of the same Indians who had once owned the land.

As the train pulled out of La Oroya, I breathed a sigh of relief and hoped the surroundings would become more hospitable as we descended into the Mantaro Valley. I was not disappointed. It was the beginning of the growing season in the valley with frequent rains that stretched from November to April. The peasants were already tilling their lands with oxen and an occasional tractor I glimpsed from the train's window. As I soon found out, the valley has an exceptionally mild climate with temperatures rarely dropping below freezing, even during the winter months from May to July. The remaining months from August to October are the dry season, with strong breezes and lots of sun.

It took about five more hours to arrive in Huancayo where the train tracks ended. We actually passed through Matahuasi, 27 kilometers before Huancayo, but I could not get off because our train did not have a scheduled stop in the small community. I reached Huancayo as the sun was setting, exhausted but excited. Edward Dew, the regional director of the Peace Corps, met me at the train station. He was a lanky, good-natured guy, who was also a student of Andean society and writing his Ph.D. thesis, "The Politics of the Altiplano," which was published soon after.

Dew took me to the Olympia restaurant for dinner, where I met a half-dozen other volunteers who worked at different sites in the city and the valley. Olympia was the best restaurant in Huancayo with great meals for a dollar or two. It was owned and run by a short mestizo man and his Indian wife who I would soon find out had two wastrel sons who squandered the family money on race cars. The restaurant was a center of local and foreign intrigue, and it was here that I would later run into a CIA agent returning from the hunt for Che Guevara in Bolivia.

The next day, Ed Dew drove me to Matahuasi with my few possessions, mainly books and a shortwave radio. There I met the mayor of the town who gave me the keys to a one-room adobe dwelling that fronted the town's modest plaza. My source of water was a faucet on the corner of the plaza, and for toilet facilities I would piss in the weeds in back of my dwelling. For more serious needs, I used the open air outhouse set about 25 paces back from another corner of the plaza. It was next to a church that was also "open air" because it had a collapsed roof. Matahuasi had no electricity because of a malfunctioning generator. I used most of my $100 settling-in allowance to buy a Coleman lantern and stove.

I received only $78 per month from the Peace Corps to cover my living expenses but life was so simple in Matahuasi that I managed to live within my budget, even given an occasional trip into Huancayo for a movie or a meal at the Olympia restaurant. I didn't mind the long nights with my lantern, as I had brought with me a large personal library of books that I had not been able to read during my college years.

Matahuasi and the central valley were distinctive from the rest of the Peruvian highlands. Just about everyone I met spoke Spanish and although the people were overwhelmingly of Indian extraction, the men had by and large adopted the westernized dress and customs of the mestizo world. They were descendants of the Huanca Indians who had long resisted Inca rule and then collaborated with the Spaniards to overthrow the Incas. This legacy made the Huancas somewhat ambivalent about their identity. I'll never forget the time a man with strong Indian features and a deep brown skin came up to me in Huancayo and said, "The United States did it right, you wiped out the inferior races in the Indian wars."

Most peasants in Matahuasi had two or three hectares, with some of the more well-to-do owning five hectares or more. There were no haciendas in Matahuasi, or for that matter, in most of the valley except for the steep slopes of the mountains and the plateau that ringed the valley. The absence of haciendas on the rich lands of the valley floor is in part attributable to the independent spirit of the Indians who resisted the Spanish seizure of their lands and labor. The opening in Cerro de Pasco of the La Oroya smelter also worked against land concentration in the Mantaro valley. The mine workers needed staple grains and produce, which stimulated commercial peasant farming in the Mantaro Valley because it was not blanketed by the toxic fumes of La Oroya. Huancayo grew as an industrial-commercial center, producing clothing and light manufactured goods for the mines.

While my specific task was to help set up cooperatives in Matahuasi, I had been formally assigned as a Community Development volunteer. Frank Mankiewicz, the first national director of the Peace Corps in Peru, had come up with the concept of community development based on his work as a lawyer and activist with the NAACP and farm workers in Southern California. Drawing on the community organizing principles of Saul Alinsky (a radical with roots in the 1930s who advocated militant, nonviolent organizing and criticized liberals for being too passive), Mankiewicz believed that volunteers in their communities could help spark significant change by being witnesses to what was happening and by weighing in on the side of those who were challenging the "rigid, class-ridden, racially tinged social structure" of the Andes. This was the most radical current in the Peace Corps. Mankiewicz and a handful of others in the Peace Corps leadership saw their mission as not all that different from revolutionaries who were trying to overturn the oppressive institutions of Latin America. As Alinsky once said, "We're talking about revolution, not revelation."

Like much of the Peruvian highlands, Matahuasi and the Mantaro Valley in the 1960s served as a social and political laboratory, an arena where anthropologists and social theorists along with Peruvian politicians, guerrilla movements and international development agencies sought to win the hearts and minds of the people. Within a week of my arrival, a Peruvian agronomist came and knocked on my door to tell me that in a month he would be opening up a governmental agrarian extension office in Matahuasi called SIPA, the Information and Agrarian Promotion Agency. SIPA offices had already been set up in other parts of highland Peru, providing agricultural advice and assistance to peasant communities. The agronomist had talked with Ed Dew in Huancayo and they had both agreed that it would be ideal if I could work with the new Matahuasi office, especially since one of its tasks was to found an agricultural cooperative.

I soon learned that the agrarian extension program was heavily funded by the US Agency for International Development (USAID). This was part of a broader US thrust in Peru in the 1960s aimed at promoting development and change, particularly in the Andean highlands, to counteract the influence of guerrilla and revolutionary movements.

I now faced the dilemma that many leftists articulated in the 1960s and subsequent decades—whether to support reform or revolution. But this struck me as a false dichotomy. Did one need to ignore all reform efforts, sitting around and waiting for the true revolution to arrive? Rather than picking one path or the other, I opted for both. While participating in the reform initiatives in Matahuasi, I invoked the spirit of Alinsky and Mankiewicz. In my own modest way I tried to help people better their daily lives while simultaneously making it clear that I identified with those who wanted to overturn the dominant order.

Events in South America in the late 1960s appeared to reinforce the view that reform could lead, if not to revolution, at least to a deepening of a radical political process. When Fernando Belaunde Terry was elected president of Peru in 1963, he positioned himself between the oligarchy that had historically ruled the country and the more leftist political forces calling for deep-rooted changes. Backed by the United States, Belaunde launched a token agrarian reform program while concentrating government spending on big ticket developmental projects, such as highways and dams for hydroelectric power and irrigation. Some new funding went to rural schools and housing projects in Lima, but support for these proved limited as the US was constantly withholding aid while trying to bludgeon the Peruvian government into granting concessions to Standard Oil to exploit new oil fields.

When Belaunde finally ceded to these pressures in 1968, and tried to hide part of the agreement with Standard Oil from the public, the military stepped in and took power. This happened in October, the month after I left the Peace Corps. The popular sectors, increasingly frustrated by the divergence between Belaunde's rhetoric and his actual social reforms, did nothing to defend the government. The new government led by a populist military figure, General Juan Velasco, expropriated most of the country's haciendas and moved against US petroleum and mining interests.

Beyond ruminating about reform and revolution in Matahuasi, I had more mundane concerns, such as how to communicate at the simplest level with the villagers. Even though I had learned some Spanish during summers in Mexico and two months of Peace Corps training, it took me almost half-a-year in Peru before I felt I could communicate comfortably in my new language.

The first friends I made were the young men who would gather at the only "*tienda*" (store) that fronted on the plaza to drink beer in the evenings. True to their reputation, Matahuasians were prone to find any excuse to declare any given day a personal fiesta. The custom was for someone to buy a liter bottle of beer and to pass it around a circle along with a four-ounce glass that everyone chugged from until the bottle was empty. Then someone would immediately order up another bottle. I could never buy a bottle and began to think that they just wanted to see the young gringo get drunk. But then I realized they were competing to see who could be the "*patron*" of a roaring good time.

These gatherings, while exposing me to more Spanish, also pointed out the limits of my new idiom. In one conversation, I related that I had eaten "*trucha*," or trout the night before. Everyone howled with laughter for the longest time and I had no idea what was going on. Finally, someone explained that because I had not learned how to roll my r's in Spanish, the word had come out as "*chucha*," the word for a woman's cunt. I had said that I had eaten cunt the night before. I didn't live that one down for the remainder of my days in Matahuasi.

Matahuasi was a sprawling community with a few cobblestone streets and many more dirt covered walks and roadways. Most of the people walked, come rain or shine, and an occasional motored vehicle rumbled through the village. I would often take long walks in Matahuasi and the surrounding countryside, just to see how people lived and worked. Most of the peasants I met in the fields would nod to me or say "*Hola*" but then continue with their work, not knowing quite how to deal with this strange young man from a faraway country.

It was during one of these long walks that I met Tito Chuquin who lived three kilometers up the road in San Lorenzo, a village less than half the size of Matahuasi. Only three years older than me, Tito had just been elected as the only Socialist mayor in the Mantaro Valley. We soon became the best of friends. Short of stature with fiery eyes, he had an ironic sense of humor and a quick mind. It was through Tito that I learned a great deal about the politics of the valley and the recent history of the left.

According to Tito, in June 1965, the year before I came to Matahuasi, a couple dozen guerrillas had begun operating in the Andamarca River basin, about 50 kilometers northeast of the Mantaro Valley. Led by Guillermo Lobaton of the Left Revolutionary Movement (MIR), they seized explosives and munitions at a mine, took over a couple of haciendas, captured a military outpost and ambushed an army detachment sent to pursue them, killing seven soldiers.

In the valley, Tito helped circulate flyers about this early spate of successful activities by the guerrillas. Unfortunately, this turned out to be the highpoint of the guerrilla campaign. The Peruvian army, under the guidance of US counterinsurgency advisers, launched a major offensive against Lobaton's guerrillas. While the guerrillas were forced to retreat deeper into the nearby jungle inhabited by the semi-aboriginal Campa Indians, the Peruvian air force began to napalm the Campas, killing hundreds according to American missionaries. US advisers then set up a base in the region and coordinated a relentless pursuit of the guerrillas. By the first week of January 1966, the guerrillas were decimated, and Lobaton was captured and killed.

What happened in the Andamarca region was repeated in the La Convencion Valley in the Department of Cuzco where the MIR also went into action in mid-1965. Headed up by Luis de la Puente, the main leader of the MIR who had received training in Cuba, this band was encircled after barely a month and Puente died in combat.

An older guerrilla organization, the National Liberation Army (ELN), decided to coordinate its activities with the MIR. In September 1965, they seized the largest hacienda in the Department of Ayacucho, and executed its owners, the Carillo brothers who were notorious for abusing the peasants who worked on their lands. The Peruvian army, preoccupied on the other two guerrilla fronts, waited until early December to go after the ELN. In a couple of weeks they captured and executed the ELN leadership, effectively eliminating the band of guerrillas.

When I arrived in the Mantaro Valley in late 1966, rumors still circulated of guerrillas operating in the nearby mountains and the jungle, but during my stay in Matahuasi there were never any confirmed reports of guerrilla actions. They had been wiped out. These guerrilla movements in Peru in the mid-1960s were part of the "*foco*" theory of guerrilla warfare that flourished throughout Latin America at the time. Inspired by the Cuban revolution, the foco activists believed that a small band of brave spirits could inspire others to take up arms and mobilize the populace against the repressive regimes of the continent.

As Luis de la Puente wrote before he went into battle in the Peruvian highlands, "the guerrillas act as catalysts of the social outburst, seed for the rebel army, instruments of propaganda and organization, as well as ideological and military schools." We now know they failed, not only in Peru but throughout Latin America. But for me and others, these guerrillas were truly heroic figures. To this day they remain tragic utopians whose only failing was to dream of a continental revolution sparked by a cadre of idealists.

8. Gringo in the Andes

"Life isn't about finding yourself. Life is about creating yourself."
–George Bernard Shaw

My years in Peru, 1966-68, were riveted with upheaval in the world at large. I listened to my shortwave at night, getting news of the ever deepening conflagration in Vietnam and the rise of the anti-war movement. I had come to Latin America, fascinated by the revolutionary movements, but with the race riots in 159 US cities and the "long hot summer" of 1967, it looked as if the United States might go up in revolutionary flames. In Detroit the urban upheaval was suppressed by paratroopers of the 82nd Airborne Division with tanks and machine guns.

At the same time, San Francisco, California with its "summer of love," seemed to presage a very different future as the youth of my age went to the Haight-Asbury near Golden Gate Park with "flowers in their hair." In Peru, I also found myself caught up in history as I experienced the wrath of the early recruits of the Shining Path guerrillas and encountered a CIA agent in Huancayo who participated in the hunt for Che Guevara.

More mundane issues predominated for me as word got out in November 1966, that a cooperative might be formed in Matahuasi. Alejandro Meza, a peasant with about eight hectares in an adjunct hamlet of Matahuasi, came to see me, proudly telling me that he had been to Wisconsin the year before, thanks to a travel grant from USAID. I was, of course, astounded to meet someone ten thousand feet above sea level in the Andes who had recently been to my home state.

Lighthearted and good-natured, Alejandro owned a John Deere tractor, one of about a dozen in the community, that he used to cultivate his neighbors' land as well as his own. I never identified with him politically as I did later on with Tito Chuquin, but he was a dedicated, hardworking man who wanted the best for his family and the community. We began colluding immediately about how we would go about setting up a cooperative.

Aside from Alejandro and the community leaders we recruited, a major force behind the cooperative would prove to be Lionel Gomez, the agronomist who headed up the newly opened SIPA office in Matahuasi. Lionel, a charming man of upper middle class origins, relished his superior professional position, although he was willing to roll up his sleeves and work with the Matahuasians to get the cooperative going. He lived in one of the well-to-do barrios in Huancayo with his wife and four-year-old son, commuting the 27 kilometers to Matahuasi.

As I would soon find out, the real control center for our activities was the regional SIPA office in Huancayo where Lionel would usually go in the morning before coming to Matahuasi. It was here that the idea for a dairy cooperative was originally hatched. Backed by international aid agencies, Lionel's bosses in Huancayo, after I left, would secure foreign assistance to set up the valley's first milk processing plant that would be linked to the cooperative.

As the planning for the cooperative was getting off the ground in Matahuasi, I was sent to Ayacucho for the Peace Corps cooperative training program. Our face-off with the angry anti-American demonstrators in the plaza in early February of 1967, proved to be predictive of what was to come in Ayacucho. The Peace Corps coordinator for all cooperative activities in Peru was Aquiles Lanao, a native of Ayacucho. A charismatic rotund man with a booming voice, he brought the volunteers to his hometown because he wanted his fellow citizens to reap the benefits of the Peace Corps expense accounts. The delegation needed housing and I swear, all of Aquiles' aunts, uncles and cousins put up at least one volunteer in their homes. When we didn't eat at our residences, we were given meal ticket discounts at a restaurant favored by Aquiles. Meeting rooms for our training sessions were also rented from his friends. Everyone, including the volunteers, enjoyed Aquiles' magnanimous and vibrant personality. But in his quest to be a patron in his home town, he was out of touch with the growing radicalism of the university students at the National University of Huamanga in Ayacucho.

The students experienced an initial radicalization as a result of protests that erupted when a military coup took place in July 1962, toppling

Peru's elected government. The protests were brutally repressed and a number of students were allegedly killed, although there was never an official report on what happened. The US government had no direct hand in the coup, but the repression nurtured a latent anti-American sentiment at the university.

Several months later, three Peace Corps volunteers were sent to teach at the university. In October 1963, one of the women volunteers struck a female student on the butt for allegedly misbehaving in class. In response, the student federation convened a student assembly and voted overwhelmingly to call for the expulsion of the Peace Corps. The volunteers were forced to resign their university positions.

Another indication of the political climate at the university could be seen in its faculty.

Manuel Rubén Abimael Guzmán, the future leader of the Shining Path, arrived in Ayacucho in 1962, to take up the post of philosophy professor at the university. Together with the rector of the university, an anthropologist, he began organizing students and set up a university program that worked in the surrounding impoverished Indian communities. A member of the Peruvian Communist party, Guzman sided with the Maoist faction when the party split and in 1965, he visited China. He refused to have anything to do with the Cuban-backed foco guerrilla movements of the mid-1960s because they enjoyed the support of Cuba and the Soviet Union. Instead, Guzman began advocating a peasant-led revolution based on the Maoist model of a long war from the countryside that marched on the cities. In the 1970s, Guzman, under the nom de guerre Comrade Gonzalo, founded Shining Path and launched a vicious and bloody guerrilla insurgency that started in the Ayacucho region.

This was the historic brew into which Aquiles Lanao dropped about thirty Peace Corps volunteers in February 1967. After our first encounter in the plaza with students throwing pebbles and oranges at us, Aquiles intoned, "Just ignore them, they are only having fun as students will."

One of the Peace Corps volunteers from Texas didn't follow that advice. "Tigre," as he was known because he had been an amateur boxer in Texas, went out drinking at one of the student bars the next weekend. I was there when one of the Peruvian students began taunting Tigre. He hauled off and clobbered the student, laying him out on the floor.

The next day, the students were once again out in the plaza demonstrating against the Americans. Aquiles counseled that we should once again ignore them, as it would blow over. He didn't even admonish Tigre, saying that he could understand what happened because the Texan had definitely been insulted and had to stand up for his honor.

The next weekend found Tigre once again frequenting the student bars. Another brawl quickly ensued and this time Tigre decked two Peruvians, sending one of them to the hospital.

The next day all hell broke loose in Ayacucho as students, professors and even some of the townspeople marched in protest against the Peace Corps volunteers. We were under siege and didn't dare leave our residences. The national Peace Corps office in Lima sent out the deputy director to assess the situation. They sent a charter plane to Ayacucho to fly out the volunteers. Tigre was sent back to Texas.

I needed to get back to Matahuasi and did not fly out, and planned to drive the eight hours journey across the Andes in a Peace Corps-owned Land Rover with Josh, another volunteer from the valley. It was a wet and stormy day as we set out. About three hours later, when we were driving on a narrow, partially washed-out road overlooking a gorge descending a thousand feet below, Josh lost control of the Land Rover. We were about to go over the edge when he managed to swing the vehicle around, slamming into the side of the mountain. We were badly shaken, and the bumper damaged, but after a few minutes we gathered ourselves together, the engine coughed and started, and we made it back to Huancayo. To this day I sometimes wonder if Comrade Gonzalo of Ayacucho might have been working his sinister black magic on the Peace Corps' Land Rover.

Back in Matahuasi, I threw myself into the cooperative work. There was, however, a slight change in plans ordered by the SIPA office in Huancayo. Instead of starting out with a dairy cooperative, an easier-to-manage supply cooperative was first set up. The thinking was that it would draw a large member base by undercutting the middle men and the merchant houses in Huancayo that sold fertilizers and pesticides to the peasants at exorbitant prices. To help stock the cooperative warehouse in Matahuasi, we secured a loan of about $40,000 from a government development bank. Our prices were less than half those of the merchants.

Based in part on what I learned in the classes at the aborted training program in Ayacucho, I was appointed the bookkeeper of the cooperative. Because Lionel Gomez didn't live in Matahuasi, I also became the principal dispenser of supplies from the warehouse, or "bodega" as it was called, when the peasants came to make purchases from the cooperative. (About half-a-decade later, two American sociologists came to Matahuasi to study the cooperative. They gave me a one-line acknowledgment in their book, noting that a Peace Corps volunteer had once served as the bookkeeper.)

As the harvest came in and the rainy season ended, the official fiestas became more frequent in Matahuasi. I would often find myself in the plaza dancing at night as a village orchestra played "*huaynos*," the traditional music of the Andes. The stars in the sky were brilliant, a million points of light glimmering down on the plaza through the thinned-out atmosphere at that high altitude. At the major fiestas, some of the local people who had gone to Lima to seek their fortune would return home to celebrate and act as *patrones* by dispensing some of their new-found wealth in the festivities of their native village.

On one exceptionally brilliant starlit night I began dancing with a beautiful, voluptuous 19-year-old girl from one of Lima's *barriadas*. She was mysterious, accompanied by no one, appearing almost like an apparition to me. After a few huayno dances we found ourselves in the single bed in my adobe dwelling that fronted on the plaza. It was a night of bliss with her, the first woman I had made love to in months, and only the second one in my lifetime.

The next day she left on the train. She gave me her address in Lima (neither of us had a phone) and we promised to see each other again. I didn't make it to Lima for months, and then it was to pick up Mary Helen. My apparition never reappeared, or at least never looked me up again. I was left with memories of the most splendid one-night stand in my life.

There were other young women who lived in Matahuasi who took an interest in me, but I found it difficult to respond to their enticements. The men in my drinking circle at the "*tienda*" were constantly taunting me to get it on with one of the girls, saying that it would be great to "*mejorar la raza*," to improve the race. I was taken aback by the racism of these comments, and also by the unseemly thought of impregnating a woman with a child that I would probably never see again once I left Peru.

In general, I had little to do with the girls in the village. One evening, Dante Chuquin, the socialist mayor's younger brother, did manage to persuade me to use the SIPA pickup to go for a ride with him and two local damsels. I did some groping and smooching, but not much else transpired. I think Dante, who was known for seducing women, went further than me. I was too worried about getting involved with someone I didn't really care about or share any common interests with. In any case, even the story of this one-night fling became the talk of the town. To my chagrin, it reached the ears of Lionel Gomez, who promptly grounded me and made sure I would never again have the keys to the SIPA pickup when he was not around.

It was about this time that Edward Dew, the regional Peace Corps director in Huancayo, suffered a nervous breakdown and returned to the

United States. I really liked him and his wife. I had been to their house for dinner a couple of times, and we talked at length about Andean and Peruvian politics. I wasn't close enough to him to understand the actual causes of his breakdown, but from my experiences with other volunteers, I began to see a number of them, for want of a better term, become "weirded out." It was a traumatic experience to try and live in a culture so profoundly different from that of urban and suburban America. Many of the volunteers became dysfunctional: They were inept at their jobs and often alienated from the Peruvians with whom they were assigned to work. When things went wrong, many of them would blame the locals, saying they were incompetent, lazy or backward.

Other volunteers would just drop out, literally and figuratively. They were lackadaisical at their work, taking life as it came, counting the days when they could return to the US, saying they had fulfilled their two years of duty. Marijuana became the drug of choice, particularly for the volunteers who lived in Huancayo. A couple of volunteers in a village about 10 kilometers from me even began to cultivate the precious herb, distributing it to their friends. I never even tried a toke while I was in the Peace Corps. I guess I was too much of a nerd at the time, not understanding the usefulness of a plant that would one day become a virtual mainstay of my life.

I did try coca leaves. At the local store in Matahuasi that fronted on the main highway leading to Huancayo, there was a huge burlap bag of coca from which one could scoop out the desired quantity of leaves and weigh them on the scale next to the bag, paying just pennies for a few grams. I could probably have purchased five burlap bags with my monthly Peace Corps salary of $78. I once bought several grams, and instructed by Tito, put several of the leaves on one side of my mouth and began masticating them vigorously. After about 15 minutes, I did notice a certain tingling and numbness in my jaw but not much else. I never became a coke enthusiast, at least not in Peru. But I did come to believe in the power of the coca leaf.

One day, a truck pulled up to the cooperative's bodega with a load of seed potatoes that we planned to distribute to the farmers. A ramp was thrown up to the truck and an Indian-looking youth, about 21 years old and weighing less than 60 kilos, began to carry 100 kilo sacks down the ramp on his back, tossing them onto the floor of the bodega. He marched up and down the ramp for almost an hour as I stood there dumbfounded by his display of stamina and strength. It could only be attributed to his constant mastication of the bulge of coca leaves in the corner of his mouth. He was able to do superhuman tasks with the coca, but it surely must have taken its toll on his physical well-being and I seriously doubt that he lived to see his fortieth birthday.

In mid-June I went to Lima to meet Mary Helen who was flying in from California. I had been in highland Peru and its villages for eight months, and I was amazed as I entered Lima with its enormous skyscrapers, congested avenues and honking horns. I felt like I had once again discovered modernity, even though Lima was one of the more impoverished capitals of Latin America.

Mary Helen and I spent a couple of days in Lima and our romance flourished once again. We then set out for Huancayo, this time in a collectivo, a taxi with five fare-paying passengers, which proved a lot faster than the train that I had taken when I first journeyed to the valley.

We decided that she would rent a house in Huancayo because the unwritten rules of the Peace Corps dictated that an unmarried American couple could not live together in a village. It was supposedly too shocking for the locals, even though most of them were not formally married, living in common-law unions. In any case, Huancayo was just about the only place in the valley where Mary Helen could find gainful employment, and I certainly could not support anyone on my Peace Corps salary in Matahuasi.

Mary Helen quickly landed a job teaching English at the Instituto Cultural Peruano-Norte Americano, an affiliate of the US Information Agency, which in turn was part of the official US governmental presence in Peru. The Institute's formal mission was to foster friendly exchanges between Americans and Peruvians. It had a library and a meeting center, but its most practical function was to provide English classes for a fee to largely middle class Peruvians.

At least half a dozen Americans, all of them males in their twenties, taught English at the Institute when Mary Helen arrived. This peculiar demographic configuration puzzled me at first until I realized the Americans were evading the draft and the Vietnam War. Bob, the director of the Institute and the longest-serving teacher with a record of three years, had invited his friends to come and work with him. When their draft boards inquired why their home-town boys were winding up in the Peruvian Andes, Bob would write a letter on official US stationary stating they were needed "to fight communism in Latin America."

Things worked out well at first between Mary Helen and me. I would usually come into town on the weekends and spend a couple of nights at her house. We'd often invite acquaintances over to her place for dinner or go out to the Olympia restaurant, meeting other volunteers or someone from the Institute.

One Monday morning in late October 1967, I went to the Olympia for breakfast before heading out to Matahuasi. An American, about 30 years old, of slender frame and ordinary Anglo features, came up to me and introduced himself as Brian Smith, a writer for the *Readers Digest*. He said he had just come from Bolivia where he had covered the capture and assassination of Che Guevara on October 9. I was enthralled by being in the presence of someone who had been in Bolivia when Che died, and when he asked me to take the day off to accompany him as a guide, I readily assented. We went to a rather poor village on the plateau of the valley known for its weavers. I translated for him, as the villagers told the story of their lives, particularly their relationship to the nearby hacendado who was known for his ruthlessness. I also talked with Brian about US politics, and told him that I opposed the Vietnam War and had no intention of returning to serve in the US military. He counseled me against taking that path, saying I would ruin my life if I became a draft dodger.

At the end of the day he invited me to travel to Lima with him in a taxi, saying he would pay my expenses for a couple of days and that we would enjoy the delights of the big city. I declined his offer saying I already felt guilty about being absent from my work in Matahuasi for a day. We parted on friendly terms and he promised to send me his articles and some publications that came from the presses of *Readers Digest*.

I never heard from him again. A few months, later I looked at a collection of *Readers Digest* magazines in the Huancayo Peace Corps office and found no Brian Smith among the authors or contributors to the publication. I was puzzled. Then I heard that *Readers Digest* was a willing collaborator of the CIA, that it would often allow agents to use the magazine's name as a cover for their real activities. I was shocked, as I realized that Brian Smith, or whatever his real name was, had been part of the CIA team that hunted down Che Guevara. When he met me at the Olympia restaurant a couple of weeks after Che's death, he was undoubtedly on an intelligence gathering mission on his way back to CIA headquarters, trying to obtain any information he could about guerrillas or restive local populations. I had been duped into helping out, although in looking back on my service as his guide, I realized that I had relayed nothing from the villagers that spoke of radical movements or guerrillas. At worst, he may have opened up a file on the dissident Peace Corps volunteer from Matahuasi, a "fellow traveler" of the burgeoning international leftist movement who refused to serve his country in Vietnam.

In October 1967, the cooperative in Matahuasi began to expand its activities into dairy marketing. With part of the $40,000 loan that the coop had secured earlier in the year, it bought a large Chevrolet pickup that was used to collect milk from local producers to sell in Huancayo to restaurants and commercial establishments. The peasants who sold their milk to the coop were not very big producers, as the average dairy herd was no more than four or five cows.

The coop leadership felt proud of this new commercial endeavor. Alejandro Meza, now the president of the coop, told me: "Alone we will never progress, but with the cooperative we are not alone. With our numbers we can make the authorities sit up and listen, convincing them to provide us with financial and technical assistance. We can escape the grip of the big commercial houses that monopolize the sale of fertilizers and the intermediate merchants who dictate the price of the milk they buy from us."

The cooperative movement in Matahuasi appeared to embody the path to development espoused by Jose Maria Mariategui, Peru's leading Marxist thinker who flourished in the 1920s. Decrying the role of the hacienda in maintaining a moribund feudal economy, Mariategui saw the communal traditions of the Indian communities as capable of ending this economic stagnation. He wrote: "In the sierras, the latifundia has preserved its feudal character intact and has put up a much stronger resistance than the 'community' to the development of a capitalist economy. In fact, when a 'community' is connected by railway to commerce and central transportation, it spontaneously changes into a cooperative." For Mariategui, these communal and cooperative enterprises, while implicitly capitalist because they were tied to the market economy, were a progressive force, capable of liberating the Indians and peasants of the Peruvian highlands. Once the hacienda was destroyed as an economic unit, Mariategui believed a cooperative, socialist economy could emerge at the national level.

As my second year in the Peace Corps unfolded, I achieved a certain distinction as one of the few "success" stories among the volunteers. The cooperative was going well, I had befriended many Peruvians, and I was one of the few volunteers who managed to live in a village without becoming despondent. In hindsight, I believe I adapted well to village life because I had grown up as a farm boy in Wisconsin. While the rural cultures of the Mantaro Valley and Wisconsin are vastly different, I had learned how to live with the solitude that is an inherent part of rural life. By day, I would bustle around in the community, working out of the coop office, and in the evening I would retreat to the seclusion of my abode. I did not mind the long quiet nights as I had brought dozens of books with me I would read by lantern light.

During the midpoint of my second year, word came down from the central Peace Corps office in Lima that I had to present quarterly reports on my work as a volunteer. This had been a formal requirement since I had come to Matahuasi, but I had refused to write anything up, suspecting that these reports might be of some use to officials at the embassy, perhaps even to the CIA. But now under duress, I picked up the current book I was reading, *Reason and Revolution* by Herbert Marcuse, and wrote a brief essay about why I thought reason would inevitably lead to revolution in the highlands of the Andes. I mentioned no names in the report, in fact I didn't even discuss the politics of Matahuasi; I simply asserted that the revolution was coming based on Marcuse' dialectical logic.

I never heard back from the Peace Corps staff in Lima, nor did they insist on any more reports. They must have thought that one more volunteer had gone mad in a remote village of the Andes.

9. Nostalgia, Lovers and Idaho Potatoes

January 30, 1968: The People's Army of Vietnam launches the Tet offensive in South Vietnam, demonstrating that there is no "light at the end of the tunnel" for the 400,000 US soldiers occupying the country.

March 31, 1968: President Lyndon Johnson makes the stunning announcement that he would not run for reelection. Demonstrators chant outside the White House, "Hey, Hey LBJ! How many kids have you killed today?"

April 4, 1968: Martin Luther King Jr. is assassinated in Memphis, Tennessee. Riots erupt in over 100 US cities.

"*Martin Luther King Asasinado*" read the headline of a newspaper I bought as my train from Buenos Aires pulled into a station in the Andean highlands of Bolivia. I sat down heavily on the steps of the train. During my year-and-a-half in South America, I had never felt a deeper loss, not only because of King's death, but also because I had not participated in the political ferment that was convulsing the United States as the Vietnam war raged on and the movement for racial justice deepened. For better or worse, it was my country and I wanted to be a part of its strife and tumult.

It was the last stage of a trip I started three weeks before in Peru. To promote volunteer sanity, the Peace Corps provided an ample travel stipend to encourage volunteers to take a trip during the month of vacation time they were allotted in their two-year stint. I opted for an excursion that started in Cuzco and then took me to countries of the Southern Cone—Bolivia, Chile and Argentina. Mary Helen went with me during the first part of the trip, serving as a great guide to the Cuzco region where she had been a volunteer several years before.

After exploring some of the ancient stone edifices of the city of Cuzco for a day, we traveled by train to the ruins of Machu Picchu. These were the days when the ancient retreat of the Inca royalty was not yet overrun by tourists and we had a great time hiking around the ruins, bumping into only a couple dozen visitors or so. That night Mary Helen and I camped out with our sleeping bags in the middle of the stone ruins, a couple hundred feet from Huayna Picchu, the prominent peak that rises above the royal city. We made love in the ruins of the city that the Inca kings had founded over half a millennium before.

Early the next morning we awoke shrouded in a light fog that soon began to lift. It was truly magnificent as rays of sunlight broke through the fog, giving a mystical air to the ruins. Later in the morning we reluctantly packed our bags to catch the train back to Cuzco. From there, we set out by bus for the southern city of Puno, caught a ferry across Lake Titicaca, spent a few days in La Paz, Bolivia and then headed south to Chile.

I have not been back to Machu Picchu since then, and doubt if I will ever return, preferring to keep this singular pristine image of the ancient Inca city forever engraved in my mind.

After more than a year of living in Peru I marveled at the relative wealth of Chile, the warmth of its people, and the heated political discussions that one overheard on the streets and in the local bars and restaurants. This was mid-March 1968, when Eduardo Frei was over half-way through his six-year presidential term and many of his promised reforms were coming up short. Workers were organizing and striking for higher wages while the peasantry demanded a meaningful agrarian reform to rid the country of its old haciendas. I fell in love with the country, the spirit of its politics and the geographic beauty of the port towns and the central valley. I knew that I would someday return to Chile.

In Chile, Mary Helen and I parted ways, she returned to Peru via plane, and I continued by land over the Andes to Argentina. Our parting marked the beginning of the end of our relationship. She had hoped that during the trip I would make a definitive commitment to her, even saying at one point, "When are you going to pop the question?"

I simply couldn't commit to marriage, there was too much in life that

I wanted to experience. To me, marriage seemed like a dead end, a trap, not the start of a new life. These feelings were not simply a typical male reflex of not wanting to make a commitment. My parents' long relationship, devoid of love and riveted with arguments and conflicts, made me fear the institution of marriage.

When I returned to Peru, I realized that there were real limits to what I could achieve in Matahuasi. Jose Carlos Mariategui's belief that the indigenous communities of the highlands could transform society via communal and cooperative enterprises did not seem to hold true in the Peru of the 1960s.

The shortcomings of the cooperative movement in Matahuasi first became apparent to me when Tito Chuquin and I tried to expand the cooperative to San Lorenzo, where he was the mayor. Much poorer than Matahuasi, few peasants in San Lorenzo had more than one milk cow, so we began to discuss setting up a communal dairy stable in which the peasants could collectivize their cattle and augment the herd by purchasing cows with a higher milk yield. We were surprised when Lionel Gomez and the SIPA office in Huancayo refused to have anything to do with the project. A marketing cooperative that worked with the mid-level peasantry was acceptable to them, but they had no interest in providing financial or technical assistance to the poorer peasantry who wanted to set up a truly communal enterprise to better their lives. Faced with these obstacles, Tito and I had to abandon our organizing efforts in San Lorenzo.

The collapse of this endeavor coincided with the appearance of a West German technical mission in the Mantaro Valley. They began talking with the SIPA office in Huancayo about setting up a dairy pasteurizing plant in the valley that would be financed by German capital. While the mission was interested in collaborating with the Matahuasi dairy coop to help secure a steady supply of milk for the new pasteurizing facility, it soon became apparent that control of the entire process was being subverted by the Germans and Peruvians in Huancayo. Even the leaders of the Matahuasi cooperative became uneasy over what was transpiring. Their worst fears were realized the year after I left when the SIPA office was closed in Matahuasi, and the cooperative compelled to move its headquarters to the district capital of Concepcion where the new pasteurizing plant was being built.

I also began to understand the limits of the cooperative in providing the peasants with seeds, fertilizers and insecticides to augment their crop yields. This package of inputs was part of the widely heralded Green Revolution that was supposed to help lift the third world out of poverty and hunger.

The emerging critique of the Green Revolution was that the use of costly inputs provided by agribusiness corporations could mainly be afforded by larger agricultural producers, while smaller producers would be forced out. In the late 1960s, I was largely unaware of this critique and I was not in the Mantaro Valley long enough to observe if the Green Revolution led to land concentration. But I did see that the peasants I worked with had their doubts about the new agricultural technologies. In the valley, SIPA and the US aid mission were pushing the use of Idaho seed potatoes, even though Peru was home to over 4000 varieties of native potatoes. Many peasants readily adopted the Idaho in conjunction with fertilizers and insecticides because they could achieve much higher yields than they did with their native varieties.

But then I saw that many of the same peasants would cultivate their native varieties in small plots next to their houses for personal consumption. When I asked them why, the common response was "Our own potatoes have more flavor and taste better to us." At home and during the fiestas, the villagers always made sure they used the local varieties, not the Idaho potato which was shipped off to the markets in Lima for less discriminating palates.

Scientific studies soon began to show that there was more to the native potatoes than taste—they were also more nutritious than the Idaho. Years later, in the 90s, I stumbled across a study of the Mantaro Valley that lamented the spread of the potato monoculture due to the cultivation of imported hybrid potatoes used extensively for the french fry industry and the Lima markets. The local varieties were being squeezed out, sharply reducing the gene pool just as these native genes were needed because of their resistance to the plagues and diseases that increasingly afflicted the more homogenous imported varieties.

Three-and-a-half decades after I left the Peace Corps, I personally became a victim of the agrochemicals of the early Green Revolution. In 2004, I was diagnosed with Multiple Myeloma, a rare blood cancer. When I researched its probable causes, I found out that there is a high incidence of this cancer among people who work with farm chemicals. Reflecting on my experience as the manager of the cooperative warehouse in Matahuasi, I realized that I had had almost daily contact with pesticides in porous paper bags, particularly a chemical called Aldrin manufactured by the Shell Corporation. Not only did I inhale the fumes every time I went into the warehouse, but with no running water nearby, I rarely washed my hands after dispensing it to the peasants who came to purchase it. Aldrin was subsequently banned for agricultural use, first in the United States in 1987, then in most of the world because of its toxic, carcinogenic effects.

Thoughts of my demise were far from my mind in 1968 as my romantic life took a new turn during my final months in Peru. I continued to visit Mary Helen in Huancayo after returning from our trip to the southern cone, but now we rarely made love. I am not sure who became unfaithful first, but I noticed that Nat, one of the teachers at the language institute in Huancayo, became a frequent companion of Mary Helen's. Gentle and personable, I liked him a lot and saw him as more of a friend than a threat. Perhaps I felt guilty about not wanting to marry Mary Helen and subconsciously wanted Nat to take up with her. But on occasions I did succumb to feelings of jealously. One evening, Mary Helen was supposed to go out with me, but instead she took off with Nat. I felt deeply hurt and confronted her the next day, asking her, "What's going on with Nat?" She shrugged it off saying, "I really love you, don't worry, I'm not involved with anyone else."

While this was going on, I met Rosa, a young woman who attended the local university and worked at the SIPA office in Huancayo. She was different from the girls in the village who had little depth. Dark-featured with deep brown eyes and a solid, attractive body, she began finding excuses to visit me in Matahuasi and we soon became lovers. She said she had another boyfriend in Huancayo but I never met him. Rosa had a dark, possessive side, and I soon came to suspect that she was using a phantom lover to make me more interested in her.

At about the time I became involved with her, I moved to another more recently constructed adobe building on the other side of the plaza. Electricity arrived in Matahuasi at about the same time, so my new accommodations seemed like a virtual paradise. It was a wonder making love to Rosa in the late afternoons. Then after she left, I would feel inspired as I read my books by the new electric lights and wrote in my diary.

One night, I went into Huancayo to take Rosa to a restaurant with a dance band. Afterwards, when I was walking her home, we ran into Nat and some of his male friends from the Institute. I was terribly embarrassed; we made small talk, then moved on. Several days later, I saw Mary Helen but she said nothing. I suspect that Nat told her about his encounter with Rosa and me, but Mary Helen chose to ignore it, probably because she felt as guilty as I did about what was going on.

My plans to return to graduate school in the fall received a rude shock when I got rejection letters from the University of California, Berkeley and Columbia University. I soon found out that I received these dismal notices because Robert Padden, one of the three professors that I had asked for recommendations, had actually written a letter of non-recommendation. A former professor of mine at St. Norbert College, Padden had helped me get into Case Western Reserve University in 1965. But in 1968, he wrote me that he had not recommended me because I was "not qualified to go to any other university." He also commented on the diary-letters I had sent to him and others about my experiences in Peru, saying "the positions you take indicate you do not have the capacity to undertake serious, objective academic work."

At St. Norbert's I was aware that Padden was a conservative but I naively thought he would respect divergent political positions and write a recommendation based on my intellectual qualifications, not my politics. Fortunately for me, in applying to graduate school, the forms I requested from Indiana University had arrived belatedly in the mail. So I filled them out, replacing Padden's name with a professor whom I trusted, and was soon admitted to the Ph.D. program in Latin American history at Indiana University in Bloomington.

In late August 1968, I took the train to Lima for my "termination proceedings" with the Peace Corps staff before flying back to the US. I said goodbye to Mary Helen and Nat on the train platform in Huancayo. We never did talk about our mutual "transgressions." I told Nat, "Take care of her, make sure she gets back to the States." They would return together in the spring of 1969, and get married. I wasn't invited to the wedding.

A few days before I left, I had a going away party along with a couple of other volunteers who were leaving Huancayo. Rosa showed up, sporting a new hairdo and an attractive dress. She was in a black mood, barely holding back her tears. There was not much I could say or do. I felt horrible as I kissed her goodbye and left the party. A few months later in the US I received a post card from Rosa with nothing more than the words, "Me Recuerdas?" Remember me? I wrote her back but never heard from her again.

As I crossed over the Andes and Ticlio Pass on the same train route that had taken me to the Mantaro Valley almost two years before, I reflected on my life in Peru and the Peace Corps. I had learned much about the real world, particularly regarding personal relations and politics. I felt satisfied with my tenure in the Peace Corps, but I now realized it was not enough to struggle for incremental changes at the grassroots level. I had to take on the entrenched institutions that dominate society. At the same time, one could not lose contact with life at the grassroots. I needed to be aware of the daily struggles of people.

I still dreamed of a radically different world. Senator Robert F. Kennedy, who was felled by an assassin's bullet on June 6, 1968, had proclaimed in his last political campaign: "Some people see things as they are, and ask, why? I dream things that never were and ask, why not?" The failures of Che Guevara and other guerrillas who died in combat while I was in the Peace Corps did not end those dreams. Kennedy and Guevara may have been enemies as one sought to advance US interests while the other wanted to undermine them in Latin America. But they had much in common: they both represented hope and a commitment to a different world.

10. Joining the War At Home, 1968-69

Come you masters of war...
–Bob Dylan

It was near dusk on Saturday, November 15, 1969 in Washington, DC. Along with several thousand other anti-war demonstrators gathered in front of the Department of Justice on Constitution Avenue, I chanted "One, two, three four, we don't want your fucking war!" and "Ho, Ho, Ho Chi Minh, the Viet Cong is going to win!" I hurled a red paint bomb at the ornate doors of the Justice building, while others burnt US flags and threw stones and other projectiles. The police lobbed tear gas and marched towards us with their batons in the air. A gas cylinder landed near me, searing my eyes and lungs. I staggered and coughed, barely able to breathe. Scores were arrested but somehow I managed to get away, barely avoiding the grasp of a D.C. cop with handcuffs on his belt.

At the behest of radical anti-war leaders, we had broken off from over 300,000 demonstrators who had assembled at the Washington monument earlier in the day to hear an array of anti-war speakers, including three US Senators. It was the largest demonstration in Washington history, organized by the National Moratorium and the New Mobilization Committee to End the War in Vietnam.

Reacting to our demonstration in front of the Justice Department, Nixon's Attorney General John Mitchell declared we were "active militants who want to destroy some of the processes and some of the institutions of our government." His wife Martha, watching us through a Justice Department window, said: "It looks like the Russian revolution." We were jubilant; this was exactly the response we wanted to provoke.

By the fall of 1969, the country was deeply divided. The peace movement had mushroomed into a multitude of diverse organizations and tendencies. Vice President Spiro Agnew, in an attempt to rally the right wing, pro-war forces, called liberals and those on the left "ideological eunuchs" and "merchants of hate." He later denounced the radical demonstrators as "effete snobs." Earlier in the year the first-term governor of California, Ronald Reagan, called on Congress to cut off federal funds to rioting college students and denounced college presidents as "slow to act, and quick to accede" to student unrest.

The domestic conflict had gathered momentum ever since I returned to the United States from the Peace Corps. Arriving at the end of August 1968, I stared in disbelief at the TV as demonstrators were bludgeoned at the Democratic Presidential nominating convention by Chicago cops under orders from Mayor Richard Daily. This was a traumatic event for the youth of Middle America, turning many of them from anti-war pacifists into radicals bent on directly confronting the oppressive institutions of our country. The Black Panthers had already galvanized many militant blacks, making this a multiracial struggle. FBI Director J. Edgar Hoover launched a series of deadly raids on the homes and offices of the Panthers across the country, ordering FBI operatives to "destroy what the [Black Panther Party] stands for" and "eradicate its 'serve the people' programs."

Indiana University in Bloomington did not seem at first sight to be a particularly auspicious place for anti-war militancy. Set in picturesque Monroe County in southern Indiana, the town of Bloomington was divided into a university enclave with about 30,000 students and a largely working-class community on the "other side of the tracks."

But it was a testimony to the strength of the anti-war and counterculture movements that they had penetrated even the citadel of Indiana University. Over a half-dozen students had been admitted to the doctorate program in Latin American history the year I arrived in Bloomington and they all opposed the war in Vietnam. One of them, Larry Richter, who would become a close friend, had served time in jail for refusing to be drafted. Another, Paul Williams, acted as the sage of an informal group of about a dozen or more graduate students who would gather at his house on the weekends to talk politics and get stoned while listening to music and watching W.C. Fields and Mae West movies.

Even the courses I took lent themselves to advancing my radical proclivities. The first semester I signed up for a seminar on the History of the Cuban Revolution taught by a contemporary historian, David Burke, who was a gifted lecturer. His politics were liberal at best but he was open-minded and allowed his students to pursue their political interests.

I opted to focus on guerrilla movements starting with the 26th of July movement led by Fidel Castro in the Sierra Madre mountains of Cuba and its progeny, the Cuban-inspired guerrilla movements that spread throughout Latin America. At about the time I took this course, Che Guevara's diary of his last days in the jungles of Bolivia was published. I became obsessed with every word of the diary, seeking to understand the mind and actions of this great revolutionary of the late twentieth century. I would on occasion lament that while I was in the Peace Corps I had not been more heroic and taken off to the mountains or jungles of Latin America to join a guerrilla movement.

Just over a month after I returned to the US, my draft board in Watertown, Wisconsin sent me a notice stating that Uncle Sam wanted me. I conferred with an anti-war draft counselor at Indiana University and told him that I had no intention of going to Vietnam, that I would sooner move to Canada or return to Latin America. He said, "Let's not go there just yet. Do you have a history of any accidents or physical impairments that might disqualify you?" The only thing I could think of was a car accident that happened when I was four years old. I was thrown out of the car window and suffered a broken right arm and right leg. Because the bone in my leg was not healing straight, the doctor had to put a metal plate with three metal pins in my leg to make sure it mended properly. My counselor pounced on this event, saying, "You should go to the physical for the draft and tell them that you have a bum leg. You can always leave the country if that doesn't work."

It was a cold morning in early November when I showed up for the physical exam at the regional draft center in Juneau, Wisconsin along with about 50 other potential draftees. On the forms I had to fill out I put down that not only did I have a bad right leg, I also had difficulty breathing because I had contracted a rare lung disease while living in the Andes of Peru, and that I had constant diarrhea due to the bad food I had eaten there. (The latter was actually true. It took me over half a year to get rid of the amoebas I had picked up in Peru). Then I got in line for a series of specific exams for my eyes, lungs, ears, etc. The attending physician for each exam checked me off on the form, saying "You're in great shape, next in line."

When they asked us to stand on one leg and then on the other, I faked a fall to the floor as I tried to balance on my right side. The observing physician merely looked at me and said "You're fine, you'll make a good soldier." When I reached the final review, I picked the doctor who seemed the most gregarious. When I got up to him, he looked at what I had written down and said, "If you have a plate in your femur, you are automatically exempt from military service." The other doctor looked up, saying: "I didn't know there was such an exemption." My physician said, "Yes, there is. All he has to do is send us an x-ray showing he has a plate in his leg."

I was ecstatic as I went outside to meet my father who was waiting to drive me back to the farm. Not known for his display of emotions, he smiled when I told him the good news and said, "You lucky son of a gun." I responded, "Well I guess I'm joining the long family line of draft dodgers," referring to our history of military deserters and draft evaders of the nineteenth century, and also to my Dad himself who had been exempted from World War II to work on the farm. We drove immediately to the doctor's office to get an x-ray of my "bad leg." I would not have to become an expatriate; I could stay in the United States and raise hell.

Because I had arrived at Indiana University from Peru at the last moment, the only lodging I could find was at a 12-story building on campus that housed graduate students. It was probably the best habitat for someone returning from a stint abroad as I could meet up with a wide variety of people, particularly at the common cafeteria where over 300 students came to dine. I probably avoided the "reverse culture shock" that afflicted many Peace Corps volunteers by befriending Latin students at the dormitory. It was there that I met Carlos Castaneda from El Salvador, a Ph.D. candidate in physics, who would provide me with an introduction to his brother in the Foreign Ministry when I later visited the country on my journey back from Chile in 1973. I also befriended two Spanish women from whom I learned just how distinct the Spanish culture and mores are from those of Latin America.

Though I tried, I had no amorous relations during my first year at Indiana University. Perhaps I just didn't fit into any woman's model of a desirable male, given my bizarre background of going from a dairy farm in Wisconsin to a village in the highlands of Peru. I developed a big crush on a Turkish woman from Istanbul, Hediye, and flirted with her for several months. But while I was writing her love letters from Wisconsin during Christmas vacation, she was falling in love with a mutual friend, Steve, who had served as a Peace Corps volunteer in Panama. He was morose and even suicidal, she gregarious and optimistic about life. Yet, despite these differences, it seemed that opposites do attract, and they eventually married.

After Hediye, I developed an interest in a polar opposite, Susan, a stunning, slender, brunette graduate student in literature who had little interest in politics and whose father had been a Presbyterian minister in India. She did not have a particularly enchanting personality, but I was mesmerized by her beauty. She showed only a lukewarm interest in me, and I became so frustrated that one night I dreamed I was a bird of prey who descended upon her, grabbing her in my talons and carrying her up to my nest for carnal relations.

Then to my dismay, Sue picked up with Sparky, a philosophy graduate student who seemed even weirder than me. One spring evening, Sue came back to the graduate dorm and effusively said, "Sparky got stoned in the park and told me to eat grass with him. It was a riot." This was a blow. Sparky had managed to touch some emotion I hadn't been able to reach in Sue.

But politics, rather than romance, remained my obsession. Richard Nixon's inauguration on January 20, 1969 infuriated me. I watched it on TV with some fellow history graduate students. Remembering my Dad who always called him Tricky Dick, I said, "Nixon will never be a legitimate president for me. He is a shifty, callous person. He will be a disaster for the country and the world." One of the graduate history students, Bill, was taken aback by my harsh rhetoric, saying, "He deserves a chance, after all another Republican president, Dwight Eisenhower, brought the troops home from Korea." I demurred, saying nothing, preferring to watch the snippets of the counter-inaugural march in Washington that drew some 10,000 people who pelted Nixon's procession with rocks, beer cans and ink-filled balloons as it rode down Pennsylvania Ave. Pigs were released at the inaugural event in front of the White House.

During my second semester at Indiana University I took a research seminar with David Burke in which I had to write a 30-plus page paper in preparation for my doctoral dissertation. I chose to write on the government of Jacabo Arbenz [[CK]]of Guatemala from 1950 to 1954, the first president of Latin America after World War II who decided to implement an agrarian reform program, nationalizing the vast idle lands held by the United Fruit Company. Because Arbenz threatened US interests and allowed the small Communist organization—the Workers Party of Guatemala—to participate in the government, the CIA orchestrated its first coup in Latin America against Arbenz, toppling his government in June 1954 and installing a military regime. As a boy in Wisconsin I actually remembered hearing about the overthrow of Arbenz, as it occurred on June 17, the day before my tenth birthday.

The coup unleashed four decades of strife in Guatemala and set the tone for US policy in Latin America throughout the Cold War years. Che Guevara, who was traveling in Guatemala on a motorbike at the time of the coup was deeply affected, writing home to Argentina, "Along the way, I had the opportunity to pass through the dominions of the United Fruit, convincing me once again of just how terrible these capitalist octopuses are.... I won't rest until I see these capitalist octopuses annihilated." A few months after the coup, he went to Mexico where he linked up with Fidel Castro to mount an insurgent attack against the dictatorial regime of Fulgencio Batista in Cuba.

In the process of my initial research at Indiana University, I discovered that the CIA had sent a special team to Guatemala to seize records and communications, particularly those of the Workers' Party of Guatemala, the Arbenz government ministries, including the Ministry of Agriculture, and the peasant organizations that were active in the countryside. The CIA made all these documents available to Richard Adams, a young professor at the University of Texas who specialized in Guatemala. When it came time to publish his work based on these papers, he realized that his academic reputation would be ruined if they remained secret and the factual basis of his treatise could not be verified. So he persuaded the CIA to deposit the documents in the Library of Congress.

These papers were copied onto microfilm, and I had Indiana University purchase a set of them to research my paper on agrarian reform. Paying particular attention to the writings of peasant organizations, I concluded that the upheaval in the countryside was not orchestrated by the Workers' Party of Guatemala or the Arbenz government. Indeed, the Workers' Party was wary of the peasants' takeover of lands beyond those of the United Fruit Company, fearing that the haphazard indigenous land seizures would destabilize the country and pave the way for an assault by reactionary forces. This fit in with the general perspective of the Communist parties in Latin America, which argued that the continent was still in a semi-feudal state of development and that before socialism could take root, capitalist relations of production would have to be established.

The most profound intellectual revelation for me did not come from the seminar or from any particular course at Indiana University but from Andre Gunder Frank's seminal work, *Capitalism and Underdevelopment in Latin America*. Focusing on the development of capitalism in Brazil and Chile, Frank argues that imperialism as a historic system created stunted, dependent structures throughout the Third World. Called dependency theory, Frank along with Samir Amin, Teotonio dos Santos, and others drew upon the work of Paul Baran of *Monthly Review* magazine who asserted that third world countries were underdeveloped because of parasitism and the draining of surpluses to the advanced countries. Unlike the Communist parties and orthodox Marxists, the dependency theorists argued that exploitative capitalist relations already existed in Latin America, that it was these very relations, not feudalism that led to impoverishment and underdevelopment.

The doctoral dissertation I would eventually write was framed by dependency theory. While doing research for it in Chile from 1971-73, I would work with Andre Gunder Frank at the Center for Socio-Economic Studies (CESO). He is one of the more memorable characters I've known in my life, always opinionated, gruff and at the same time engaging. One of my friends dubbed him "Gunder Thunder." He could easily offend you until you realized that his banter was his way of provoking conversation and debate. He had his foibles but I admired his tenacity and his brilliance as he usually turned out scores of articles every year.

The ferocity of the Vietnam War continued unabated under Nixon and radical politics in the United States flourished. In June 1969, I attended the ninth convention of the SDS at the Chicago Coliseum, along with some 2000 others. It was a tumultuous event. Anyone could participate, and the four days of meetings included Wobblies, Spartacists, Black Panthers and a plethora of radical groups. The two largest fractions were the Maoist Progressive Labor Party (PL) which wanted to take over SDS and the Revolutionary Youth Movement (RYM) wing of SDS. The latter issued a manifesto based on a lyric from a Bob Dylan song, "You don't need a Weatherman to know which way the wind blows."

The rancorous convention soon degenerated into chaos. When the Progressive Labor Party (PLP) moved to take it over, they were vehemently denounced by the Panthers, who reveled in sexism, calling for "pussy power." Led by Bernadine Dohrn, the Weatherman Faction then seized control of the microphone, staged a quick vote to expel the PLP by 500 to 100, and walked out of the coliseum with their band of 500 adherents. By the next day, there were two SDS organizations. The Weatherman Faction soon evolved into an underground organization, while SDS never held another national convention until it was resurrected in 2006.

I was dumbfounded by the experience. My sympathies were with the Weathermen who wanted to "bring the war home" because of the deadly US slaughter in Southeast Asia that was killing millions of innocent people. Sabotage and violent anti-war acts at home were definitely in the air. I had even engaged in abstract conversations with my fellow history graduate student, Larry Rector (who had been a Peace Corps volunteer in Chile), about taking out the electric power plant in Bloomington, Indiana. And yet there was something about the harsh rhetoric of the Weathermen that put me off. Slogans like "death to the pigs," meaning police and corporate leaders, didn't seem the best way to win friends and political allies at home.

Before the conference, the Peace Corps had asked me to go to Mexico City to train volunteers during the summer of 1969, offering to cover all my expenses plus $500 per month, which seemed like a magnificent sum at the time. Larry Rector was also contacted by Peace Corps headquarters in Washington to help train new volunteers in Puerto Rico.

But I had another offer that summer. Shortly after I had returned to the United States in 1968, I had joined the Committee of Returned Volunteers (CRV), an organization comprised mainly of radical ex-Peace Corps volunteers who asserted that US imperialism was the main enemy that had to be combated to overcome underdevelopment in Latin America. The Committee contacted the Cuban government and received an invitation to send a delegation to visit their country. While Larry accepted the Peace Corps offer, I didn't bother to respond. After the SDS convention, I took off for Cuba via Mexico. I had definitively turned my back on any career that would take me into the sphere of US government service, and would now be marked for life as a radical.

11. Cuba: Encountering a Spartan Utopia

Disembarking at the Havana airport I saw giant billboards proclaiming: "Long Live Socialism" and "A Socialist Consciousness Creates Wealth." I was barely 25 years old when I landed in Cuba in June 1969, but my political and intellectual journey to the island had begun five years before. At St. Norbert College, I had abandoned my belief in the other-worldly paradise of Catholic doctrine, taken up Latin American studies, and begun to believe that the Cuban Revolution might be constructing some semblance of the humane, earthly utopias envisioned by the likes of Thomas More, Karl Marx and Che Guevara.

The Cuban revolution captured the world's imagination. A small band of guerrillas fighting in the mountains for just two and a half years galvanized the country, triumphantly marching into Havana on January 1, 1959. The new government immediately embarked on a series of radical reforms that were unprecedented in the history of the Americas. It launched a campaign to end illiteracy, implemented an agrarian reform program, expropriated most of the holdings of Cuba's upper class and the multinational corporations, and opened up free medical and education facilities for the country's populace.

Moreover, it was a story of David versus Goliath, a small island of seven million people standing up to the world's leading imperial power. I, and many others on the New Left, instinctively identified with the Cuban revolution not only because of its utopic ambitions but because it was a victim of US aggression. After the US launched the Bay of Pigs invasion in April 1961, Cuba was second only to Vietnam in inspiring sympathy and solidarity among the ranks of the New Left.

At college in 1964, I had read William Appleman Williams' *The United States, Cuba and Castro* which laid bare the long history of US intervention in Cuba. To free itself from the United States and the stranglehold of the multinational corporations, the revolutionary leadership turned to alternative trade and economic partners among the socialist bloc countries, particularly after the United States cut off Cuban sugar imports in 1960 as the revolution radicalized. What made the Cuban revolution even more striking was its willingness to take Soviet aid while refusing to follow the dictates of Soviet leaders, even ousting pro-Soviet figures from the Cuban leadership in 1962.

It was this bold experiment in socialism and its independence from the Soviet and eastern Europeans that made Cuba such an attractive model for the New Left in the 1960s. Most of us mobilized against the Vietnam War, but because of the destruction rained on North Vietnam, the country was hardly in a position to undertake the construction of a utopian society. But the Cuban revolution, after a brief insurgency, took over an economic infrastructure that was largely intact.

As part of the US government's efforts to isolate this bold revolutionary experiment, ordinary American citizens were not allowed to travel freely to the island. I went to Cuba via Mexico with a twenty-member delegation of the CRV. We all risked being prosecuted, sentenced to jail time, and hefty fines under the Trading with the Enemy Act. Mexico was the only Latin American country that did not bow to US pressures and sever diplomatic and commercial relations with Cuba. At least in its foreign relations the Mexican government still maintained a semblance of its non-intervention policy that dated back to its early twentieth century revolution when US troops invaded the country.

However, the Mexican security and migration authorities at the airport in Mexico City showed no signs of revolutionary solidarity with Cuba. We were detained for the day, our passports were confiscated, and we were told "Cuba is not a desirable country to visit." When we walked around the airport, we were followed by security agents who tried to hide behind cement pillars and make it look like they were innocently reading newspapers. It was hilarious. Finally we got our passports back with a full page stamp saying, "Salida a Cuba," Leaving for Cuba. Wishing to complicate our return to the United States, the Mexican immigration officials had inserted the phrase because they knew the Cubans did not stamp the passports of visiting Americans.

We were warmly greeted at the airport by representatives of ICAP, the Cuban Institute of Friendship with the Peoples, which hosted visitors and delegations from around the world. We were transported to our residence in Havana in a Soviet-made minibus that would become our principal mode of transportation when we visited other parts of the island. ICAP gave us a choice of several places to stay, including a hotel. We chose a student residential complex in the Miramar district of Havana that housed poor high school scholarship students who came from the Cuban countryside. We were assigned to a three-story house that used to belong to a wealthy family who fled to Miami in 1960.

A large number of Americans, famous and not so famous, had visited Cuba during the first decade of the revolution. Black Panthers, academics, anti-war activists and many others had come, some of whom were on the run for evading the draft or for involvement in politically-motivated crimes in the United States. The CRV was among the first delegations from the US to do volunteer work in Cuba while witnessing the revolution. We helped pave the way for the Venceremos Brigade that would bring thousands of Americans to Cuba in succeeding years to engage in volunteer labor.

The revolutionary fervor was palpable as soon as we arrived and we barely slept during the early days. We wanted to hear and absorb everything we could about Cuba. The first night we drilled Manuel Lee, the ICAP representative in charge of our delegation, with questions until 3 a.m. The agenda for our visit seemed quite flexible and open-ended. We could request visits with virtually any government agency, institution or organization in Havana, and we were told that travel would be arranged to visit different provinces on the island. Lee said, "We know there are dissidents who work against the revolution. You will probably see and converse with them, but you will also encounter many, many more Cubans who are with the revolution and are struggling to construct a new society."

Cuba was an incredible and bewildering experience for me. I wanted to believe that a "new man and woman" were emerging with the revolution. In the diary I kept, most of my ruminations were over whether Cuba was creating a new person. Over four decades later, reflecting on my summer in Cuba, I find myself still trying to sort out my experiences, digging back into the political literature of the period and calling old acquaintances who were in Cuba at the same time.

1969 marked a unique period in the revolution. The previous year, Fidel Castro and the Cuban leadership had declared a "revolutionary offensive," the "opening act" in an effort to simultaneously build socialism and communism. They rejected the Soviet position and that of many classical Marxists who argued that in countries of economic scarcity the market place as well as differential wages had to be used in the socialist stage in order to allocate resources and build a productive economy. Once relative abundance was achieved under socialism, the orthodox Communists argued, a society could pass into the stage of communism in which wages were equalized and Marx's dictum could be implemented: "From each according to his ability, to each according to his needs."

Fidel, in critiquing the two-stage approach, drew upon Che Guevara's earlier arguments that the use of market mechanisms even under socialism meant maintaining the capitalist system of exploitation. If a new society was to be built based on social justice, equality and the end of alienation in the work place, the market forces had to be suppressed.

In line with this position, 1968 saw the nationalization of whatever remained of private industry and commerce. Some 56,000 small businesses were taken over, and even farmers' markets were eliminated. These measures, it was believed, would eradicate individual selfishness and foster a communist consciousness among society as a whole. To mark the triumph of the simultaneous passage to socialism and communism, Fidel declared that in 1970, through popular mobilization, Cuba would harvest 10 million tons of sugar, double the harvest of some of the earlier years of the revolution. This, he claimed, would launch Cuba onto a plane of economic self-sufficiency. Thus, when our delegation set foot on the island, the country was in the midst of a massive mobilization to plant and cultivate the sugarcane needed to achieve that goal. We soon found ourselves weeding, culling and fertilizing sugarcane plants alongside brigades of Cubans who were transported from their urban jobs to work in the fields. I distinctly remember cutting down weeds with a machete on July 26, the day commemorating the beginning of the revolutionary struggle 16 years before. Even Fidel was working in the sugar fields instead of giving his traditional speech at Havana's Revolutionary Plaza.

Havana showed the strains of a city where the resources were diverted to the countryside. Since the early days of the revolution the focus was on the development of agriculture and the rural communities. The mystique of the revolution held that it had originated in the rural areas, in the Sierra Maestra mountains especially, and it was there that a new society would begin to take shape. Under the old regime, Havana had been the center of wealth and opulence while the people in the countryside languished in poverty, seen as little more than disposable appendages to the sugar-dominated economy. As a spokesman at the agrarian reform institute told us, "The revolution wants to break the historic cycle that has strangled Latin America. The metropolitan centers suck the wealth out of the countryside. People here now know the importance of agriculture and working in the fields, to not look down on the countryside as a backward place that needs to be escaped from."

This approach made sense to me after working in the Peace Corps in the Andean mountains where people fled to Lima and the other major urban centers to escape poverty and rural deprivation. Historically, capitalist industry has always arisen at the expense of the peasantry, as the Enclosure Acts of the 17th, 18th and 19th centuries in Great Britain demonstrated, by driving peasants off their commonly-held lands. The Cuban effort to reverse history also broke with the experiences of Eastern Europe and the Soviet Union, where the peasantry in the early and mid-20th century was often treated harshly in the drive to produce food for the urban centers and the emergent industrial work force.

Havana, which had been the favorite Caribbean haunt of the mafia and many American tourists in pre-revolutionary days, was now a Spartan-like city. Vedado, the old center of elegant restaurants, hotels and night life next to the Malecon—the historic walkway that fronts on the sea—had been transformed. One night we visited the Tropicana, once the jewel of the nightclubs of Havana and the Caribbean. Now it was little more than a relic of the past with its dimly-lit interior and tacky chairs and tables. Afro-Cuban musicians and dancers performed the old acts of the 1950s in front of a sparse audience.

In Miramar, where we stayed, the big fortress-like mansions of the wealthy had been turned into schools, prenatal clinics and multiunit housing for working families. None of the buildings had been painted since the revolution. Paint was simply not available. There were few cars on the streets and those that did circulate, except for government vehicles from the Soviet bloc, were exclusively of pre-1959 vintage. The mansion where we resided was dilapidated, although still structurally sturdy. I'm sure the oligarchic family that once owned it would have thrown up their hands in horror if they had come back to see it.

The effort to equalize the distribution of food and basic commodities between the city and the countryside meant the standard of living had dropped precipitously in Havana. Even brooms were not available as the broom factory was shut down because it received no raw materials. Food was distributed with ration cards and everyone had to stand in long lines to get their monthly quotas. Unlike the rest of Latin America, no one went hungry or was begging in the streets, but there was a good deal of grumbling and pockets of discontent throughout Havana.

For me, the burning question was whether a "new man" could emerge in the midst of these difficult revolutionary conditions. In his famous essay, "Man and Socialism," written in early 1965, Che Guevara argued: "In this period of the building of socialism we can see the new man and woman being born. The image is not yet completely finished—it never will be, since the process goes forward hand-in-hand with the development of new economic forms."

In the crucible of action, the revolutionary regime sought to forge a new person and a new political culture. Emphasis was placed on the importance of immersion in revolutionary activity in the mass organizations, the neighborhood Committees for the Defense of the Revolution, the armed forces, the Communist Party, and the schools. With the exception of the party, one did not need to be "pure" in order to join; it was precisely through voluntary participation that change would take place.

Our visit to Cuba was slated for only three weeks but due to the disarray and lack of planning at ICAP, which characterized most government agencies, we wound up spending almost a month and a half in Cuba before we finally caught a sugar boat headed for Canada. I was delighted. This gave us a lot of unplanned time to meet and talk with people, often on our own with no guides or assistance from ICAP.

I met many Cubans who were indifferent and some who were outright hostile to the revolution and its ideals, including young people who believed the revolution was a farce. In our delegation, Paul Williams, an ex-Peace Corps volunteer from Chile whom I had befriended at Indiana University, seemed to have a special facility for finding those who were disillusioned with Fidel and the revolution. An engaging person with maroon-colored hair and a striking mustache and sideburns, Paul identified strongly with the counterculture current of the 60s generation. From the beginning, Paul was far more of a skeptic about the Cuban revolution and the project of creating a new man than I was. He saw the party leaders and activists as mouthing slogans and rhetoric that meant little for people's real lives.

I became enamored with another member of our delegation, Carollee Bengelsdorf. She was an attractive, intelligent woman of my age, whom I flirtatiously tried to capture the attention of, but to no avail. She later told me that she was so perplexed by her visit that she did not communicate very much. She introduced us to Edmundo Desnoes, a famous Cuban writer who had written the existential novel *Memories of Underdevelopment* about alienation in Cuba. It was released in 1968 as a movie by the Cuban Film Institute. She would later marry him. In 1994, she published *The Problem of Democracy in Cuba,* perhaps the best single book on the struggle for democracy in the revolution, although I believe that her interpretation of the 1960s fails to capture some of the enthusiasm and serious intent of the leadership to spawn an authentic popular democracy.

Paul introduced me to Afro-Cubans who practiced a syncretic religion that melded old African religious practices with Catholicism. Their forms of worship, referred to as Santeria, involved black colored figurines that merged African deities with traditional Catholic saints. In old Havana at dusk one evening we were invited into a home with a room filled with figurines surrounded by many candles, particularly red ones. We talked to a middle-aged woman and a younger man who explained the significance of the different saints as well as the wall paintings with black religious figures on them. In the conversation that ensued, it quickly became apparent that they were at best indifferent to the revolution. The woman said: "We want to carry on with our Santeria practices and our own history, we don't feel the new government relates to our beliefs and real needs. Its words and promises mean little to me and my family and friends."

With Paul, and also on my own, I met discontented youth who were in high school or just out of school who usually hung around the hotels and the Malecon. I was not impressed by my conversations with them. One 18-year-old complained: "We don't have the music we want, even the Beatles recordings are difficult to get a hold of." None of them talked of serious vocations they wanted to pursue in life. They just wanted to escape, to go to the United States to enjoy the material luxuries they didn't have in Cuba.

This Contrasted sharply with my experience on the Isle of Youth, known as the Isle of Pines before the revolution. Two-thirds the size of Rhode Island, the island had been known for its large prison complex where Fidel Castro had been jailed after his abortive attack on the Moncada Army Barracks on July 26, 1953. In 1966, the government began phasing out the prison and the first contingents of young people started to arrive to clear the land and begin planting citrus trees while continuing their schooling.

Here was the idyllic setting to create among the youth the new man and woman that Che Guevara had called for in 1965: "Our task is to prevent the current generation, torn asunder by its conflicts, from becoming perverted and from perverting new generations. We must not create either docile servants of official thought, or scholarship students who live at the expense of the state—practicing freedom in quotation marks. Revolutionaries will come who will sing the song of the new man and woman in the true voice of the people." By 1969, there were an estimated 20,000 young people on the Isle of Youth from all walks of life, some of them delinquents sent from the mainland, and others leading students in their classes who volunteered to take up Che's challenge to develop a new, selfless person.

After a five-hour ferry ride to the island, we spent five days living with young people in their teens and early twenties. The camp had an energizing, contagious spirit—the closest I have ever come to feeling I was living in a truly collective, communist-like community. Everyone at the camp rose at 5:30 in the morning and after a quick breakfast, headed for the fields. They often sang as they worked, returning at 11:00 to the camp as the scorching sun bore down on them to have lunch and do some homework assignments. At two in the afternoon they headed back to the fields and returned at six. Then they began five hours of classes, catching dinner between sessions, and often wrapping up the day with small gatherings to discuss politics, to socialize, or to listen to music, some of it provided by their own youthful musicians. The meals were all prepared by rotating teams who lived in the camp. Of course, they were not the best cooks in the world—lots of bland rice and beans, maybe a bit of meat, and heavily sugared fruit drinks. But the young people in the camp had no trouble downing large quantities of whatever was served up, given the immense amount of energy they expended.

My experience was very different in Havana, but even in a city known for its complainers and dissidents, most of the people I met supported the revolution. We talked to many people in the government, in the Communist party and in the local organizations who voiced a determination to construct a new society, free from the greed of capitalism, where wealth and goods were equally shared. They took pride in their new country, its commitment to universal education, the end of illiteracy, and access to free medical care. They talked about their hopes for a new and better life in the future. Fidel was lionized in Havana and throughout the country. The people believed in him, and when there were complaints or things went wrong, the common refrain was "If only Fidel knew!"

On a visit to the University of Havana, mid-way through the trip, I met Alicia, a student majoring in political science. She came to see me at our residence in Miramar and we soon wound up making love on the patio-like roof. On hot summer nights, with a soft breeze blowing, it was actually cooler than sleeping in a bedroom. Slight and soft spoken, she told me: "I support the revolution, appreciate the education and the opportunities that are opening up for me, especially given my poor family. But I am not a militant in the party or the university." She did not display the revolutionary enthusiasm of the young people I met on the Isle of Youth, probably reflecting the sentiments of a wide number of people in Havana.

We sadly parted ways at the end of the trip, realizing we would most likely never see each other again. Carollee subsequently told me that she believed Alicia was hoping I would invite her to come to the United States. I am not sure this was true but it would make sense. The appeal and illusions of life in the rich country to the north—with more opportunities, no lines or shortages of basic necessities—is a dream that gripped many people, even supporters of the socialist revolution in Cuba, as well as tens of millions of people living under more dire conditions in the rest of Latin America.

The cornerstone of the new society at the community level was the Committees for the Defense of the Revolution (CDR). We visited several of the CDRs in Havana, usually in the evenings when everyone was home from work. Although the opponents of the revolution claimed the CDRs were set up to spy on neighbors, to me they appeared to be vehicles for community participation in which spirited discussions took place. Any resident in the neighborhood could join the committees and participate in the meetings. They elected their leaders, mobilized people for specific tasks, and engaged in discussions about the problems the local community faced.

Through the CDRs we attended People's Courts presided over by judges selected by the community. The session we heard centered less on guilt or innocence than on the social circumstances that led to the commission of the crime being tried. In one case, we witnessed a man accused of not supporting his family, of drinking too much and not taking care of his children. He was reprimanded, sent to do a month of "volunteer" work in the sugarcane fields, and ordered to change his behavior. I'll never know if this had any effect, but certainly public shame must have caused him to do some rethinking about his life.

During our first month we visited many of the showcases of the revolution's achievements. We went to schools and medical facilities, talked to children in the classroom and saw ordinary women waiting for pregnancy exams in clean, newly-built clinics. We strolled up to the Habana Libre, formerly the Hilton Hotel, and stood in line at the Coppelia, the famous ice cream dispensary that boasted of having surpassed the 26 flavors of Howard Johnson. Like everyone else, we had to wait in line, often for an hour or more. For us, it was a way of meeting ordinary people, most of whom were friendly and curious. They could scarcely believe we were from the United States, as so few Americans had visited their country since the revolution. They queried us as much about our society as we did about theirs.

I did encounter dogmatism among party officials and hardliners who had no tolerance for diversity and independent thinking. We visited the newspaper *Granma*, which reflected the hard edge of the revolution. The paper was little more than a propaganda rag, and its editor criticized gays as "deviants," and declared that "dissidents should be disciplined, and forced to work in the fields or put in jail."

But there were many other prominent figures that we talked to who held more open and tolerant positions. The magazine *Pensamiento Critico*, founded in 1967 at the Department of Philosophy of the University of Havana, reflected the innovative and diverse thinking that was taking place within a new generation of revolutionary thinkers. It represented a "heretical" approach to Marxism, imbued with the thinking of the New Left that shook the world in the 1960s. It broke sharply with the model offered by the Soviet Union and orthodox Marxism, seeing itself as part of a new revolutionary process.

We met with its main editor, Fernando Martinez Heredia, who talked of "practical ways to create a new society relevant to Cuba." *Pensamiento Critico* also worked closely with the Insituto del Libro, founded in the same year, which published many of the writings of authors then in vogue among the New Left, such as Herbert Marcuse, Antonio Gramsci, C. Wright Mills, and Louis Althusser, as well as intellectuals who wrote on the conditions in Latin America and put forth new theories of imperialism and revolution, such as Andre Gundar Frank, Theotonio dos Santos and Rui Mauro Marini. *Pensamiento Critico* was particularly noted for its Third Worldist perspective, drawing on the early writings of Franz Fanon. The school of thinking that led to the founding of *Pensamiento Critico* had crystallized already in Havana in 1966 at the Tricontinental Congress, a meeting of intellectuals and activists from Asia, Africa and Latin America.

They, in many ways, represented a new International, a world-wide revolutionary approach distinct from the Third International set up by the Soviet Union in the 1920s. Subsequent gatherings in Cuba that reflected this new thinking were the Organization of Solidarity of the People of Asia, Africa & Latin America (OSPAAL) in 1967, and the first conference of the Continental Organization of Latin American Students in the summer of 1968.

The editors and writers of *Pensamiento Critico* reflected an approach that diverged sharply from the Schools of Revolutionary Instruction, the arm of the Communist Party set up to train young cadres. As Richard Fagen reveals in his seminal work, *The Transformation of Political Culture in Cuba,* the schools, founded in 1960, had a dogmatic approach, compelling students to memorize parts of, rather than think creatively about, the texts of Marx and Lenin. The battle between the two approaches gave rise to the *"polemica de los manuales,"* a debate about the appropriateness of Soviet-inspired textbooks and training methods at the Schools of Revolutionary Instruction. In 1968, the Cuban leadership resolved the debate in favor of the approach of *Pensamiento Critico*, shutting down the Schools of Revolutionary Instruction. Commenting on the limits of the Schools in March 1968, Fidel said, "Just when you think you have a truly developed revolutionary, you find that what you have is a militant who does not understand many of the most serious problems of the contemporary world."

Given that I was a student of history bent on getting a doctoral degree, I was very much interested in Cuban historiography. With the revolution, history became a field of study rich in foment and critical debates. The more orthodox Marxist historians had taken over the School of History at the University of Havana, while another more innovative group of historians worked in other government positions, publishing in diverse mediums. I befriended one of the latter historians, Manuel Moreno Fraginals. His study, *"El Ingenio,"* The Sugar Mill, had been published in 1964. I looked him up at his office in the Ministry of External Commerce where he served as the Director of Information. A soft-spoken, warm reflective man now in his late 40s, he had left Cuba in the early 1950s for political reasons, returning in 1959 with the revolution.

Not only did we discuss El Ingenio, which he was in the process of revising and expanding, but also his essay, *"Historia como Arma,"* History as a Weapon, which had started circulating in 1963. It called for "a new way of seeing the past," and was highly critical of the historians at the University of Havana. He told me they "do little original historical research, often simply taking the texts of pre-revolutionary writers and repackaging them with Marxist rhetoric."

Moreno was particularly disgruntled with the tendency of these historians to see all of Cuban history only through the prism of foreign domination. He felt this approach ignored the complex social relations and internal class dynamics of Cuba's sugar economy. He excoriated the university historians who turned 19th century history into a simple "Cuban-Spanish conflict," that lauded the Cuban sugar plantation masters who supported independence while under-emphasizing the "profound sense of class struggle, the confrontation between producers and merchants," and "the silent tragic figures of half a million slaves."

The university historians tried to suppress the publication of "El Ingenio," and it was only through the intervention of Che Guevara, who admired Moreno's work, that it saw the light of day. In our conversations, he also critiqued government economic policies. From his position at the

Ministry of External Commerce, he came to believe that "the decision to focus on harvesting 10 million tons of sugar in 1970 is ill-advised and could lead to economic difficulties;" a prediction that unfortunately would prove all too true.

My own experiences in Cuba also raised questions about the economic viability of some of the projects of the revolution as along with other members of the CRV I labored in the "*cordones verdes*," the greenbelts around Havana. The idea behind these fields ringing the city was to produce food for urban consumption. One of Fidel's brainstorms for the greenbelts was to grow a new variety of coffee there that could endure Havana's harsh heat, not needing the cooler climate of valleys and mountains where most of the world's coffee is grown. As I weeded the young coffee plants it was clear to me that the project was a failure. The plants in the sun were stunted or shriveling up and dying, while the few plants that happened to be under a tree or in a shaded area were much larger and thriving. Years later, I found out that the planting of coffee around Havana was abandoned.

Another of Fidel's much ballyhooed projects was his idea that the native zebu cattle could be crossed with imported Holsteins to produce a new disease-resistant cow that would be a high milk producer. We visited the main farm experimenting with this new breed of cattle, run by Fidel's brother Ramon Castro. I inquired about the average milk production of the cows and was told that it was seven liters. I was stunned. This was almost identical to the production of the scrawny cows in the Andes where I had worked as a Peace Corps volunteer, far short of the 40 liters of milk that Fidel had boasted his new breed of cattle would produce. I theorized that the genetic cross had resulted in the opposite of what had been expected: the new strain had the low milk production of the zebu while being vulnerable to the udder diseases that afflicted non-native cattle like the Holsteins.

But these economic miscues did not dampen my upbeat mood as I left Cuba in early August. Looking back from the ship at the picturesque Havana harbor guarded by the historic Spanish El Morro fortress, I was determined to return in a year or so to learn more about the revolution and perhaps do my doctoral dissertation under the guidance of Fraginals. It was not to be. The following summer, I got a Ford grant to do exploratory research on my dissertation, but my entreaties for a visa at the Cuban-interest section of the Czechoslovakian embassy in Washington, D.C. led nowhere. Nor did I receive any response to the letters I wrote to Moreno. I was apparently not important enough to merit the attention of Cuban officials who made visa decisions. I would subsequently find out that Moreno had fallen out of favor with the government because of his criticism of the economic policies and his friendship with Jose Lezama Lima, a Cuban poet who wrote about his homosexuality.

I would not make it back to Cuba until December of 1976 when I went as a writer for the journal of the North American Congress on Latin America (NACLA). I found a world very different from the Cuba I had visited six years before. It now seemed like the grey, bureaucratic communist societies of Eastern Europe. Instead of being hosted by ICAP, we were met by officials of the Cuban Communist Party who put us up at a hotel and scheduled our visits with government and party officials. Gone was the spirit of the 1960s. There was little or no discussion of the new man and woman, only talk of institutionalizing the revolution and the economy.

The 10 million ton sugar harvest had been a failure, falling far short of its goal. Fidel, in a speech on July 26, 1970, accepted blame for what happened and promised to reorganize the economy. Material incentives were restored and Cuba joined COMECON, the socialist trade bloc led by the Soviet Union. Cuba now acknowledged that it was only in the stage of "the transition to socialism." An underdeveloped country could not leap directly into communism.

Regardless of what stage of economic development the country's leadership declared it was in, the real tragedy is that the cumulative economic failures of the 1960s had direct consequences for the country's morale. By the 1970s people had grown tired of the economic hardships they were enduring, and many no longer responded to the exhortations to work harder for the greater good of society. As Bengelsdorf reveals in her book, during the year of the 10 million ton harvest, the worker absentee rate was 29 percent. Perhaps the majority of the people still believed in a "new man and a new woman," but the fact that a significant minority did not even bother to show up for work severely crippled the output of the entire economy, making it impossible to continue with the model that relied on the popular *consciencia* or consciousness.

This economic failure and popular exhaustion cast a pall over the entire country. The free-thinking, open society of the 1960s came to an end. *Pensamiento Critico* was shut down in 1971. In the same year, Herberto Padilla, a dissident intellectual, was imprisoned, leading to an outcry among leftist intellectuals abroad, as well as within Cuba. The Cuban constitution of 1976 strengthened the role of the Cuban Communist Party over the governmental bureaucracy and the economy, proclaiming that the party is "the highest leading force of society," responsible for "organizing and guiding the common effort towards the goals of constructing socialism."

112

To its credit, the new path chosen in Cuba did differ somewhat from that of Soviet communism in that the new constitution also enshrined "popular power." At the local level, people elected representatives of their choosing to the municipal assemblies. These assemblies were empowered to administer many of the local social and economic activities, from schools and movie theaters to local economic enterprises like bakeries, restaurants, hotels, and bus services.

Over one-third of the country's economic activities fell under the control of the municipal assemblies and institutions of popular power. But the overall direction of the economy and the allocation of resources were still set at the national level. The Council of State headed by Fidel made policy proposals that were approved by the National Assembly, both of which were dominated by the Communist party.

The shift in domestic policies did not alter the determination of the Cuban leadership to pursue a revolutionary foreign policy. Most of the guerrilla movements in Latin America had been defeated in the late 1960s by repressive dictatorships and US counterinsurgency. However, Cuba continued to promote socialist and anti-imperialist policies abroad. In late 1975, in response to the request of the newly independent government of Angola, Cuba sent over 35,000 combat troops to help turn the tide against counterrevolutionary forces supported by the apartheid government of South Africa with the backing of Secretary of State Henry Kissinger.

In my own work and travels around Latin America in the 70s and 80s I continually ran into Cuban involvement and support of the most progressive and revolutionary political movements on the continent. In November 1971, I witnessed Fidel's extended visit to Chile when he traveled the length of the country with President Salvador Allende at his side. Fidel did not lecture Chileans about the correct path to socialism, rather he appeared to be struck by the relative prosperity of Chile compared to Cuba and lauded the democratic struggle that had led to the first elected Marxist government in the Americas. He spoke openly of the threat of US imperialism to the Chilean effort to construct a democratic socialist society, and when Allende died on September 11, 1973, in the Chilean presidential palace, he held a machine gun that Fidel had personally given to him.

Then in the early 1980s, as I became involved in Nicaragua and the Central American revolutionary movements, Cuba pushed for the unity of the diverse leftist factions, providing critical intelligence, military and logistical assistance in the fight against the US-backed regimes of the region. Two decades later, the progressive governments of Venezuela,

Bolivia and Ecuador, bent on "re-founding" their nations and constructing "socialism of the 21st century," consulted with Fidel about the Cuban experience and received special missions of Cuban doctors and teachers who usually worked in the most impoverished, rural areas of their countries. Also, over the decades, tens of thousands of political activists have found refuge in Cuba, and an untold number, like myself in 1989, received critical free medical care that our own societies failed to provide.

Cuba may not have constructed the utopian society that many of us desired. I think it's wrong that Fidel and the Cuban leadership have never stood for national elections, that the right to free speech is curtailed, and that many opponents have been tossed in jail. But the government has never had to put down a popular revolt or used security squads to eliminate opponents. Cuba has been far more stable and egalitarian than any other Latin American society, thus providing a foundation for pursuing progressive, anti-imperialist policies abroad.

Perhaps this is the most that can be expected from a revolutionary society that has survived for over five-and-a-half decades just 90 miles from the shores of the United States. Fidel Castro can certainly be criticized for holding on to power until his health declined, far too long for any single leader to run a government, thereby preventing a new generation of leadership from emerging. But from a historical perspective, Fidel's survival and support of revolutionary forces around the world is testimony to his strategic genius, making him perhaps the greatest of the revolutionary leaders to emerge in the late 20th century.

12. Weathermen on a Sugar Boat, Nixon's War at Home

"Rebellion is born of the spectacle of irrationality, confronted with an unjust and incomprehensible condition."
—*Avi Sagi*, Albert Camus and the Philosophy of the Absurd

When our delegation of the Committee of Returned Volunteers (CRV) arrived at the Havana port at dusk in early August 1969, our Cuban hosts told us that we would be going on a sugar boat to Canada with about 15 members of the Weatherman faction that had briefly taken over the SDS convention in Chicago just months before. We were selected at the last moment because a delegation from Puerto Rico representing the independence movement had refused to board the ship, saying the Weathermen were "political crazies," privileged white youth who had no realistic sense of American politics. We soon found out that the Puerto Rican perspective was pretty much on the mark.

Bernardine Dohrn, who had led the walkout at the Chicago Convention, was the de facto leader of the group. Strikingly good looking, she had grown up in a prominent family not far from my hometown in the upper class Milwaukee suburb of Whitefish Bay. She went to the University of Chicago, ultimately getting a law degree.

The ship we boarded had to go to the Cuban port of Cienfuegos to load up with sugar. The holds of the boat needed to be cleaned out and we were asked to assist the crew. Most of our delegation, even our ardent critic of the Cuban revolution, Paul Williams, helped out, although he also used his time in the ship's holds to smoke the last of the marijuana he had somehow managed to procure in Havana. A few of the Weathermen also worked, although most of them claimed they were too busy "planning for the revolution." Some of them also used drugs, although every morning they were disciplined enough to rise and practice calisthenics of a militaristic bent. The Cuban crew didn't understand them. One of the more benign comments by a sailor was that they were "politically immature." When we rounded the southeastern end of Cuba going by the US military base at Guantanamo Bay, Dohrn grabbed a bull horn and yelled out: "This is a shipload of revolutionaries returning to your country."

There were two members of the Weatherman delegation I talked to at length and grew to respect, Diana Oughton and Ted Gold. Diana, the great granddaughter of the founder of the American Boy Scouts, joined SDS at the University of Michigan in 1966 after having served in a Guatemalan indigenous community from 1963-65 as a volunteer for the American Friends Service Committee, a Quaker organization. In my conversations with her she was always deadly earnest, revealing a more profound grasp of politics in the United States and Latin America than anyone else in the Weatherman delegation. I understood the logic that led her to become a militant in reaction to her experiences in Guatemala and the horrors of the Vietnam War. As she said, "How can one not respond with violence at home to stop the daily atrocities of the American empire?"

Ted Gold captured national media attention as an SDS leader of the non-violent occupation of Columbia University in April 1967, protesting the university's policy of permitting the Marines and the CIA to recruit students on campus. He soon became one of the leading SDS intellects. While he believed the left needed to study the texts of the great revolutionaries, he said, "Marxism is a method and a tool, not a dogma." He was a founder of *New Left Notes*, and worked extensively in educational projects in the poor communities of New York. Joining the Weatherman faction before the 1969 convention, he went on to Cuba that summer. He related to me how deeply impressed he was by his conversations with representatives at the Vietnamese embassy in Havana about the US war and destruction of their country. "We have a responsibility to use the most militant means possible to stop the US war," he said.

Excepting those two individuals, I found the rest of the SDS delegation to be superficial and rhetorical at best. They usually behaved as if they were having a big party on the ship. Bengelsdorf told me, Bernadine had her "toy boy" and many of the others engaged in communal sex, which appalled the mores and sensitivities of the Cuban crew.

After about a week on the ship, we arrived at the Port of St. John, Canada at around midnight. A group of about a dozen Weathermen were awaiting us, including Bernardine's "steady boyfriend." The Canadian authorities told us that we would have to wait for the immigration officials to arrive in the morning to disembark, but the Weathermen would hear none of it. They started taunting the Canadian Mounted Police, calling them "pigs" and other slanderous epithets. Bernardine's boyfriend even jumped on board along with others, provoking a mini riot.

The next morning we left the ship and were, of course, followed around by the Canadian police. Several Weather people went to a hotel and were kicked out when they started smoking marijuana. I said goodbye to Diana and Ted and the members of my delegation and headed out of town as quickly as possible, catching a ride in a car with a couple of North Americans who crossed over into Maine. US customs waved us through at the border without a glance at our documents or our luggage. I was delighted to keep my illegal collection of Cuban revolutionary posters and Cuban cigars, which I subsequently doled out to friends.

At the beginning of September, I returned to Indiana University to continue my doctoral studies. Before I left the Cuban sugar boat, the Weather people had urged our delegation to attend the planned Days of Rage in Chicago in October to "bring the war home" and to protest the trial of the Chicago Seven, comprised of leading radical leaders like Tom Hayden and Abbie Hoffman who were charged with causing the riots at the Chicago Democratic convention the year before. I was tempted to go, but my studies and my questions about the politics of the Weathermen kept me in Bloomington, Indiana. My instincts proved right. Some 300 demonstrators rampaged through the streets of Chicago, thrashing business buildings and automobiles, and bursting into high schools, urging students to join them. They wanted to set off an urban riot instead, they alienated most of Chicago's population.

I don't know if Diana and Ted were in Chicago, but I was shocked five months later when the newspaper headlines proclaimed they had died in an explosion at a Greenwich Village house in New York when a pipe bomb went off. I was deeply upset. However misdirected the politics of the Weathermen may have been, two of the most serious and intelligent people in the SDS had blown themselves up in the struggle to bring the war home.

From 1969 to 1971, the US really did feel like we were bringing the war home as the country was in turmoil and appeared to be on the brink of a profound upheaval. Richard Nixon became President in January 1969, after proclaiming in his campaign that he had a "secret plan" to end the war. Nothing could have been further from the truth. He and Henry Kissinger accelerated the aerial war, carpet-bombing harbors and cities in Vietnam and Laos, killing tens of thousands of innocent civilians. They were true war criminals. Then in November, Seymour Hersh published the story of the massacre of My Lai in which over a hundred Vietnamese unarmed men, women and children were slaughtered by a US Infantry unit under the command of Lt. William Calley, Jr.

On April 30, 1970, Nixon announced he was expanding the war in Southeast Asia by sending US troops into Cambodia, claiming it was a major staging area for the Viet Cong. This sparked massive student demonstrations across the United States, leading to the Kent State massacre of four students on May 4 by the Ohio National Guard and then, 10 days later, to the shooting of two students at the predominantly black Jackson State University in Mississippi. The war truly had come home, even to the Midwest and the South, as the nation viewed the events on national TV. I was astonished by the unfolding events, believing that we were living through a turning point in US history. Even Watertown High School in Wisconsin was caught up in the national upheaval where about 150 students demonstrated against the war in front of the school's main entrance. My sister Ann, a sophomore, was suspended from school for three days.

In the fall of 1970 I applied for a Fulbright Fellowship to do my dissertation in Peru on the rise of the coastal sugar plantations and the role of foreign capital. No Fulbrights were being granted for Cuba, even if I could secure a visa to do research there. As Peru had a populist military ruler who had just expropriated many of the plantations, I thought it would be one of the more interesting countries in which to work, although I was also keeping an eye on Chile as the Popular Unity coalition was about to be voted into office on a socialist platform.

13. An Epiphany Begets a Utopian Vagabond

The sound of silence...
—Simon & Garfunkel

On October 4, 1970, Janis Joplin died of a drug overdose. I was enthralled by her music, particularly the album released before her death, "I Got Dem 'Ol Kozmic Blues Again, Mama," in which her white blues style emerged. It was even more pronounced in her posthumous best-selling releases, "Me and Bobby McGee," and "Mercedes Benz." Her death shocked me, leading me to think about where my life was headed.

I heard of her death the following morning, a warm and beautiful fall day in Bloomington, Indiana. I had just left a classroom filled with a couple hundred students where my dissertation adviser, John Lombardi, had given a lecture that he had urged me to attend. I felt alienated by the experience. The idea of lecturing to a large number of students several times a week with little real dialogue just didn't appeal to me. Plus, I reasoned that once I had my Ph.D. in hand, the best I could probably do would be to get a teaching position at some small isolated college or university in a state like Nebraska or Alabama. I might escape the large classes of a big university, only to wind up living in a small town with a social life not all that different from the Midwestern farming community where I grew up.

I was still determined to get my Ph.D. degree, but I would use it as a handle to become an intellectual vagabond committed to radical politics, traveling to Latin America, maybe becoming a guest lecturer at a university for a year, or best of all, becoming a member of one of the alternative

New Left think tanks that were opening up in the United States and Latin America. I would undoubtedly live on or near the poverty line with this life style, but at least I would be living life to its fullest.

I made a number of trips to Washington, D.C. for demonstrations and strategy sessions on the war over the coming months. On an early trip I met Katherine, who had a downtown apartment, and wound up staying at her place on subsequent visits. It was largely a relation of convenience, not passion. She liked the sporadic encounters and companionship, and I, of course, appreciated the free lodging and love-making.

One night, around the end-of-year holidays, things got out of control at a party at her house as I engaged in my first and only multi-sex encounter. Gary, who I lived with and Terry, his girlfriend had driven with me to D.C., also accompanied by Chris, a woman who had made moves on me back in Bloomington. After a few joints and some wine, things came together for us and we escaped into a bedroom. She made love intensely, almost too intensely, humping me virtually every second. I'm not sure if it was her style, or if she was simply seizing the long sought-after opportunity. A couple of hours later I became enthralled with a sensuous girl from Washington and she began playing footsie with me, even allowing me to stroke her back and touch her breasts. But her boyfriend was present and she was still coherent enough to know what limits to set. Later that evening I bedded down with Katherine and we made love. She said nothing about the events at the party.

The farm boy from Wisconsin who had been a virgin until 21 had become a libertine. My erotic encounters with women became an integral part of a broader passion to travel, to struggle for a better world, to search for Utopia, and to explore life in all its manifestations.

At about this time I read Hermann Hesse's *Narcissus and Goldmund*. In a story set in early Renaissance Europe, Goldmund is sent by his father to study at a monastery where he befriends Narcissus, a young monk and scholar. After a few years of learning in which he develops a talent for art and sculpturing, Goldmund goes out to collect herbs one day when he meets a married farm woman and makes love to her in the fields. He returns to the monastery, but soon realizes that his destiny is to pursue his passion for life and art in the wider world. He roams Europe, barely surviving on his artwork and by taking on scholarly tasks, as well as simple day-to-day jobs, always catching the eyes of women he meets along the way. For him, his many loves were openings to the world, enabling him to better appreciate life and deepen his understanding of art.

Goldmund's approach to life during the Renaissance was reflected in the zeitgeist of the rebellious 1960s with its opening to new experiences in love, life and politics. Moreover, I was still affected by the unhappy marriage of my parents, where they both felt entrapped by circumstances in a dreary life. The main catch I saw in Goldmund's life was that around the age of 40, given the more rapid aging of people in early Europe, he found that the women of the world were no longer as interested in him as before. But Hesse gives his main character an out: he returns to join his old friend Narcissus at the monastery where he produces some of his greatest works of art, finally dying peacefully in his arms, worn out by his travails in the real world.

Given the advances of nutrition and health care, I thought I could perhaps make it to 60 with a Goldmund-like life style. After that I couldn't imagine my existence. I really didn't think I would go on to a more creative life by withdrawing from the world to some archive or library. In fact, I came to believe, or perhaps even hope, that my adventures would lead me to a premature death, maybe from a bullet fired by a US trained counter-insurgent, or an airplane crash. My prediction almost came true earlier than I expected: at the age of 45 I nearly drowned in a body surfing accident in Nicaragua. I was saved at the last moment and resurrected in a wheel chair, only to face another major health crisis just short of my 60th birthday.

After my experience in Cuba with the CRV delegation, I became more active in the organization. In February 1971, I went to reside in a cold, windswept Chicago for six weeks as the CRV representative organizing a "Conference on Anti-Imperialist Strategy and Action." I worked closely with Frank Teruggi, who represented the radical Chicago Area Group on Latin America. Frank was a wiry, intense person, whom I could never get a smile or a rise out of. He was a hard worker, totally dedicated to the struggle against the empire. I would meet him again in Chile in 1972. He was murdered by the Chilean junta shortly after the military coup against Salvador Allende.

Documents on Teruggi later forcibly declassified reveal that the CRV came under surveillance in 1971. The FBI stated: "CRV is a national group composed primarily of returned Peace Corps Volunteers who espouse support of Cuba and all Third World revolutionaries and oppose United States' 'imperialism and oppression abroad.'" I found this one of the few FBI covert reports that accurately captured the true mission of the targeted organization and the conference.

The three-day conference in Chicago was a great success. About 300 people attended the different workshops we had organized. There I met Mike Locker, my first contact with the NACLA. He flew in from New York to run a workshop on imperial strategies in the hemisphere and to push NACLA's monthly periodical, then called the *NACLA Newsletter*. Mike called it "scholarly propaganda, persuading people through facts and information that what you feel is true and correct, not through rhetorical flourish and ideological citations." I liked Mike's sharp mind and gregarious personality and began to think that I might someday want to work for NACLA, which had one office in New York and another in Berkeley, California, both of them run as collectives.

Returning to Indiana University after the conference I hit the books, taking my Ph.D. preliminary exams in late April. Just days later, before I knew the results, I took off for Washington, D.C to participate in the massive May Day 1971, demonstrations designed to shut down the federal government and stop the war.

14. Levitating the Pentagon and Jail Time

Having failed to end the Vietnam War with protests that started in 1965, the militant anti-war leaders in 1971 decided to mount the most aggressive non-violent assault possible on Washington, D.C. Putting together the May Day Tribe coalition, they called for people to converge on Washington on Monday, May 3, to "shut down the government." This would be achieved by groups of protesters blocking all the major intersections and bridges in the capital to stop workday traffic from entering the city.

I showed up the Friday before and camped out with the main contingent of demonstrators assembled at West Potomac Park, not far from the Washington Monument where rock music and marijuana abounded as did planning for the takeover of the city. On Sunday, some of us decided to engage in a bit of political theater by going out to Arlington, Virginia, to levitate the Pentagon. While we were chanting and humming in Virginia, the Nixon administration canceled the park permit and the police, dressed in riot gear, stormed the park, firing tear gas, knocking down tents and hauling people away.

We reassembled at churches, universities and homes around the city for the assault on the city. Early Monday morning I headed off with a group of demonstrators to block an intersection near the Roosevelt Memorial Bridge that led into the center of Washington. It was not long before a phalanx of police descended on us from all four streets leading into the intersection, arresting everyone, even those on the sidewalks. About 50 of us were detained and forced on to a waiting bus. In front of me in the line being pushed onto the bus were two dumbfounded college fraternity types who I am convinced were simply visiting Washington. Because the jails were already filled with demonstrators, we were taken to an emergency detention center that was part of the RFK Stadium complex. As the day wore on, we were joined by thousands of other detainees from the hit-and-run battles going on in the streets.

It was later disclosed that the Nixon administration had militarized Washington in the days leading up to May 3 to thwart our efforts to shut down the government. Ten thousand Federal troops, including 4,000 paratroopers from the US 82nd Airborne Division were brought in to back up a 5,000 Metropolitan Police force and 2,000 National Guard troops that were already in the city. At one point, troop transport planes were landing at the rate of one every three minutes at Andrews Air Force base in nearby Maryland. Washington was literally under siege.

By Monday evening the guards at our open-air detention center began moving us into other enclosed areas. I was hauled over to a high school gymnasium where I camped on the floor with several hundred demonstrators. The next day, they had judicial clerks in the gym to process us on misdemeanor charges. If we paid $10 bail and gave our fingerprints we would be released on personal recognizance with a court date.

Most of us refused to leave, not wanting to go on record for what we thought were wrongful charges, and also intending to keep the jails and detention centers full. On Tuesday night, however, I and several other detainees noticed that those who did go through the legal processing received a white slip of paper with a number on it and were allowed to go out a gym exit door after passing through a hallway that had several phone booths lining it. We cut out similar slips of paper, wrote down fake numbers, made believe we wanted to make phone calls, and then handed the slips to the guards at the door.

I was free! About midnight, I crashed at Mary Mullarkey's house, an old friend from college who worked at the Department of the Interior and would later become Chief Justice of the Supreme Court of Colorado. Katherine had given up her apartment the month before. I never saw her again. The next morning, I awoke early and heard news of further demonstrations. I knew I would probably be busted again but I thought it's the least I can do, given that the Vietnamese are dying every day in the war against the United States. As fate would have it, on Wednesday, May 5, John Kerry, the 2004 presidential candidate and a leader of the Vietnam Veterans Against the War, was also in Washington leading a peaceful demonstration that I joined. After a while, some of us left to join a demonstration aimed at blocking access to Capitol Hill where Congress was in session. I gathered with about 150 protesters at the entrance. House Representatives Ronald Dellums and Bella Abzug came out to address us and decry the war.

After they left, we began chanting anti-war slogans again and moments later the police showed up with bullhorns, telling us we had to leave or we would be arrested because our "noise was disrupting the work of Congress." We refused and about a hundred of us were arrested. This time we were carted off to the bowels of the Washington jail system, with about 30 people placed in small crowded holding cells. Once again, most of us refused to be legally processed and leave. We had virtually no access to bathroom facilities and no ventilation. The place became an overheated cesspool and word got out about the conditions. On Thursday night a judge visited us and ordered that we be put in smaller cells that held two apiece.

It was interesting to see that once we were split up into pairs, our morale broke down and most of us, including me, were processed and left the jail on Friday night. I did hear that one demonstrator was held for over two months for refusing to give his name. We were given court dates, but did not return for them. ACLU attorneys took over our case and filed a class action suit for the violation of our right to free speech and the right to assemble in front of Congress. The case dragged on in the local courts for well over a year, with a jury finally deciding that indeed our civil rights had been violated and that we were not disrupting the work of Congress. A key piece of evidence presented on our behalf was tape recordings of a performance several weeks earlier by the Texas Drum and Bugle Corps playing in front of Congress. The noise decibel level on those tapes was much higher than the noise we were making as demonstrators.

Each of us received monetary awards depending on the time we were held in jail, with $10,000 being the maximum if we were held for over 48 hours. I had spent just over 50 hours. The Justice Department, of course, appealed the case all the way to the Supreme Court and in 1975 I finally received a check for $2,000. I had a big party in Oakland, California, and used the rest to pay off some debts.

Returning to Bloomington after being released from jail I was notified that I had passed my preliminary Ph.D. exams with flying colors. I also received a letter saying I was an alternative candidate for a Fulbright Fellowship. My love life was as fragmented and diverse as ever. I even took up with a woman who was a cokehead. The lease on my house expired in early June. Unbeknownst to the landlord, I figured out a way to move into the basement where I stayed for a few more weeks. I then took off for Washington again, this time to do research in the historical archives at the Library of Congress on US commercial relations with South America to facilitate the start of work on my doctoral dissertation.

In late July, the Fulbright Commission notified me that I had been moved up from the alternate list to become the recipient of a two-year grant to do my dissertation on the coastal sugar plantations of Peru. I wrote back to the commission saying I had decided to change my topic to Chile where I would do a study of Chilean industrialization in the 20th century and its relationship to foreign capital.

The commission refused my request, probably not wanting any more Fulbright scholars in Chile under the Marxist government of President Salvador Allende. The United States had already begun its informal blockade of the Chilean economy. In September, I flew to Lima, Peru. There I checked in with the local office of the Fulbright Commission, and set up a joint P.O. Box with an old friend in Lima where I would receive my Fulbright payments. Then I flew off to Chile to begin work on my dissertation, having my semiannual checks forwarded to me in Santiago. My encounter with Allende's Chile and a democratic revolutionary experiment had begun.

UTOPIA FETTERED

15. The Long Trek Home from Paradise Lost

"I rebel, therefore I exist."
–Albert Camus

The story of my odyssey opened in this book with the event that shook my life forever—the bloody overthrow of Salvador Allende on September 11, 1973, the first democratic socialist president in the Americas. I left Chile in early October on a long trek back to the United States. I crossed the Andes into Argentina, taking buses to Buenos Aires and then up to the capital of Brazil where I caught a cheap flight to Panama. Virtually penniless, I started hitchhiking up the Pan American Highway hoping to make it to California. I spent my first night camping on the beach in a Panamanian hamlet. The next night found me in San Jose, Costa Rica and early in the morning, after a rest in a no-star hotel, I headed off to the northern border, crossing into Nicaragua.

I confess to not being particularly enamored with Nicaragua from the start, being taken aback by its abject poverty, harsh terrain and climate. The landscape is bleak and arid in Rivas, Nicaragua's southern-most province that I crossed into from Costa Rica. The foliage increased as I traveled closer to Managua, but then a wall of heat hit me as I entered the capital. Managua's climate is always sweltering, hot and humid for half the year and hot and dry for the other half when dusty winds kick up. If you are lucky, you may feel a slightly cooling breeze blow over the city in late December and early January.

Less than ten months before, on December 23, 1972, a devastating earthquake had shaken the country, killing over 10,000 people and destroying the old downtown area that fronted on Lake Managua. I saw only a few severely damaged high-rise office buildings still standing amongst the rubble, while impoverished barrios ringed the outskirts of Managua. There tens of thousands of people lived in tents and haphazard dwellings. Semi-naked children, many with distended bellies, ran around in the dirt-covered streets.

The devastation and poverty I saw were due in large part to the fact that the ruling Somoza family had pilfered much of the international relief assistance after the earthquake. The clan, backed by the United States, had dominated the country since the mid-1930s when Anastacio Somoza Garcia, the head of the National Guard, assassinated Augusto Cesar Sandino, the leader of a guerrilla army. For years, Sandino had used hit-and-run tactics to strike against the occupying US marines until they withdrew in 1933. Some called it the "War of the Mosquito." A series of negotiations with the rebels led to a truce and after one session in Managua on February 21, 1934, Somoza arrested Sandino and his fellow insurgent leaders with the complicity of the US ambassador and had them executed.

The Somozas came to dominate the country's economy, taking over some of the richest lands that produced coffee, cattle and cotton for export. The family owned textile companies, sugar mills, rum distilleries, the merchant marine line, Nicaragua's only airline, and the country's largest pasteurized milk facility. Many national and foreign companies were squeezed for payments in return for economic concessions. By some estimates, the personal wealth of the country's reigning scion in the mid-1970s, Anastacio Somoza Debayle, called "Tacho," stood at US \$400 million, the largest in all of Central America.

As I departed Managua after a couple of days, I told myself this is one of the last places in the world I would ever want to visit again. Even though Chile was dominated by Pinochet and a military junta, there is no comparison between the countries, I thought. Chile's trade unions, its democratic tradition and the rich array of leftist political parties meant that it, rather than Nicaragua, would soon throw off the yoke of oppression. Almost exactly five years later, in October 1978, I would find myself flying into Managua. Nicaragua, not Chile, was on the brink of revolution.

After leaving Nicaragua, I traveled by land through Honduras and then into El Salvador. My first encounter with the country in 1973 had a twist. At Indiana University as a graduate student in 1968 I had met Carlos Castaneda who was working on a Ph.D. in physics. Very friendly and affable, he came from an upper middle class professional family in San Salvador. We became good friends and he told me that if I ever wound up in his native country I should look up his brother Ricardo who worked in international law and collaborated with the foreign ministry.

Exhausted and destitute, I looked up Carlos' brother in the phone book when I reached the outskirts of San Salvador. I called his home and was put in touch with him at his office. Ricardo told me to wait where I was, that he would send a vehicle to pick me up. To my surprise, I was met by a chauffeur-driven limousine and taken to his home in an ostentatious neighborhood in San Salvador where he lived with his wife and two children, replete with a swimming pool and half-a-dozen servants. Ricardo was no longer simply an international lawyer, he was now the second highest ranking official in the Ministry of Foreign Relations.

El Salvador was relatively tranquil in 1973 with a veneer of prosperity as the multinational corporations invested heavily in a country with an industrious, subservient labor force. As a Chamber of Commerce brochure proclaimed, "If you tell a Salvadoran to plant rocks and harvest more rocks, he will do it." It is the most densely populated country in Central America and the oligarchs then still derived much of their wealth from agriculture, particularly coffee. Two percent of the population controlled 60 percent of the land. *"La Chusma"* or "the rabble," as the lower classes were disparagingly called, lived in miserable conditions. Fifty-eight percent of the people earned $10 a month or less, while 70 percent of the children under five years old were malnourished.

The year before I arrived had been tumultuous. In rigged elections in 1972, the oligarchy-backed candidate, Colonel Arturo Molino, stole the presidency from Christian Democrat Jose Napoleon Duarte who had campaigned on a platform of modest reforms. Spontaneous protests erupted but Duarte, who was already known for his lack of political backbone, refused to call on his followers to contest the election results in the streets. Then Colonel Benjamin Mejia, who read poetry to his troops (shades of Hugo Chavez in Venezuela over two decades later!), arrested the incumbent president for violating the Salvadoran constitution by upholding the fraudulent election results. The revolt was quickly crushed, Duarte was blamed, and after three of his fingertips were cut off, he was sent into exile. Less than a decade later, when he came to power under US tutelage and turned a blind eye on military atrocities, Duarte would hold up his fingers to seemingly prove his bravery.

Influenced by the Cuban revolution, Salvadoran guerrilla movements took root in the early 1970s, led by two unusually controversial figures in Salvadoran history: Joaquin Villalobos, the head of the People's Revolutionary Army (ERP), and Salvador Cayteano Carpio, known as Marcial, who broke with the Communist Party at the age of 50 over its pursuit of electoral politics to found the Popular Liberation Forces Farabundo Marti (FPL). The ERP initially captured public attention with its kidnappings of members of the oligarchy for hefty ransoms while the FPL focused more on building popular organizations among the masses. Marcial became known as the Ho Chi Minh of Central America.

When I first arrived in El Salvador, the aura of repression from the previous year had abated somewhat. The capital city of San Salvador did not appear as bleak as the earthquake-devastated Managua that I had just come from. Ricardo Castaneda, while acknowledging the simmering discontent in his country, argued, "El Salvador is changing for the better. We are building a new country." He represented a new generation of technocrats who thought they could bring some level of civility to the oligarchic-military regime. After listening to my account of what had happened in Chile the month before, he proudly proclaimed, "See, I was right when I convinced my government to allow some Chileans to take temporary refuge in the Salvadoran embassy after the coup in Santiago." I didn't bother to challenge him by pointing out that this hardly compared with the actions of the Panamanian, Italian and other foreign embassies in Santiago which accepted hundreds of Chileans seeking refuge and then allowed many of them to take asylum in their countries. After a couple of days I left and was driven in Ricardo's chauffeured limousine up to the Guatemalan border. Then it was life on the lam again as I grabbed the first of several buses up to the Mexican border, accompanied by Mayan-speaking Guatemalans replete with bags of beans, corn and caged chickens.

About a week later, I caught a two-day train that took me to Mexicali on the California border, and a day-and-a-half later I hitchhiked into the Bay Area. I crashed with my friend Glenn Borchardt, who had lived on the farm across the road from me where I grew up. He had moved to San Francisco the year before with his wife Marilyn who had been a classmate of mine in high school. Glenn had a Ph.D. in soil sciences and worked for the state of California as a geologic and earthquake scientist. Marilyn ran a foster-parenting organization. They had a two-year-old adopted daughter, Nina. I began living with them and we soon agreed to rent a house in Oakland, which we eventually wound up buying.

I came to Berkeley to work for NACLA, a radical research center that put out a monthly publication. I was determined to use a pen to do what I could to foment international opposition to the Chilean dictatorship. I did not believe the struggle for a socialist utopia was lost. The left needed to regroup and learn from this historic setback. I dedicated the next seven years of my life to taking part in this task at NACLA, an endeavor that would take me through many twists and turns in my political and personal life.

16. Tribulations at Home and in Latin America

"Change does not roll in on the wheels of inevitability, but comes through continuous struggle."
—Martin Luther King, Jr.

As I walked into the NACLA office in Berkeley in late October 1973, I was warmly greeted by Fred Goff. I had first met him in Chile the year before when I picked him up in downtown Santiago on my Yamaha motorbike and we rode out to my place in El   on the eastern outskirts of the city overlooking the   River. We had a great fish   with a couple of friends. Fred is one of the most engaging persons I have ever known, with an exceptional ability to listen and relate to your interests. Months after talking to him, he brings up past conversations and personal matters that you don't even remember telling him. He also has extraordinary administrative and editorial skills, talents sorely needed then by organizations like NACLA.

Fred was the son of a Presbyterian minister who had served in Colombia and graduated from Stanford University in Latin American studies. He joined a fact-finding US delegation that went to the Dominican Republic after the Johnson administration sent in the Marines in 1965 to repress a popular uprising. Upon returning to the United States, Fred along with others formed the North American Congress on Latin America in New York, putting out its first newsletter on Latin America in 1967. The word "Congress" soon became a misnomer as NACLA evolved into a research and publication center run by a collective staff, first out of a Manhattan office, then another office in Berkeley set up by Fred when he moved in 1971.

The founding of NACLA reflected the broader rise of new left centers and publications in the United States in the 1960s and early 1970s, which also included the Middle East Research and Information Project (MERIP), The Insurgent Sociologist, Radical America, and the Union for Radical Political Economics (URPE). They contributed to the intellectual renaissance of the period, rethinking many of the truisms of the Old Left, as well as exposing the exploitative role of multinational corporations and the interventionist strategies of the US empire.

At NACLA, I went to work as an understudy to Elizabeth Farnsworth who had written and edited "New Chile," an outstanding and widely read work on the Allende years. It depicted the popular struggles unleashed by the government as it sought to construct a socialist society while exposing the efforts of the CIA and the Nixon administration to destabilize and overthrow President Allende and the Popular Unity coalition. After his historic speech to the United Nations on December 4, 1972, denouncing the informal economic blockade and US efforts to topple his government, Allende, in response to questions at a press conference, declared: "If you want to know how the United States has affected Chile, just read 'New Chile' by NACLA."

Elizabeth is another charming persona like Fred; vibrant, very talented and able to win your immediate confidence by showing an interest in your perceptions and concerns in life. After leaving NACLA, she went on to become a regular correspondent for *The Nation* magazine and later a reporter for the PBS News Hour. Elizabeth also later produced and directed a superb documentary film on Judge Juan Guzman, the first Chilean magistrate to prosecute Augusto Pinochet in the early 2000s.

At NACLA I began trying to write for the "real world." The Ph.D. process turns students into academic scribes, writers of dissertations and journal articles in an obscure and turgid language that is only understood by professors and university elite. Elizabeth had published in the *San Francisco Bay Guardian* and suggested I write a piece on Chile for that alternative weekly magazine. It was a flop, even though I redrafted it many times and cannot recall if the *Guardian* finally ran it or not. But under Elizabeth's and Fred's tutelage I persevered and finally did begin to hone a more accessible writing style.

My companion in Chile, Elizabeth Patelke, had returned to her parent's home in Lake Bluff, Illinois. She was devastated by the coup in Chile and the murder and disappearance of friends and was suffering traumatic depression, not knowing what to do with her life. After a month or so, I persuaded her to come to California to live with me and Glenn and Marilyn. Although there was always a certain distance between us because she was more domestic-minded and less engaged in the world than me, our relationship was rekindled as we found love and solace with each other based on the bonds we had forged in Chile. For the time being I was content to be monogamous as I focused on my work and the political challenges unfolding in the world around me. Elizabeth got a job in another organization that Fred set up, the Information Services on Latin America (ISLA). It clipped and recompiled the major US newspaper articles on Latin America, distributing them to other left organizations as well as to professional associations and writers who subscribed to ISLA.

With the rise of dictatorships in Chile and Latin America, which controlled three-quarters of the continent's population by the mid-1970s, NACLA served as a bridge between the solidarity organizations in the United States and the struggling oppressed Latin American societies. We would write about the resistance of underground movements, their differing analyses of the political conditions they faced, and the role of the US government in backing the dictatorial regimes.

I also became active in Non-Intervention in Chile (NICH), an organization with close ties to NACLA. The offshoot of a precursor organization founded (before the coup) in April 1973 by Eric Leenson (who would become a lifelong friend), NICH became the main solidarity organization on the West Coast. It denounced the systematic human rights violations taking place in Chile, provided any help it could to the imprisoned and impoverished victims of the dictatorship while working with Bay Area trade unions and other grassroots organizations to press for changes in US policy towards Chile.

Bob High, whom I had met in Chile where he worked as a mathematics professor at the University of Chile, also returned to Berkeley and became the new head of NICH. I had last seen Bob just two weeks before the coup at a Sunday barbecue fiesta at Charlie Horman's house. Charlie and Bob, largely oblivious to the hubbub around them, were playing the highly cerebral game of Chinese Go. Three weeks later, Charlie was dead.

Tall, lanky and austere, Bob never knew where his next rent check was coming from. He was a Trotsky-like figure of the solidarity movement, constantly reading political theory, traveling and always thinking strategically about the best way to advance the movement. I admired him, went camping with him in the California Sierras on occasion, and remained a friend of his until the day he died in a river rafting accident in Chile in early 1993 at the age of 40 while trying to rescue a fellow rafter.

NACLA and the solidarity organizations participated in the broader political debate among the left in the United States and Latin America about how to seize the political initiative. Most of the leaders and organizations on the left still believed that a new epoch of social and political upheaval had begun in the 1960s. In this view, 1968 marked a historic turning point. The world was engulfed in a series of political and social revolts of which the most dramatic were the Paris uprising in May, the Prague spring of "socialism with a human face," the student uprising in Mexico, and the political turmoil in the United States, which reached its peak at the Democratic convention in Chicago.

However, none of these movements or uprisings was victorious. Indeed, they each met with defeat in the same year: President Charles de Gaulle weathered the general strike and remained in power in France; Soviet tanks rolled into Czechoslovakia; students were slaughtered in Tlatelolco Square in Mexico; and Richard Nixon won the presidential elections in the United States. And yet, the events of 1968 changed the world. They were similar to the revolutions of 1848 in Europe (which precipitated the flight of some of my German ancestors to America) in that although the revolts failed, they marked the beginning of an entirely new political era. The genie could not be put back in the bottle. The social movements and political forces unleashed in the 1960s questioned not only the existing political systems, but also the social values and relations that exist between races, sexes, communities, nations, and individuals.

Placed in historical perspective, the political upheavals of the 60s and early 70s had two important effects on US society. On the one hand they nurtured the development of an array of radical and Marxist thinkers, many of whom were able to secure positions in universities or alternative research centers where they influenced subsequent generations. Simultaneously, the social discontent and political questioning of this period enabled a number of powerful social movements to arise and expand. The Black and civil rights movements, the rise of new trade unions like the United Farm Workers in California, the emergence of feminism and the National Organization of Women (NOW), the development of the environmental and gay rights movements—these social movements, together with the anti-war and solidarity organizations, made up a powerful and permanent force for change in the United States that the right wing has been trying to roll back for decades.

NACLA in the 1970s was caught up in this political cauldron, trying to help push forward a radical agenda and appropriate political strategies. In spite of the rise of the dictatorships in Latin America and the Nixon administration, we believed the shift to the right was temporary, that the very brutality of the dictatorships, like the repression of the Batista regime in Cuba in the 1950s, would foment new guerrilla movements leading to new revolutionary victories.

17. Rejoining a Dysfunctional Family

Soon after returning to California, I began to rekindle my family relations, making several trips to Wisconsin. I found that I was a part of a family that had become completely dysfunctional. The relationship between my mother and father had reached a breaking point while I was in Chile. They quarreled incessantly. My father, Hubert, spent less and less time at home, going to the bars, working as a farm organizer, and becoming marginally involved in the Civil Rights Movement in Milwaukee. He began to mentor young black kids, often bringing them home to do paid work on the farm. My mother, Rita, was outraged; she felt he was neglecting his own family, spending time with them while leaving my younger brothers to do the chores.

Despite the ongoing pleas of my mother that began before I left for Chile, I refused to become involved in their fracturing marriage. But when I returned home from Chile, I began to talk more with my six siblings than I had when living with them. My favorite was Ann, 10 years younger than me. When I was in college, I brought home books for her to read. I remember giving her John Dewey's thin tome "Liberalism and Social Action." I doubt if she understood much of it given that she was still in grade school, but she was impressed by the fact that her oldest brother took an interest and tried to discuss what was going on in the world with her.

My oldest sibling, Marie, moved to Madison in the late 1960s and after briefly attending a Catholic women's college, went to the University of Wisconsin. I did try to see her on occasion, but she would have nothing to do with me. She intensely disliked me because I had picked on her and bullied her incessantly when we were growing up on the farm. It took decades for the psychological scars to heal between us.

My relationship with my brother Joel, eight years younger than me, has been contentious at times and complicated. The most industrious and entrepreneurial in the family, from the time he was a little boy he always wanted to be a "success," promising my mother that when he grew up, he would build her a new house. Joel won my father's favor when in school because unlike me, he threw himself wholeheartedly into helping out with the chores and field work. But in his late high school years, more fiercely independent and willful than I was, Joel went from father's favorite to classic rebellious son. He decided that he had worked enough for his dad who was increasingly absent from the farm—drinking at the two bars three miles down the road in the small community of Richwood, leaving Joel at home to do the evening chores.

By his senior year, Joel had started his own rock band, made fake ID cards for his classmates who couldn't get into the Watertown bars and become involved in petty drug dealing. For an irreverent look, he stole altar boy cassocks from St. Henry's Church to outfit his rock band. Given that Joel was helping out less than ever with the chores, Dad got angrier than Mother over the theft and called the sheriff who came out at supper-time one evening, searched the house and arrested Joel for having false ID cards. Fortunately, no marijuana was found in the house because Mom had already found it in his room and flushed it down the toilet, compelling Joel to find a more secure hiding place. The parish priest didn't press charges for the altar boy clothes, which in any case weren't found at the house. Joel was held in jail for a couple of days before being released. The sheriff decided it wasn't worth it to prosecute for the false IDs, especially given that it was Joel's first offense. Joel graduated and moved to Madison in the summer of 1970, took a few courses at the university, and soon became involved in more remunerative business activities. Like me, he was a rebel, but of a different type, working on the more lucrative margins of the new alternative society.

The final crisis in the relationship between my parents began in 1970. My mom refused to tolerate her husband's ever-increasing drinking problem, fearing that they would lose the farm as the debts piled up. She tried to get one of Hubert's brothers who lived in Nebraska to come out to talk to him, but to no avail. She next went to support meetings for spouses and friends of alcoholics, trying unsuccessfully to get Dad to go to Alcoholic Anonymous meetings. She then talked to the parish priest and convinced Hubert to participate in counseling sessions. She thought it was working out and I even remember getting a letter from her in Chile saying, "Your dad loves me again." But after a while, he refused to go to any more sessions and turned silent, stonewalling any efforts by Rita to talk with him. One night she became so furious with him that she smashed and fractured a cast iron frying pan on the stove.

Mom finally forced the issue by filing for a two-year separation in March 1972, just before Easter. I was in Chile enjoying the last days of summer, but in Watertown it was a snowy wintry day and the schools were dismissed early before the roads became impassable. Ann had stayed home that day and as Dad started packing his bags he told her, "Mom doesn't want me here anymore." My younger sisters Miriam and Del Rey were called off the bus as it was about to depart St. Henry's and ordered by the priest to remain in the priory. He told them our parents were separating and they should wait until Dad had left. My younger brother Fran, a freshman in high school, took off with friends, hoping to spend the snowy day having fun indoors with his buddies in town.

A couple of hours later, Mom picked up her two daughters at the priory. When they arrived home, Dad was still packing and he retreated to the bedroom. Miriam, already a straight-talking eighth-grader went up to him and asked, "How come you're leaving; is it because you don't love us?" Dad, who always had problems directly expressing his feelings replied, "Who said I don't love you?"

Dad moved to a run-down hotel in Watertown, the only one he could afford. He would come out every morning to do the chores and then go back in the evenings. My dad's relationship with his sons was always better than with his daughters, and Fran stayed with him at the hotel for a while. But the room was too small and with only one bed. Fran soon found himself dejectedly splitting his time between staying with mom and crashing with friends.

This was the dire, unhappy situation I found when I began to visit Watertown in late 1973. There was little I could do. I conversed with my sisters. Ann was in the best shape, about to take off for Madison and the university in the fall; Miriam had found a certain inner stability which she would carry throughout her life. I felt close to Del Rey, a sweet, quiet girl, and tried to play the nice big brother to her. She was the most devastated by the family breakup. Fran, like his dad, was a boy of few words, easygoing and nice with lots of friends, but not disposed to probing or dealing with his inner feelings.

Mother said I should go and talk to dad, which I did, but not with her agenda of trying to get him to rectify his life so they could reconcile. I did establish some of my old rapport with him but as usual, it was difficult to draw him out, to get him to express his feelings and thoughts. He began going to Milwaukee more frequently, visiting the Black kids and their families that he had befriended in earlier years. I believe he identified with the suffering and difficulties in life of the mostly poor Black families he took up with.

This dismal family situation made me believe more than ever that one could never attain happiness in marriage or family life. Fulfillment could only be found in one's work, adventures, and a continuing quest for the exotic in life.

18. Agribusiness, Left Politics, New Lover

Love and knowledge led upwards to the heavens
But always pity brought me back to earth;
Cries of pain reverberated in my heart
Of children in famine, of victims tortured
And of old people left helpless.
I long to alleviate the evil, but I cannot.
And I too suffer.
This has been my life; I found it worth living.
—Bertrand Russell, Autobiography

At NACLA in Berkeley I found purpose in my work as I wrote about the situation in Chile and Latin America. I also participated in collective discussions about new directions for the New Left in the United States as well as in Latin America. At first these were healthy discussions, but a certain sectarianism soon took hold as we became engulfed in intense debates over the "correct" ideological position. The US military was experiencing defeat in Southeast Asia and the government was suffering splits in the political leadership as evidenced by the Watergate scandal but, nonetheless, the left was unclear what needed to be done at this historic moment.

Susanne Jonas, a piano prodigy and a brilliant political scientist with a Ph.D. from the University of California, Berkeley, joined NACLA before my arrival. She staked out the country of Guatemala as her area of expertise, becoming a life-long writer and expert on the country, committed to the struggle of the Guatemalan people and their revolutionary organizations against a succession of US-backed regimes. When I joined NACLA in 1973, Susanne was in the midst of coordinating the publication of "Test Case for the Hemisphere: United States Strategy in Guatemala, 1950-1974," a seminal study of the US-backed coup of 1954 and US support for the authoritarian regimes that came to dominate the country.

Drawing on the experience of the Cuban revolution, in which a small band of guerrillas led by Fidel Castro overthrew the Batista dictatorship, Susanne and many other political activists began to study the Bolshevik revolution in Russia, believing it could provide lessons that were germane to the United States. They came to view its leader, Lenin, as a powerful thinker and actor who through his iron will and clear vision was able to persevere and lead the Bolshevik party to power. They proposed that likewise, the only way to transform the United States would be to build a Leninist-type party that could serve as a vanguard to mobilize the rest of society.

Susanne became obsessed with NACLA's relations with other political organizations in the United States and abroad. As a highly respected organization on the left we were often asked to endorse political statements and demonstrations by other organizations. At first, the discussions over these endorsements seemed fairly innocuous and just plain tedious as Susanne and a few others in NACLA compelled us to engage in weekly debates over which political organization had the "correct line" and merited our endorsement and support. I soon became disgruntled, often petulant at the meetings, feeling like I was wasting my time; I would much rather be writing and doing something more productive.

As time went on, Susanne recruited others—both old and new members of NACLA—to her Leninist position. I had allies on the collective staff, but they soon opted out of the debate. Michael Klare, a gay activist on the collective and a first-rate analyst of the Pentagon and its international strategies, like me, felt that the discussions were a waste of time. He soon abandoned the staff meetings to focus on his work and subsequently got a research fellowship at Princeton University, eventually leaving NACLA to carry out his research and writings in a more academic setting. Elizabeth Farnsworth also began to pull away from NACLA, although in her case, it was perhaps more personal as she had a second child and wanted to pursue other interests in life. That left me as the sole holdout at the NACLA collective meetings. Fred Goff did not adopt the Leninist perspective; indeed it is even doubtful if he was a Marxist, but due to the respect he commanded in the organization and his refusal to confront Susanne and the others, he remained above the fray trying to mediate the differences.

I reacted badly, often sulking at the meetings and engaging in "unsocial" behavior, unable to articulate a clear political perspective that differed from the Leninist approach. But I continued my work at NACLA, still feeling that it offered the best outlet for me to continue writing on the struggles of the Latin American peoples and the atrocities of the US empire. I also persevered because I knew that the NACLA collective in New York had a political stance similar to mine. In our joint annual gatherings we would usually shake Fred into siding with us and holding back the Leninist assault in order to ensure the overall survival and effectiveness of the organization.

While in the midst of this sectarian battle I launched a new project, Agribusiness in the Americas. Drawing on my farm roots and my rural experiences in Latin America, I became part of the burgeoning radical critique of US corporate and agricultural policies. For most of the 20th century these policies had decimated peasant societies, compelling them to abandon their lands and work as wage laborers on plantations and agribusiness enterprises that produced cheap food for the global markets. My research for the project often took me away from the oppressive atmosphere at NACLA as I went to Washington, DC to interview policy makers and traveled to Latin America to witness firsthand the struggles of the peasantry and the inroads made by US agribusiness corporations. To the chagrin of the Leninists on staff, I also became an effective fundraiser for the organization as I garnered research funds for the critique of agribusiness and the work I was doing on human rights issues. The National Council of Churches and emergent progressive foundations and donors began to support our work.

My interest in starting the agribusiness project was nurtured by what I saw happening to our family farm when I visited Wisconsin, even as my parent's relationship entered its final throes. The two-year trial separation ended in divorce in June 1974. My Dad could now finally realize his lifelong dream and sell off the farm as the only way to divide up the assets. The 160-acre farm they had owned for over two decades was sold for $160,000. That was a lot of money in 1974 and more than my parents had ever expected. The bulk of the funds went to pay off bank debts. The remainder was split 60-40 between my parents as the divorce property laws were still based on patriarchy and the false belief that the man was the main breadwinner. My Mom bought a nice house in Watertown for $20,000 where she went to live with her two youngest daughters, Miriam and Del Rey. She got a job as a nurse's aide at the Watertown hospital for a meager salary. But with the house fully paid off and a small nest egg left over, she could live decently.

Dad paid child support of $90 per month for each child. He moved to Milwaukee, got a factory job, joined a union organizing movement, and bought a big house in the Black area of the city. Never good at managing his money, he put his trust in a shifty stockbroker who took him to the cleaners, leaving him with very little savings.

During the 1950s and '60s, Europe and Japan had become major economic powers, winning an ever-increasing share of the global market for their manufactured products. In 1971, Nixon launched the New Economic Policy (NEP), which took the US off the gold standard and devalued the dollar. The NEP was designed to overcome the first US trade deficit by increasing grain and agricultural exports.

Just as the United States began to break down agricultural trade barriers in the name of "free trade," the Soviet Union experienced a cold summer that destroyed much of its grain crop and purchased one quarter of US grain exports in 1972. This caused an explosion in grain prices on the international market. The five giant trade corporations, led by Cargill of Minnesota, made enormous profits as they used their insider information to buy cheap grain reserves and obtain US export subsidies. This led to Congressional investigations of the grain corporations, but it also caused a trickle-down effect for smaller farmers as land values began to increase over the next two years. My parents lucked out, catching this boom in the land cycle price, alleviating in some small way the back-breaking work they had endured for decades in trying to make ends meet and keep food on the table for their seven children.

This unfolding global shake-up in grain and agriculture was grist for the first NACLA Report on agribusiness. While I was in the early stages of working on that report, Patricia Flynn, a strikingly beautiful woman walked into the office trying to find out about volunteer work. As the collective was engaged in another dreary meeting, I had slipped out and was the only one in the front room to talk to her about NACLA and the agribusiness project. About one year older than me, Pat lived with Leon Klayman, a bohemian over 10 years her senior. Leon's lifestyle was probably closer to Goldmund's than mine, being a penniless artist who engaged in guerilla poster art work on behalf of the homeless and the social movements in San Francisco. The year before, Pat and Leon had returned from a year-long trip in which they took their Volkswagen bus on a ship from New York to Venezuela and then drove all the way down the South American continent to Chile and back again. Pat was currently finishing her Master's degree in international relations at San Francisco State University.

I have never liked being a solitary writer, always preferring to entice others to work with me on a given project. So it was natural for me to suggest to Pat after a couple of meetings that we might work together. Possessing a very creative and agile mind, she became a co-equal with me in the project and within months, we jointly published *The US Grain Arsenal* in October 1975. Leon made a block print for the report cover— a portrait of Henry Kissinger in the guise of the Statue of Liberty holding up a sheath of grain in place of the light that's a beacon to immigrants.

Although we weren't fully cognizant of it at the time, the *Grain Arsenal* outlined the early stages of the rise of neoliberalism and globalization. US multinational corporations in the 1950s and '60s had begun outsourcing their production, particularly to Europe, where they began manufacturing durable and consumer commodities to sell back to the US market. These multinationals, along with agribusiness corporations then began touting "free trade" as a solution to the world's problems, asserting that capital as well as all commodities should be free to flow around the world, breaking down national tariff barriers that stood in their way.

The impact on workers or the explosion of hunger and starvation in the third world countries were irrelevant to the free traders. As an assistant secretary of agriculture for international affairs, Richard Bell, told me in an interview in 1975, "Our primary concern is commercial exports.... We can't subordinate our commercial exports to needy people." Dan Ellerman, who worked under Henry Kissinger on the National Security Council, declared: "To give food aid to countries just because people are starving is a pretty weak reason." Earl Butz, the secretary of agriculture who had worked for the likes of Ralston Purina and Stokely-Van Camp stated publicly, "Hungry men only listen to those who have a piece of bread."

As Pat and I wrote in the introduction to *The US Grain Arsenal*: "Economic integration under capitalism is also having detrimental effects on US working people. Because of the growing internationalization of capitalist production, the multinational corporations no longer rely as heavily on the purchasing power of US workers to sustain their economic growth. Thus, higher food prices and the resultant decline in the standard of living for North Americans are acceptable to the multinationals, especially when these changes are part of a strategy to prop up the US empire and to aid the international expansion of the corporations. The treatment of the US worker as only one of many market inputs explains why Secretary of Agriculture Butz pushed ardently for foreign grain markets while simultaneously calling for a reduction in the Food Stamp program."

Even though I had a satisfying, largely conflict-free family life with Elizabeth, Glenn and Marilyn, I soon became restless. I guess I was permanently afflicted by the Goldmund syndrome and the need to live life on the lam, always exploring in the broader world.

Taking another page out of Hesse's *Narcissus and Goldmund*, Glenn came to play a Narcissus-like role for me. Very intelligent and mentally agile, Glenn would talk with me for hours on end, usually at the dinner table, about science, politics, philosophy, Marxism, infinity, all the great concepts of life. But he was my opposite in lifestyle. Except for hunting and camping trips, he was a stable homebody, totally dedicated to Marilyn and his marriage. She was his first and last love. He went to work every day, followed the rules of the state bureaucracy, even when he felt that he had a better idea or was being taking advantage of by his superiors.

Elizabeth was a very sensuous person and we had a satisfying sexual relationship. But she was quiet, and we engaged in few animated conversations. A stillness settled over our relationship. When I had first met her in graduate school as a student of Slavic Studies at Indiana University, I had thought she would educate me on one of the areas of the world of which I was largely ignorant. But once she left school, she dropped all interest in the region, hardly ever discussing the achievements, failures or news coming out of the Soviet Union and Eastern Europe.

I became bored with my home life. I remember, on my 31st birthday I left my car parked in front of the house and took off on a hitchhiking trip up the northern coast of California. I simply wanted to meet and talk to people from all walks of life, to find out about their singular experiences in the world.

When I had returned from Chile, I began to work about one day a week on construction for an old high school friend, Jim Schmitt who had found his "fortune" in California, building houses and additions as a contractor. The money, $50 a day, was useful, as I got very little from NACLA. But more importantly, I enjoyed the experience of getting out of the office once a week to clear my head and just bang away with the hammer, the nails and wrecking bars.

I think Pat and I both instinctively sensed that a sexual liaison was inevitable from the first moment we laid eyes on each other at the NACLA office. Stunningly beautiful with dark hair and dark brown eyes, she had an Italian-Mediterranean complexion and a slender physique that she inherited from her Italian-American mother, belying her father's Irish genes.

Her family history was fascinating. Her mother, Matilda "Mattie"

Mele, was a child of the Roaring Twenties. Born in Washington, DC, she went to California at a young age to work as a secretary for Frank "Porky" Flynn who, along with Artie Samish, ran the liquor lobby in the state capitol of Sacramento. It bought and sold politicians to fix liquor prices for the public. They also lobbied on behalf of other business interests, including the petroleum corporations. The rewards for Samish and Flynn were concessions on parking lots and other activities in Reno and Las Vegas, along with insider tips on getting stocks.

For some unknown reason, Mattie went to Chicago after a few years to meet John Ryan, an acquaintance of Frank's who controlled the slot machines in the Windy City. She wound up marrying him, but continued to return to Sacramento every summer. When she turned 40 she became pregnant with Pat by Frank Flynn. Mattie returned to live with Ryan while continuing her annual visits to California with her new babe in arms. Then at the age of 45, she got pregnant with Pat's sister, finally divorcing Ryan and marrying Flynn.

Several years later, the Feds investigated the business activities of Flynn and Samish and indicted them for tax evasion. While awaiting trial, Frank suffered a heart attack and died when Pat was 10 years old. The Feds seized a sizable portion of the family inheritance but there was still plenty left over for Mattie to clip stock coupons, live in the upscale neighborhood of Pacific Heights, San Francisco, and send her daughters to good schools. Pat used the inheritance from one of her Dad's concessions on the Harrah's parking lots in Las Vegas to help defray the costs of attending Smith College.

Pat, who had a stormy relationship with her Mom, introduced me to Mattie early on. We hit it off. She was an elegant and entertaining woman. We would remain grand friends until the day she died at the age of 93.

As Pat and I were engaged in the final stages of producing *The Grain Arsenal*, the sexual tension between us became unbearable. My house and her pad with Leon were naturally out of bounds, so one day Pat said, "I have a great idea. Let's go over to my mother's place in Pacific Heights." Mattie was gone. In her early 70s she had married for a third time to a Jewish retail auctioneer in Reno where they lived part time. In the apartment's living room, under the big bay windows, Pat threw a cot-like mattress on the floor. Then we undressed, lay down and caressed each other's bodies, making ravenous love as the warm afternoon sun began to set over the Golden Gate Bridge.

19. Imperial Decline and a Dysfunctional Left

At the end of April 1975 refugees were being airlifted from the roof of the US embassy in Saigon to waiting ships where the helicopters were unceremoniously dumped overboard to make room for more incoming flights. The US debacle was complete, and while the victory belonged to the Vietnamese, our anti-war organizing, protests and militant actions starting in 1965 had played no small part in bringing the war to the end. Coming in the aftermath of Watergate and the resignation of Nixon the year before, the US political establishment was in disarray as it withdrew from Southeast Asia. More importantly, the defeat gave rise to what some on the US right referred to as the "Vietnam Syndrome," the unwillingness of the American public to send troops to foreign lands.

Adding to the woes of the US empire were reports in late 1975 and early 1976 of Cuban troops arriving in Angola to help defend the newly independent Marxist government against counterrevolutionary forces supported by the apartheid regime of South Africa with the backing of US Secretary of State Henry Kissinger. An island 90 miles from the shores of the United States had the audacity to do what the US imperial leaders and empires past thought was their sole prerogative—send a military force to a distant continent.

Among the investigative skills I learned at NACLA was an ability to do power structure research. NACLA's Research Methodology Guide, put together principally by Fred Goff, Michael Klare and Mike Locker, was one of the key publications that helped the left analyze the relations between the corporate elites and US political leaders. Thus we began to track the Trilateral Commission immediately upon its birth in 1974. It represented an effort by the more moderate and liberal groups of the establishment to try to reconstruct the fractured consensus in US foreign policy. Comprised of major corporate, political and even academic figures, the term "Trilateral" reflected the inclusion of elite representatives from Europe and Japan. The Commission's platform held that new Third World challenges could be met only if the leading capitalist nations strengthened their multilateral ties and forged a common front for dealing with the emergent process of globalization. In the United States, the Commission included figures like David Rockefeller, Cyrus Vance, Zbigniew Brzezinski, and a rising political star, Governor Jimmy Carter of Georgia.

The conclusion of the Vietnam War also had major repercussions for the US left. The anti-war movement came to an end with some of its leaders and activists migrating into the solidarity organizations, some of which supported the resistance in countries like Chile and Argentina. A parallel and somewhat overlapping movement, drawing on the radical political perspectives that had emerged in the 1960s, continued the process of trying to construct political alternatives to the entrenched system of rule by the Republican and Democratic Parties. The search for a new utopia continued.

Within the left there were two major currents. The New American Movement (NAM) and a like-minded publication, Socialist Revolution, captured the more moderate tendency that I supported. We believed that given the uniqueness of American history, patient organizing at the grassroots level was needed to mobilize people to push for a socialist agenda, primarily through work among the emergent social movements and in the electoral arena.

The other current was comprised of a plethora of more militant organizations, some old and some new, most of them Marxist-Leninists. The Weather Underground continued to carry out sporadic bombings, targeting military and corporate property. But most of the Marxist-Leninist organizations were nonviolent, trying to win adherents in the labor movement and the trade unions, particularly among Third World workers, although their membership, if it grew at all, tended to come from the white middle class.

Within NACLA, we were, of course, elated by the end of the Vietnam War. At the same time we anguished over what was happening in Latin America with the military governments decimating the internal resistances and consolidating their hold on power. As we continued to collaborate with the solidarity and oppositional movements, NACLA adopted internal security measures to protect our contacts, both those in exile as well as those who traveled to and from their home countries. Nothing that would compromise anybody in the resistance was discussed in the office because of the possibility that our offices were either bugged or under surveillance. As Jon Frappier, who was in charge of security in our office, said: "We can't be sure what the government is doing. But we need to act as if our phones are tapped, our office is bugged, and some of us may even be followed."

Our fears that "Big Brother" was watching were confirmed in the early 1990s when NACLA secured its files under the Freedom of Information Act. While many pages were blanked out, it was possible to discern that the NACLA phones in the 1960s and 70s had been tapped and that there was indeed extensive surveillance of the organization's activities, including monitoring of our bank accounts.

More importantly, the assassination in Washington, D.C. of Chilean Orlando Letelier, who had served in a variety of high level positions in the Allende government, brought home the reality that death squads could reach into the heart of the United States. I had talked to Letelier at his Washington office at the Institute for Policy Studies just months before his death. He was one of the most congenial and humane people I have ever met, representing the more moderate tendency within the exiled community that was not involved with the armed resistance.

Given the vibrant role that San Francisco and the Bay Area played in the rise of militant politics in the 1960s, it remained a magnet for the more radical political tendencies as the anti-Vietnam War movement began to wind down. The most bizarre group to emerge was the Symbionese Liberation Army (SLA) in Oakland that burst upon the scene in November 1973 with the shooting of Dr. Marcus Foster, the Black Oakland superintendent of schools. I barely noticed the organization's emergence, but a few months later the group captured the attention of the entire nation when it kidnapped heiress Patty Hearst. In captivity, Hearst became a convert to the SLA and under the *nom de guerre* Tania, participated in a bank robbery in San Francisco, yelling "Up against the wall mother fuckers!" She and two others were subsequently arrested and in a trial in 1976 she was found guilty. It marked the effective end of the SLA, as an earlier shootout in Los Angeles had annihilated the core of SLA. From its start, with the slaying of Foster, I had little sympathy with the bizarre activities of the SLA and it was largely repudiated by the left in the Bay Area as well as the rest of the country.

This was the backdrop to the political debate in NACLA over the appropriate political strategy for the left that had begun in 1974 and 1975. It only deepened as the decade wore on. In the mid-1970s,

Marlene Dixon, a charismatic, demagogic woman came to the Bay Area from McGill University in Canada where she had been a radical feminist. She founded the League for Proletarian Socialism in San Francisco circa 1975, renouncing radical feminism and fiercely attacking the more moderate currents of the left, like the New American Movement. Dixon proclaimed that they were "anti-working class, anti-communist, petty bourgeois reform movements." I heard Dixon haranguing at a weekend political summer gathering of the League in Sonoma County in 1976, "These groups have the blood of the working class on their hands." Susanne was the first member of the NACLA staff to fall under Marlene's sway and began pushing the line of the League within NACLA, winning others over to her position.

Pat and I continued to advance the work of the agribusiness project with even more intensity, deciding to focus on the Del Monte corporation, which had its headquarters in San Francisco. In this study, as well as in the earlier case study of Cargill that had appeared in the US Grain Arsenal, we employed the tools developed in NACLA's Research Methodology Guide, scouring newspapers, business publications and corporate reports for information on how corporations function and their ties and influence within the US government.

In the case of the earlier work on Chile, Farnsworth and others had interviewed US government officials to augment information gathered from the corporate and print media. In the agribusiness project, we began to perfect the technique of interviewing corporate and US government officials by posing as "objective" researchers. In my trips to Washington, D.C., I would use my Ph.D. from Indiana University to say I was doing postdoctoral work for a book on agribusiness. The era of the Internet was hardly a flicker in the minds of Bill Gates and Steve Jobs, so my recent writings or credentials could not be checked out.

I found that most government and corporate officials like to talk about themselves, their work and their supposed achievements in office. I would usually mention my origins as a Wisconsin farm boy and that along with my appearance in a rumpled sports coat disarmed them, making them feel they could help "educate" this naïve Midwesterner. Richard E. Bell, the Assistant Secretary of Agriculture for International Affairs— who told me in 1975, "We can't subordinate our commercial exports to needy people"—was particularly interested in assisting me when he found out that we both had graduated from Midwestern universities and had been members of 4-H clubs. I had no qualms about deceiving the rich and powerful, knowing that they had trampled on others to get where they were, participating in one way or another in the exploitation of the impoverished and dispossessed peoples of the world.

Cargill, the largest privately owned corporation in the world, was renowned for its secretiveness. However I managed to obtain interviews with one of its officials in Washington and another retired executive in Minneapolis who helped me understand the inner workings of the corporation. I then decided to push my luck, to go into "the belly of the beast," showing up at Cargill's global headquarters, an elaborate 63-room replica of a French chateau near Lake Minnetonka, just outside of Minneapolis. Ushered through several gates, I was finally able to sit down with the head of public relations, hoping he would give me access to higher executives. A straight-looking Midwestern business type about my age, dressed in a dapper suit, he somehow saw through my ruse and after about 15 minutes, tossed me out on my ear saying he believed "I was up to no good." In my long subsequent career of interviewing corporate, government and Pentagon officials, he was the only person to directly call me for my genteel deception.

In September 1976 we released the NACLA Report, "Del Monte: Bitter Fruits." It, too, was based on interviews with corporate officials, this time in San Francisco. But even more importantly, we conducted field work and interviews on Del Monte's banana plantations in Guatemala and its investments in the Bajio Valley of Mexico. The country visits were also important because they enabled Pat, an excellent photographer, to take pictures that enlivened the pages of the report.

When we visited the Bajio Valley 200 miles north of Mexico City, we found a rich agricultural valley endowed with fertile soils and a mild climate. A plethora of foreign agribusiness corporations dotted the landscape with their canning facilities and produce-packing plants. Del Monte, the largest and most influential with over 5,000 employees, had contracts with an unknown number of agricultural producers covering thousands of hectares for commodities like peas, sweet corn and asparagus. The canning plant in the valley turned out the largest variety of fruits and vegetables of any of Del Monte's facilitates in the world.

The work force, three-quarters women, was paid the minimum wage. Eva, in her mid-20s, who had worked for the company for six years, told us, "I don't work at Del Monte because I like it—I have to feed my children." She added, "There are no real unions to represent us, only the sham unions backed by the government who could care less about our salaries and working conditions." We visited a Del Monte hiring haul for temporary seasonal workers where we saw hundreds of people gathering at six in the morning. As one woman said, "If I don't get work today, how will I eat?"

The conditions of the field workers were exceptionally difficult since they were employed by the newly emergent class of Mexican agribusiness entrepreneurs who contracted with Del Monte and didn't even pay the minimum wage for 12, 16 or more hours of back-breaking work. The boss of one gang of workers harvesting asparagus wouldn't even let us talk to them, saying: "They've got to toe the line, that's what we've got them here for." When we queried Del Monte Vice-president William Druehl in San Francisco about the dismal wages and labor conditions in the valley, he assertively replied: "Labor is one of the main factors that has to be kept under control."

As Pat and I wrote in the introduction to the Bajio article, titled Canned Imperialism: "Around the world, agribusiness corporations are moving into regions that are struggling with the problems of malnutrition, poverty and land distribution. The corporations usually pose as saviors, claiming that their fertilizers, tractors, hybrid seeds and food processing plants will help solve the Third World's problems by expanding food production and providing employment opportunities. However, as this study of the Bajio Valley in Mexico shows, the modern agribusiness corporation accentuates the extremes of wealth and poverty, turns out highly processed foods that are priced beyond the reach of most of the country's population, and forces peasants off their lands."

The foggy late summer day in Berkeley when the newly printed copies of the Del Monte Report arrived in the NACLA office marked a high and low point in my life. I looked at the immaculate white cover of the report with a Del Monte symbol and a print of a bent-over field worker hoeing, just as the staff began to assemble in the room for our weekly collective meeting.

Fred was the first to speak, saying, "Roger, the rest of the collective members feel that you can no longer work with us."

Susanne piped in: "We are trying to take the organization in new directions and you are an obstructionist."

The rest of the staff was tallied, almost like a jury reading a verdict that had been decided behind my back. I was removed from the collective, designated an "associate staff member," able to write and research for NACLA but not allowed to participate in its political or organizational discussions. It was one of the most painful experiences of my adult life. I felt inadequate, thinking that perhaps I possessed some character flaws that didn't enable me to work cooperatively with other people.

A few months later, Susanne left the staff to work directly under Marlene, leaving behind her sympathizers on the staff to argue vehemently that NACLA should adopt the political line of the League and become an adjunct publication. Then, at the beginning of 1977 Nancy Stein, the only remaining woman on the collective, also left along with Bill Felice to join the League. With just four male staff members left, developments took an unexpected turn. Pat Flynn was the only woman available. The male staff grilled her for two days but in the end they had no alternative but to bring her into the collective. Possessing perhaps an even more tenacious personality then I do, she became known as "Stand Pat Flynn," as she vehemently fought the takeover efforts of the League. The only non-League sympathizer among the four males, Fred Goff, continued to hover above the fray, hoping to prevent the collapse of the organization.

20. Dole's Banana Republic Politics

In June 1977 Tim Dramin, a founder of a kindred organization in Canada, the Latin American Working Group (LAWG)—which also put out radical analyses and publications on Latin America—visited the Bay Area. He headed up the San Jose, Costa Rica office of the Canadian University Community Overseas Organization (CUSO, a French acronym). An international development organization with Canadian government funding, Tim's office supported volunteers and research projects in the Central American countries and Colombia.

A lanky gregarious Canadian possessed of immense energy, he always had a twinkle in his hazel eyes and an easy chuckle. We hit it off at first sight and he offered to help fund a field trip to Honduras, Costa Rica, Colombia and Ecuador to further the study of the impact of international agribusiness. It was an immensely productive trip. Then in 1978, after an international phone call, Tim agreed to help finance my trip to Nicaragua and Central America, this time to survey the burgeoning revolutionary movement in the region, as well as to deepen my work on agribusiness.

Pat and I took off in November, 1977, first for Costa Rica and Colombia to do field work for another NACLA agribusiness report. On the way back I stopped off alone in Honduras to investigate reports of a scandal over the repression of striking workers on plantations of Castle & Cooke (known today as the Dole Food Company). Using Tim's contacts, I met Vanessa Parks, a volunteer for an international education and overseas program.

Climbing the cobblestone streets of Tegucigalpa to get to Vanessa's house at night, I met a striking woman with short blonde hair, about my age, of Anglican aristocratic descent, who in addition to her volunteer and organizing work, was beginning her doctoral studies in sociology. We conversed for hours about Honduras and the world. She would play a central role in my life several years later in Nicaragua in the midst of the Sandinista revolution.

The next day I flew off to the port town of La Ceiba, an enclave of Castle & Cooke's where Vanessa had recommended I talk to Phil Berryman, an ex-priest, now married and serving as a Catholic lay worker. He briefed me on the struggle of the workers and the strike, set up a couple of interviews with union members who told me of the arrest, imprisonment and torture of 200 plantation workers in March 1977. After that I headed off to interview an executive at the Castle & Cooke headquarters in La Ceiba who readily accepted my explanation that I was an academic researcher doing work on a book on agribusiness in Latin America. I left the port town the next day, going to Tegucigalpa and taking a plane back to California. Phil Berryman was shocked at this bold American who believed he could fly in and out in two days, capturing the complex reality of the social conflict shaking the plantations.

I surprised even myself, immediately writing a NACLA Update article released in the December, 1977 NACLA Report titled "Union Busting: Castle & Cooke in Honduras." The story attracted broad attention because events in Honduras were part of an unfolding international scandal involving US agribusiness corporations holding vast plantations abroad. The drama read like a page out of early 20th century history when the banana companies busted unions and bought and sold generals and presidents at will, leading to the term, "Banana Republics." In 1975 Eli Black, the chairman of United Brands, the only other major banana corporation operating in Honduras, jumped to his death from his 40th floor office in New York. At the time of his suicide, the corporation was under investigation for paying a $1.5 million bribe to the Honduran military President Oswaldo Lopez Arrellano in exchange for low export taxes. After Black's death, the revelation of the bribe led to a military coup in December, 1976. But the new president, General Alberto Melgar Castro, simply opted to change corporate masters, selecting as his senior legal advisor the head of the law firm representing Castle & Cooke in Honduras, while another member of the same firm became Minister of Labor.

Castle & Cooke desperately needed the assistance of the military government. A company executive in La Ceiba told me that the new militancy in the trade union movement along with the worker takeover of several plantations led Castle & Cooke to "consider pulling out of the country" in 1975." But the army came to the company's rescue, arresting and jailing 200 striking union leaders, installing a new subservient union that signed a contract with Castle & Cooke in June 1977. As one plantation worker said to me five months later, "We haven't seen the contract and have no idea what its terms are."

The corporation's nefarious activities were backed up by official company documents I obtained and later publicized revealing that Castle & Cooke made regular payments to Honduran military officers, customs officials and local newspaper reporters.

The army also moved to bust one of the worker-run plantations that had been legally recognized as an Associative Enterprise when the workers took over idle plantation lands in 1974. Melgar Castro ordered the army to occupy the plantation, arresting the Enterprise's leaders, charging them with "mismanagement of funds" and "communist control." The army then hand-picked new leaders who immediately signed a 10-year agreement binding them to sell all of their production to Castle & Cooke. One worker on the Association lands said to me, "These were our lands historically and now again as we reclaimed them as a cooperative association. We invested our sweat and blood in these abandoned fields to make them productive. And now the military steps in and tells us we have to sell everything to Castle & Cooke regardless of whatever price is offered to us."

In spite of the wave of repression, the spirit of resistance among the plantation workers awed me. As one worker who had been imprisoned and fired after 27 years with Castle & Cooke told me: "We have suffered heavier blows from the banana companies and recovered. We will do the same again."

One of the officers in the army whose star rose with the new military government, Colonel Gustavo Alvarez Martinez, also received payments from Castle & Cooke. He attended the US run School of the Americas and worked closely with the US embassy as "our man in Tegucigalpa." From 1979 to 1981 he was head of a special battalion that captured, tortured and assassinated suspected Honduran leftists. Then, as chief of the Honduran military, he worked with US Ambassador John Negroponte from 1981 to 1984, coordinating the CIA-sponsored contra war against the Sandinista government that was run out of camps on Honduras' southern border with Nicaragua. The death squad operations against Hondurans by Alvarez continued with the US embassy's connivance. Negroponte, of course, vehemently denied his involvement, although documents and witnesses conclusively prove that he knew of the death squads. This, of course, did not derail his diplomatic career, as he later assumed high-level positions in George W. Bush's administration as ambassador to Baghdad during the US occupation and then as Czar of US intelligence operations. Alvarez Martinez suffered a more ignominious fate as he was assassinated in 1989 by a group called the Popular Liberation Movement, which issued a communiqué upon his death calling him a "psychopath."

21. Transitions: Amorous and Organizational

I wasn't completely conscious of it at the time, but my travels to Mexico, Central America and Washington, D.C. were in part driven by the desire to escape the battles at NACLA. My personal life was also in turmoil. For about half-a-year after Pat and I became involved, we kept our relationship secret. Given that we were working so intensely on the agribusiness project, we had a good cover story for spending so much time together. But with our joint trip to Guatemala and Mexico in June 1976 it became impossible to maintain the facade.

Leon, Pat's companion was probably the first person to intuit what was going on. But he did not confront Pat, in part because his bohemian-like life style meant he did not believe in monogamy, nor was he a jealous, possessive type of person. On a couple of occasions I did detect a glare from Leon when the three of us got together but he continued to talk with me about his art work, politics and whatever was happening in the world. Leon also worked with others in his guerrilla poster art brigade, among them a bright, blue-eyed blonde from Australia, some twenty years his junior. Pat, to her consternation, came home one afternoon and found them in bed together. She was outraged but obviously had no basis to take a "holier than thou" attitude. Pat and Leon continued to live together for months afterwards.

For me, the situation with Elizabeth was much more difficult and painful. She was clearly no female version of Leon. She was not given to expressing her feelings so I am not sure when she began to figure out what was going on. Also, at the start of our relationship at Indiana University in the Spring of 1971, we had not expected each other to be monogamous and in fact, both of us had had other relationships.

But this had changed when she came to live with me in the Bay Area in late 1973. Our experience in Chile together had forged deep bonds between us, in spite of our differences and silences. I couldn't bear the thought of breaking up with her, of never being intimate with the woman who had shared important parts of my life for five years. Ending the relationship would be like cutting out part of myself and all the experiences we had together. I remember one time when we were walking up a hilly sidewalk in our neighborhood, we heard someone say in a loud voice: "When are you two non-producers going to do something with your lives?" We looked at each other startled, and then laughed as we realized he was talking to his dogs in the yard.

I must have repressed it, but I can't even remember when we first talked openly about my relations with Pat. In August 1976 Glenn and Marilyn went camping in the California Sierra's with Elizabeth. Marilyn came back and told me "Elizabeth was very upset, she didn't say anything about you to us. She just went off hiking and brooding by herself."

Our bedroom was on the second floor of the house and it was shortly after Elizabeth returned from the camping trip that she told me: "I think its best if I move downstairs, to the extra room." The situation, of course, resolved nothing, making it no less painful when we had dinner together or simply when we saw each other entering and leaving the house. Occasionally, we would even still make love on the second floor. We couldn't forget the past and neither of us had the courage to abruptly end the relationship. Neither of us could deal with the thought of never seeing or loving each other again.

Pat, even though she was still living with Leon, was not happy with the situation. Given her more assertive nature, she stormed into the house one night confronting Elizabeth and me as we were sitting in the living room watching a movie on TV.

Shortly after that, in early 1977, Elizabeth and I had a house meeting with Glenn and Marilyn. Elizabeth decided to move out, not out of deference to me as a male holding on to the domain but because I had a relationship with Glenn and Marilyn that went back decades. They agreed to buy out her quarter share of the house, making her a generous offer that eventually enabled her to buy a house on her own.

At almost the same time, the crisis in NACLA reached a boiling point. Under the direction of Marlene Dixon, now referred to by many of her detractors as "the guru of a political cult" and "a body snatcher," the League recruited members from other small left organizations in the Bay Area.

Marlene exerted an entrancing, almost primordial hold over the

League's members. One rainy winter night I was invited along with the NACLA staff to the League's main office in San Francisco. It was eerie to see how Marlene did all the talking while Susanne, Nancy, Bill and others stood by, hanging on her every word. She sounded almost like a preacher, first thundering in a loud voice about how "Our challenge is to build a vanguard organization to fight for the working class" and then lowering her tone as if she were confiding in us to say "NACLA can really help us with its research and talented members."

Given that most of those who joined the League were of white middle class origins, my belief is that they felt guilty about their class backgrounds. Given Marlene's working class roots, they always deferred to her as the only one who could speak with authority. As I once heard Susanne say: "We have to use our skills and abilities for the working class. They have suffered and are the only ones who can make a revolution."

As I later found out, one of the reasons for the meeting was that under the influence of Marlene, a NACLA West Labor project was being set up to put out a NACLA Report that echoed the League's views on the US Labor movement. Pat and I were excluded from all discussions and deliberations on the Report. Two of the three authors of the Report, Nancy and Bill, were already members of the League. This was unprecedented in the annals of NACLA history, not only because the Report's content was guided by a secretive Leninist party, but also because it had nothing to do with Latin America. Titled "Bosses and Bureaucrats," it asserted that the mere negotiating of contracts by US trade union leaders, called "contract unionism," betrayed the workers by forcing them to submit to the discipline of capital. The corporate owners, along with the labor bureaucrats, were allies who jointly exploited the workers. Mainstream labor leaders and reformers were "two wings of the same vulture" feeding on the bones of the working class.

Pat and I were powerless to stop the Report. But under the division of labor between the two coastal offices, all Reports were first printed in Berkeley and then shipped to New York for distribution to subscribers. When the east coast staff read the Report, they exploded. Led by Janet Shenk and Steve Volk—whom I had met in Chile during the Allende years—the Manhattan office simply refused to send out the Report. Volk, after reading it, declared: "Absolutely not! Unacceptable!" They sent back their comments, insisting upon the elimination of the more strident parts. The printed copies were shredded and a new toned down Report was sent out, although it still reflected the position of Marlene Dixon and the League, i.e. trade union leaders who engaged in contract unionism betrayed the workers. Even the sources for the Report were wrapped up in the League's secretiveness. The last paragraph in the introduction to the Report that was finally sent out to subscribers declared: "In our analysis of contract unionism as a system of disciplining the working class, we have relied heavily on as yet unpublished material of the League for Proletarian Socialism. We thank them for their assistance."

At the joint NACLA annual meeting in 1977 Pat and I voted with the east coast staff to make it a NACLA policy that no one who worked at NACLA could be a member of a disciplined political organization. However, there was no real way to enforce it, because supporting the League position did not necessarily mean that one was a "disciplined member." But the handwriting was on the wall. The political crisis was tearing NACLA apart and the two offices, "separate but equal" could not survive for long. Fred Goff began to build an alternative organization in 1977 called the Data Center, which became the repository of NACLA's extensive research files. The Center hired a separate staff, led by two new recruits—a married couple from my home state of Wisconsin—who had no ties to the League.

At the meeting in New York in the summer of 1978 after several horrendous, conflict-ridden sessions, the de facto leaders of the two offices, Fred Goff and Steve Volk took a walk together.

Fred relates: "We talked about the tension and whether it was going to be an amicable or an antagonistic split. I told him [Steve] I wanted it to be an amicable separation and that I would work to implement that." NACLA-west was to be shut down as a co-equal office. What went unspoken in this agreement was that Pat and I could continue to work in the west office as a subsidiary of NACLA in New York. But Fred was setting up his new bailiwick at the Data Center, and the three remaining members in our office, who were joining the League, detested us so much that they refused to countenance our presence as NACLA representatives in the Bay Area. Their price for an "amicable separation" was complete annihilation of what remained of the NACLA west coast office.

Pat and I were invited, even courted, by the Manhattan staff to move to New York and help consolidate the organization there. We agreed in principal to join, but neither of us was enthusiastic about life in the Big Apple. For the next year we continued to work and produce reports for NACLA, now in offices out of the Data Center. It was actually one of the more pleasant times in my life, "free at last" from the recriminations and sectarian politics of the League for Proletarian Socialism.

UTOPIA UNLEASHED

22. The Sandinista Insurgency, 1978

During our year-long stay in California before moving to New York, a political crisis erupted in Nicaragua as the Sandinista Front stepped up its guerrilla war against the Somoza regime. In October 1978 I found myself flying over Nicaragua's volcanoes heading for Managua International Airport, breaking the resolution I had made five years earlier when I had hiked across the country on my way back to the United States from Chile. Then I had perceived an abjectly impoverished society ruined by an earthquake and under the heels of the long entrenched Somoza dictatorship. I saw no reason to ever return.

But it was precisely the earthquake and the ensuing corruption and diversion of relief aid that had kindled the fires of discontent and resistance to the regime. When I arrived, talk of a revolution was in the air. Two months earlier, one of the three factions of the Sandinista National Liberation Front (FSLN), the Terceristas, had occupied the National Palace during a session of the Somoza-controlled Congress, taking 2,000 hostages. Comandante Zero (Eden Pastora), achieved international fame as the leader of the assault, but it was Comandante Dos, 22-year-old Dora Maria Tellez, who astutely conducted two days of negotiations with Somoza that led to the release of 60 imprisoned FSLN guerrillas, the dissemination of an FSLN manifesto, and a ransom of a half million dollars. They were guaranteed safe passage to Panama and Venezuela and throngs of people lined the streets and cheered as the rebels passed by in a bus headed for the airport.

Just over two weeks later, on September 9, a series of insurrectional uprisings took place in several major Nicaraguan cities. Abandoning their fear, Sandinista insurgents faced off with Somoza's tanks and artillery, attacking with Molotov cocktails, home-made bombs, revolvers and hunting rifles. The muchachos, as they were called, tore up brick road blocks made in Somoza's factories to build barricades to resist the assaults of the hated National Guard. Their faces covered with red and black bandannas, which became an insignia of the Sandinistas, many irregular combatants, including women, laid ambushes for Somoza's soldiers.

Desperate to suppress the revolt that was spreading to other cities and towns, the National Guard used its savage special forces to assault rebel positions on the ground and launched an air war, dropping five-hundred-pound bombs, white phosphorus and napalm on the muchachos. Finally, the Guard rolled in with heavy tanks, crushing the rebels who resisted from rooftops, doorways, open windows and their improvised barricades.

When I arrived in October 1978 the conflict still smoldered. Tense soldiers stood guard around banks, public buildings and commercial centers while troops armed to the teeth drove up and down the streets in military vehicles. A grim and defiant populace went about their business during the day. While few people ventured out at night, fearful they would be apprehended and shot, clandestine organizers met and planned while guerrillas carried out hit-and-run attacks.

Not defeated in spirit, the Sandinistas began organizing for a new assault on the dictatorship. The international community was horrified by the brutality of the regime. Even the United States under President Jimmy Carter pressured Somoza to negotiate with the opposition and to stop some of its more barbaric acts of repression. Earlier in 1978 the Broad Opposition Front (FAO), a coalition of diverse groups opposed to Somoza, had tried to strike a deal with him that would lead to his gradual removal, but it was floundering as I arrived in Nicaragua.

In Managua I met Orlando Nunez with whom I would develop a close personal working relationship that would span a decade-and-a-half. Bronze-skinned with penetrating green eyes, Orlando cut a strikingly handsome Aztec-like profile. Possessed of immense charm and charisma he is one of the most brilliant people I have known. He was born in a rural community to a small rancher and man-about-town who had about a dozen kids with various women. Orlando's mother, like mine, was a local teacher. She was the matriarch of her immediate family comprised of Orlando and three sisters.

Barely 18 when he started driving a truck, Orlando quickly saved up enough money to go to Europe. In Spain he became part of an anarchist group opposed to the Franco dictatorship. Then he went to Paris to study, participating in the May uprising in 1968 that almost toppled the government of Charles de Gaulle. In the mid-1970s he returned to Nicaragua where as part of the resistance he was soon tossed in jail. Exiled to Costa Rica, he returned to Nicaragua within a year. In the midst of all this he worked on his Master's thesis, a study of the agrarian proletariat on the cotton plantations in western Nicaragua. Our mutual interest in agribusiness led me to initially contact him, although it quickly became evident we both had much larger agendas that would lead us to collaborate in the coming years.

Our first meeting was curious, almost comical. I called Orlando and he suggested we meet at Managua's only fast food restaurant, a Central American imitation of McDonalds. As we sat in one of the plastic booths and talked, I was taken aback by Orlando's lack of caution. He spoke loudly and boldly, saying "We have been hit hard by the brutal repression of September, but will triumph in months;" going on to describe in detail the resistance taking place in different towns and cities around the country. I kept looking around thinking one of Somoza's security agents would soon appear and haul us away. But nothing happened. Orlando is simply fearless and possesses a sixth sense about what is safe or not safe to do in a given setting.

The restaurant where we met fronted on the road to Masaya, an old artisan and indigenous town about 20 kilometers from Managua. This stretch of the road in the capital had become the new main street of Managua in the aftermath of the earthquake. After talking to Orlando, I ventured over to the old center of the city, almost two kilometers away. It still remained unoccupied, much like I had seen it five years before, only now an occasional cow grazed on the vegetation that had sprung up among the ruins.

Set back on the edge of these new pastures was the Intercontinental Hotel where I stopped for a drink at the bar. The hotel has a unique Maya temple-like design that withstood the violent earthquake. It served as the favored watering hole for journalists, as well as international executives and the local elite. The eccentric business tycoon, Howard Hughes, had taken up residence in the penthouse at the top of the hotel in February 1972, and was airlifted out from the roof in a helicopter when the earthquake struck at the end of the year.

Alongside and to the west of the Intercontinental Hotel, many of the old upper class homes were being rebuilt. Not too far behind and to the south of the hotel lay Somoza's infamous bunker, where he would spend his last days before fleeing to his sugar mill outside of Managua where his airplane, loaded down with booty, took off from his private airfield.

Orlando had suggested that I get in touch with Carlos Fernando

Chamorro, the son of Pedro Joaquin Chamorro, who had been assassinated by Somoza 10 months earlier in January 1978. Carlos would also become an intimate friend in the coming years. His father, who owned the major opposition newspaper, had been a national gadfly opposing the Somoza regime with his reporting and editorials.

His death sparked the first major revolt against Somoza, led by dissident business leaders who were constantly being squeezed by Somoza. They shut down most of Managua's businesses. The people took to the streets, not just to mourn Chamorro's death, but to express their own deep-felt revulsion against the regime by pelting stones at the police and assaulting some of Somoza's businesses along the northern highway of Managua. Most notably, they attacked Somoza's plasma center, which literally sucked the blood out of poor people in exchange for two dollars a pint.

I met Carlos Fernando in the editorial offices of La Prensa which were bustling with activity. About 25 years old, he had recently returned from Canada where he majored in economics. Gifted with an exceptionally inquisitive mind, Carlos immediately began querying me about everything from Jimmy Carter's policy towards Somoza to the leftist debates in *Monthly Review*, an independent Marxist magazine in New York. Not only that, he displayed a talent for details and a quest for new techniques and technologies, skills that explain why nine months later, when Somoza was overthrown, he became editor and director of the Sandinistas' daily newspaper, Barricada.

Unlike Orlando, who remained semi-independent of the three factions of the FSLN while collaborating with all of them, Carlos Fernando had joined the more ideologically-driven faction of the Sandinistas, the Proletarians. Particularly active in Managua, the proletarians recruited many of the country's intellectuals as well as sectors of the urban working class. One evening Carlos took me to his mother's home where he lived and I met Victor, a young organizer among the itinerant workers of Managua. We talked for hours about his experiences. He recounted many atrocities as well as Sandinista ambushes against the soldiers of the regime.

Just months later Victor would be captured by Somoza's secret police at night and taken down to the shores of Lake Managua where his bullet ridden body was found the next day. Less than a year later, when I returned to Carlos's house, it was almost like a funeral parlor. His mother, Violeta Barrios de Chamorro, who would one day become president of Nicaragua, had pictures and memorabilia of her martyred husband displayed around the house, while Carlos had kept many of the books and clothes of Victor, emotionally unable to dispose of them.

After my meetings in Managua in 1978, I headed up to the second largest city, Leon, which had mounted a fierce resistance to Somoza in the September uprising. I took a colectivo, a taxi with four other passengers, where we all paid a fixed fare for the ride. About mid-point between Managua and Leon on the highway, we were stopped at a National Guard checkpoint. The only foreigner in the car, I was ordered to get out by the commanding officer. He demanded to see my passport. As he leafed through it with a scowl on his face, I decided to bluff, saying I worked with the US embassy as a Peace Corps volunteer. My ruse failed as he told the taxi driver to go on without me. I don't know what possessed me, but I said "No, Capitan" in Spanish, grabbed my passport and jumped into the taxi. I half expected a hail of bullets to follow me, but for some inexplicable reason we drove off without further ado.

Eight months later, in June, 1979, ABC reporter Bill Stewart was pulled from his car on the same highway between Managua and Leon and summarily executed by the National Guard as a video camera recorded his death. The incident caused an international uproar and led Carter to cut off all aid to Somoza, including arms shipments. As far as I could tell from the news reports at the time, it was at virtually the same checkpoint where I had been stopped.

23. Transitions and the New Revolutionary Agenda

The Nicaraguan trip opened up a new stage in my life. For the next decade Nicaragua and Central America would be at the center of my quest for a revolutionary utopia. I also reasoned that if the US imperium could be diverted and stopped in its tracks in Central America, than the Chileans would have a better chance to end the oppressive reign of Pinochet and renew their quest for a socialist revolution. A combination of these insurgencies might even herald in the continental revolution envisioned by Che Guevara.

Leaving Nicaragua in October 1978 I stopped in New York where the NACLA office was in the final stages of producing the Report, "Nicaragua in Crisis." The bulk of it was written by Alejandro Bendana, then working on his Ph.D. in history at Harvard University. A Nicaraguan who had spent many years living in the United States he spoke impeccable English and at first glance appeared to be just another clean cut American graduate student.

My conversations with him were the beginning of what would be a long personal and working relationship. In July of 1979 with the fall of Somoza he became the Interim Ambassador in Washington and then worked in New York, first as head of the Nicaraguan Consulate and then as ambassador to the United Nations. Given his extensive knowledge of the United States, he was eventually called back to Managua to work in the Foreign Ministry. There he became the second highest ranking official in the Nicaraguan Ministry of Foreign Relations, often being interviewed on Ted Koppel's Night Line in the mid and late 1980s as the US crisis with Nicaragua deepened.

I talked most extensively in New York with Judy Butler, a vivacious and very affable member of the NACLA staff who wrote the fourth section of "Nicaragua in Crisis" on US policy. A night owl like me, we would spend the evenings discussing her article and then often go out for a bite to eat at the Irish pub on the corner street. A very gregarious woman, she discussed with me the personalities and interactions of the staff. I looked forward to transitioning to New York, especially after my wrenching experience with the NACLA staff in California.

Back in the Bay Area, I went to work on the NACLA report titled "Carter and the Generals: Human Rights in the Southern Cone" that would be my swan song to the remnants of the west coast office. Harking back to my first years with NACLA, I wrote it with a "solidarity team" comprised of Bob High and David Hathaway, both close friends from my days of living in Chile, and Eugene Kelly and his partner, Andrea Halez, who wrote under the pseudonym Amalia Bertoli because of her close relationship with the Argentine resistance.

In his inaugural address in January 1977 Carter had declared: "Our commitment to human rights must be absolute." Changes in US policy did occur under Carter in line with the pronouncements of the Trilateral Commission founded in 1974 that wanted to forge a new consensus in US foreign policy that broke with the real politick of Henry Kissinger. Carter appointed human rights advocates to key positions in the State Department who tried to pressure Augusto Pinochet in Chile and other dictatorial regimes in Latin America to clean up their acts and begin a transition to democracy. The administration believed that the harshness of the dictatorships would only lead to the growth of new radical insurgent movements that would undermine the more centrist political forces that would collaborate with the United States.

But as the bureaucratic skirmishes unfolded among Carter's foreign policy advisors during its first two years, it became clear to our research team that the new administration was just as determined as the old to retain maximum flexibility in dealing with the dictatorial regimes of the southern cone. Bob High, with his six years of day-in and day-out solidarity and organizing work, pointed out "the last thing the Carter administration wants is to have its hands tied by human rights legislation."

Even Cyrus Vance, the Secretary of State, who was considered a leading advocate of human rights in the administration, declared: "Whenever possible, we will use positive steps of encouragement and inducements." He added: "We must be realistic... it is not our purpose to intervene in the internal affairs of other countries." The echoes of Kissinger's pleas for flexibility in the face of the human rights measures of past years were inescapable.

Congress, led by Senator Edward Kennedy and others in 1977, tried to pass human rights legislation to automatically force the government to vote against any loans to dictatorial regimes extended by international lending agencies. The Carter administration insisted on loopholes in this legislation, of which the most important declared that the president could override it when "national security interests" were involved.

Andrea Halez of our team portrayed the most notorious case of US support for the Argentine military junta, which murdered and "disappeared" over 30,000 of its citizens, surpassing the atrocities of the Pinochet regime by a factor of over 10. In the summer of 1978, the junta applied to the US Export Import Bank for $300 million dollars to finance a dam and power project. Under pressure from State Department human rights advocates the loan was denied. But then, as Andrea found out: "US multinationals, along with Argentine business and government officials, streamed to the US Embassy and called the White House, claiming that Argentina's economic development and their business interests as well would be jeopardized if the project were not approved." In September, Carter backed down and the loan was approved.

My work for "Carter and the Generals" sharpened my belief that Washington, D.C. was not a place where I wanted to live and work and heavily influenced my decision several years later when I was pressured to move to the capital to become involved in research and lobbying against the US Contra War in Nicaragua. As I argued at the time of the human rights report: "When Carter was elected, scores of groups representing church, community, veteran, labor and other constituencies were pushing for a complete end to aid to the dictators. What changes Carter has wrought do not come out of his administration's principles or Washington lobbyists but out of these grass roots activities that take place across the country."

At the end of 1978 Pat moved from her flat with Leon in San Francisco to a house in Berkeley. As Pat acknowledged, "Our split was fairly amicable, as we banded together against the landlord to hold on to the place as long as possible because he had never carried out even the simplest repairs or maintenance tasks." They forced him to exhaust all eviction procedures with the city and the courts while they stopped paying rent.

Once in Berkeley, I spent most of my time at Pat's place, although I still had a room and a quarter share in the house in Oakland I had bought with friends. Deciding to sell my share, we appraised the house, and since the 1970s marked a real estate boom in the Bay Area, I went from having virtually nothing in my bank account to possessing a small nest egg in six short years. Not wanting to fritter it away, I began looking around for a small place to buy in the countryside. At heart I was still a farm boy and longed for the country. I finally found a rural house in upper Sonoma County, six miles in the hills above the Pacific Ocean in a rural area called Annapolis, about a two-and-a-half hour drive from the Bay Area. It was early summer when I visited the place. I fell in love with it immediately. Tall redwood trees stood near a sizable house painted a red barn-like color. I could smell the trees and the vegetation, even in the dry summer air. There was a paved road in front of the property with a mail box, but hardly anyone drove by. It had a pleasant stillness, broken only by the occasional chirping of a bird or the noise of some busy insect going about its work.

From the start of our relationship, Pat and I both recognized that we were two very independent people. We loved each other but wanted to keep our lives from becoming too intertwined, and part of this meant keeping our own spaces and finances separate. So, while I was buying my place in Annapolis, Pat bought a house in Oakland near the historic Grand Lake Theater. We did not move to either Annapolis or her house in Oakland before we left California, renting both places out. We didn't even discuss the issue of which place one or both of us might return to when we came back from New York, although for us the property purchases in part represented an attempt to prevent the Big Apple from seducing us with its fast-paced life and infinite opportunities.

As Pat and I were now in our mid-thirties, the idea of getting pregnant was a consideration in both of our minds as we made love. We began to "play around," to test fate, with Pat putting in her diaphragm less frequently as we approached the days of the month when we knew she was fertile. Finally, the inevitable happened and she became pregnant. We were both glad, in large part because we now knew that we were both capable of procreating. But we also knew the timing was wrong. We were heading off in a few months to a new life in New York and a new baby just didn't fit into the scenario. I went with her to a clinic for an abortion and while it was a sad moment, we both knew that we could one day have a baby when the circumstances were more propitious.

In July 1979 we departed for New York from Berkeley in Pat's Honda Civic station wagon. It was a spectacular trip as we drove across the country taking the more northerly route along Highway 90. We camped out in the Grand Teton National Park in Wyoming and then headed for the Badlands in South Dakota. I did not do cocaine very often but had my best coke high ever as we pulled off the road in the Badlands National Park. Standing on the edge of a plateau that looked out over a vast gulch with pinnacle-like rock formations of diverse shapes and sizes pushing skyward, I was overawed, saying: "We must be on the sunlight side of another planet. It's astounding." The rains and storms of previous millennia had washed away the soft crater ash below, leaving only the hard rock pinnacles standing in a virtual desert, almost as monuments to gods of ages past.

Next it was on to Wisconsin where we visited my family for a few days. Fortunately it didn't take on the aura of Pat being introduced as my prospective "bride," as she wasn't the first woman I had brought home. Besides, my mother and dad were getting used to their children's frequent turnovers in boyfriends and girlfriends with none of them resulting in permanent bonds. The unstable and dysfunctional relationship of my parents was carrying over to the next generation.

As we drove from Wisconsin to New York the Sandinistas in Nicaragua were launching their final offensive to overthrow the regime of Anastasio Somoza. Pat and I were frantically trying to dial the news stations on the radio as we drove and if we stayed at a hotel we made sure we had a TV so we could watch the nightly news. The day before we arrived in New York, July 19, Somoza fled the capital and the Sandinistas raised their revolutionary banners over the city. This historic event, far more than our stay in New York, would shape the next decade of our lives.

24. Life in the Big Apple

Pat and I drove into New York City on a balmy summer afternoon after our trip across country and parked in front of Judy Butler's apartment who welcomed us to her "humble abode." It was located on the fifth floor on West 99th street in upper Manhattan, and our stay there was to be only temporary until we found our own place.

Even though I thought we were prepared for life in the Big Apple, we were in for some rude surprises. On the first morning I stepped into the elevator and saw that someone had taken a crap in the corner. The next day it was still there, and as I left the building, I ran into the "super" (the building superintendent), and said, "Have you seen the shit in the elevator?" His response was, "We'll have to see what happens to it." At least he was honest. The next day the dung was still there. It gradually disappeared as the many people using the elevator stepped on the corners of the excrement, carrying out its particles on the soles of their shoes.

Several days after our arrival, Pat's Honda Civic was broken into and the high-quality stereo radio she had installed for our cross-country trip was stolen. We went to the local police precinct where the attending officer treated us as a nuisance, shoving some forms at us saying, "Fill out these papers, so I can get on with things." We needed the forms to file an insurance claim but we got nothing, as the insurer told us, "You have no witness to prove that someone else besides you removed the radio." In any case, it was supposedly our fault for leaving the car parked on the open street.

We quickly learned just how hostile New York is to the car culture. Katha Pollitt puts the best face on this anti-car bias in her memoir, Learning to Drive: "The rest of America might deliquesce into one big strip mall, but New York City would remain a little out-post of humane civilization, an enclave of ancient modes of transportation—the subway, the bus, the taxi, the bicycle, the foot."

The next words in Pollitt's paragraph cut to the core of Pat's and my experience in the city: "Having a car in New York was not liberation but enslavement to the alternate-side-of-the-street parking ritual, to constant risk of theft." And Pat and I could throw into this trying mix a large number of parking tickets, dings on the Honda due to over-aggressive New York drivers, and dented fenders as cars tried to squeeze into tight parking spaces in back or in front of us.

After about a month, Pat and I found an apartment in Brooklyn Heights on the corner of Prospect Park, a nice second floor flat in a brownstone building. Andrea Halez, who had moved to New York a few months after finishing work with me at NACLA West on the human rights report, became our roommate. It was a 45 minute commute to the NACLA office in Manhattan on the subway, but at least our car could rest more easily when we left it behind in Brooklyn.

Almost immediately after arriving at NACLA I found myself and the organization under fire by Castle & Cooke, best known for its line of Dole Foods and its worldwide network of banana and pineapple plantations. Two years before, I had visited its Honduran operations where plantation unions had been busted and worker-run cooperatives broken up. On the night before I left the country I was given documents pilfered by company employees, which revealed that Castle & Cooke had made regular payments to Honduran military officers, customs officials and local newspapers in exchange for help in repressing the plantation work force and other related business favors. I wrote a story about these sordid activities and released the documents to religious and public interest organizations in the United States engaged in a national campaign against Castle & Cooke.

The company responded by red baiting. Castle & Cooke president D.J. Kirchhoff asserted that NACLA, along with the "Kremlin" and "terrorists" were leading religious groups and other respectable organizations down the path of revolution. In Barron's, a weekly business magazine, Kirchoff wrote: "The seeds of this slanderous "Yankee go home" attack were sown by a Marxist, tax-exempt New York- and Oakland-based organization called the North American Congress on Latin America.... NACLA research may simultaneously appear in attacks against your company at stockholders' meetings, in the straight and underground press, in the hostile press at your overseas locations and in the journals that NACLA itself publishes and distributes."

Elated at having provoked such an outburst by one of the world's largest corporations, I pointed out in the pages of the NACLA Report that Castle & Cooke never directly responded to the documented bribery charges: "Like any good corporate citizen caught with its hand in the till, the company publicly claims that its actions are above reproach." I was informed that off the record its representatives told some of its church critics that "making payments to military officers and local officials is the only way that business can be conducted in a country like Honduras." Of course, following these "local customs" facilitated the arrest and imprisonment of workers making salary demands that affected the company's bottom line.

The anti-corporate sentiment that had emerged in the 1960s still permeated the public sphere and I concluded in my article that "Castle & Cooke has good reason to be worried, as do the other corporate giants that dominate the economy. The fact that Kirchhoff feels threatened by an organization like NACLA (whose total budget is less than half of his own annual salary) is a sign of the corporation's loss of public credibility. NACLA and the company's other critics are not a 'carping melodramatic elite' as Kirchhoff alleges, but are a part of a growing popular groundswell of disaffection."

Aside from providing a base to spar with corporate America, the NACLA New York office proved to be an exciting crossroads in 1979, drawing visitors from around the world with fascinating experiences and stories to relate. Not long after Pat's and my arrival, two journalists came from Nicaragua, Susan Meiseles and Alma Guierrmoprieto. They held the NACLA staff mesmerized for hours as they talked about the early days of the Sandinistas in power. Susan, an American, was already recognized as an outstanding photo journalist of the Sandinista revolution, while Alma, a New York Latina from Mexico, could not write fast enough to keep up with the demand of established newspapers for her coverage of the Sandinistas. She would later become the quintessential "establishment" journalist as a staff writer for the New Yorker magazine.

In October, Daniel Ortega, who sat on the five member junta of the Government of National Reconstruction and was one of the nine leaders of the Sandinista National Directorate, visited New York after first stopping off in Washington to meet with Jimmy Carter. Through my connections at the National Council of Churches I was invited to a gathering with him of about a dozen people at an apartment on the upper west side. It was a strange meeting, not at all like what I had expected of a man who had just helped lead a country to the first revolutionary victory since Cuba 20 years before. He was quiet, hardly said a word, appearing almost intimidated by the people around him. I sat on the same couch as he did, with a simply dressed pregnant Nicaraguan woman between us. She had no official role, and although I assumed that the child she bore was his, I am now not so sure because it was not Rosario Murillo, his primary relationship at the time who would later become his first lady as president.

This was the only time I ever spoke a few words (of no import) to Daniel, although over the years I would see him at large receptions and gatherings in Managua, as well as at public rallies and speeches. There he would be more talkative and animated, but I could still see the Daniel I first met in New York. He was the converse of Fidel Castro, never appearing really comfortable with people around him, and invariably giving public speeches that had people leaving in droves. His genius that made him "primer entre pares" among the nine members of the National Directorate and in the government was his ability to reflect and strategize quietly with a few close advisers, especially Rosario. Once he had his thoughts organized, he single-mindedly imparted them in a strategic and coherent manner to his ministers and the other leaders of the Sandinista Front.

In late October, I took the first of two trips to Nicaragua that would be the basis for a NACLA Report on Nicaragua to be published in late spring of 1980. Upon my arrival I immediately looked up two friends from my trip to the country the year before: Carlos Fernando Chamorro, who was now the editor and publisher of the Sandinista daily newspaper, Barricada, and Orlando Nunez, who was setting up CIERA, the Center for Research and Studies of Agrarian Reform, a think tank of the Ministry of Agriculture and Agrarian Reform. These were heady times in Nicaragua. There is nothing like experiencing the first days of a revolution when the transformation of a government affects all levels of life, from what one thinks about politics and the world to how one relates to friends and family. A whole new world opens up, even for visitors who are willing to take the time to try to understand the complex experience unfolding around them.

Tim Draimin, who would co-author the NACLA Report, joined me in Managua. He took me over to the "Jesuit House," the home of about a half-dozen radical priests. They had supported the resistance to the dictatorship and now held varying formal and informal positions within the government and the revolution. Given their influence, and the backing they had as part of a prestigious international religious order, they were dubbed the "parallel government." So influential, they could make even the most pretentious of the Sandinista leaders sit up and take notice of what they said and did. The most renowned was Fernando F who served as Minister of Education. The most dynamic was Xabier Gorostiaga, an immigrant from the Basque region of Spain. Eight years older than me and slight of frame, he looked like a wizard with his graying hair and finely trimmed beard. The word "charismatic" doesn't do him justice. He could charm politicians, international funders, peasant leaders, intellectuals, ambassadors and even presidents, making an indelible impression on whoever he met.

An economist by training, he was installed as head of the Planning Ministry in the first provisional government. After several meetings with him at the ministry, he took me aside and said, "Roger I'm going to give you all the access you want to documents and information you need about the economic and political policies of the government. In return I would like you to cooperate with me in constructing an international network of scholars and activists to open up a broad discussion of new policy alternatives."

I was bowled over by his appeal to me as well as the audaciousness of his vision. In 1981, Xabier resigned from the planning ministry and began to build a research and publishing center in Managua that created an international complex of affiliated centers and institutions in Central America, the Caribbean, Canada, the United States and Europe. I became one of his point men in the United States.

At the Jesuit House I also ran into Peter Marchetti, a priest from the Midwest, whom I had first met in Chile in 1973 just days after the military coup when he performed a marriage ceremony for a Chilean woman and an American, friends of mine who were about to fly off into exile in Venezuela. The same age as me, Peter was perhaps a reflection of what I might have done in life if I had not broken so sharply with the Catholic Church in my college days and become an atheist. As far as I could tell, Peter never followed the orthodox beliefs of the Church. He once told me, "I have my own syncretic religion that draws on native indigenous beliefs, Buddhism and Marxism." Breaking the Church's rules also meant Peter had his dalliances with women. He became a "native," deeply enmeshing himself in the Central American struggles, traveling and living over the next two decades in El Salvador, Honduras and Guatemala, as well as Nicaragua.

Peter came to California once in the early 1980s and almost succeeded in recruiting my father to drive a bus to Guatemala loaded with arms for the guerrillas. In Honduras, in the 1990s Peter fled the country after the US embassy's political attaché, who personally despised him, said, "We have hard information that you are marked by the death squads. Get out while you can because we don't want your friends claiming we are responsible for what will happen to you." Peter opted to go to Guatemala, a country even more notorious for its extra-legal murders carried out by units of the military.

My closest relationship in Managua unfolded with Orlando Nunez. In physical appearance we were polar opposites, he a Nicaraguan of Mayan origins and me a Germanic-American. But our minds clicked, we were both Marxists who wanted to break with dogma in our writings and work. We came from humble roots and rose to study at the major universities of the world, Orlando even more than me as he wrote his dissertation at the Sorbonne University in Paris. We joked that we were the "peasant-intellectuals" of a global revolution that would (never) take place.

On my October trip I also looked up Susan Meiseles, whom I had met in New York the month before. Housing was difficult in Managua given all the foreigners, and Susan and I often stayed at a Sandinista house appropriated from a Somocista in a barrio at "Siete Sur," seven kilometers south of what used to be the old center of Managua before the earthquake struck in 1972. With only one bedroom, we sometimes slept in the same large bed. Our relations were purely platonic. Susan was a fascinating and exciting woman who had her share of lovers, but we were almost like brother and sister, never developing a physical attachment.

I also stopped off at Alma Guierrmoprieto's house to pick her reporter's brain about what was happening in Nicaragua. There I ran into Vanessa Parks, her roommate, who I had first met in Tegucigalpa, Honduras, a couple of years before. This time there was an immediate erotic tension with Vanessa. We conversed for hours, went out to restaurants just to hang out and exchange thoughts on what was happening in Nicaragua and the world. One day we took a trip in her jeep to the Pochomil beach on the Pacific Ocean, an hour from Managua. We did not make love, but we were enthralled with each other: We walked on the beach, laughing and talking as the sun set, watching its rays create an incredible display of colors that reflected off the sand, the ocean waves and the evening clouds that hung in the sky. As we later drove back to Managua in the starlight stillness of the humid night, it felt like we were in an enchanted paradise.

After my return to New York from Nicaragua, I became involved in a political polemic with James Petras, a leading essayist on the left whom I had looked to as a mentor and had visited at the University of Pennsylvania before I left for Chile in 1971. In the October 1979 issue of *Monthly Review*, the leading magazine of the independent left in the United States, Petras published "Whither the Nicaraguan Revolution?"

He asserted that the Sandinista Front would not lead Nicaragua to socialism, arguing that one of the three tendencies, the "Terceristas" was pushing the revolution in a social democratic direction and that the government was "bourgeois reformist." The other two tendencies, the Prolonged People's War and the Proletarians were playing a secondary role as "the loyal opposition."

Based on my conversations with Orlando, Carlos Fernando, Vanessa, Xabier and others in Managua, I knew that socialism was the goal of all three tendencies. In September 1979 a conclave of several hundred members of the Sandinista National Liberation Front met for three days to draft a document that affirmed the revolution's commitment to Marxism Leninism and to the construction of a socialist society led by the National Directorate. The governing Junta of National Reconstruction, which had been set up with the victory in July, was viewed as a "tactical project" of the revolution along with the "mixed economy" that included "patriotic" sectors of the bourgeoisie, as well as the newly expropriated enterprises run by the state. Never officially released, the "Document of Seventy-Two Hours" nonetheless circulated throughout the capital causing a stir, particularly among the more moderate political currents affiliated with the two non-Sandinistas who sat on the five-member junta.

In my response to Petras in *Monthly Review* titled "Nicaragua: The Course of the Revolution," I did not mention the internal document, merely asserting that Petras' "view of the revolution is simply contradicted by the reality of events since the victory.... Developments in Nicaragua demonstrate that the bourgeois reformists are not in control of the government and that the Sandinista Front and the popular sectors are leading the country forward on a revolutionary socialist trajectory."

The response was overwhelmingly favorable to my article, perhaps in large part because the Left, after wandering in the wilderness and suffering setbacks for two decades, simply wanted to believe that a new revolutionary government was taking hold in the center of the Americas. Publicly, the Sandinista leadership did shift back and forth in the coming years over its use of the term "socialist," but this was largely a response to the constantly shifting political and diplomatic terrain the revolution confronted. The Document of Seventy-Two Hours had laid out a project that largely imitated the Cuban model. But neither geography nor the course of history would permit "another Cuba." To begin with, Cuba was an island while Nicaragua had porous borders to the north and the south that made it difficult to control the economy as well as armed bands of counterrevolutionaries.

Even Fidel Castro recognized early on that Nicaragua was no Cuba, encouraging the National Directorate to follow a distinct trajectory. Thus the "mixed economy" became a long-term strategy for the survival of the revolution instead of a temporary stage, while the unfolding threat from the United States compelled the Sandinistas to search for broad political alliances both at home and abroad without compromising the ultimate goal of constructing an egalitarian society. There would be many policy debates and discussions among the Sandinistas and their supporters in the years to come, but the Sandinista revolution never became a "bourgeois reformist" project as it stood its ground against US imperialism.

25. A Militant in the Sandinista Revolution

It's all over now, baby blue...
Bob Dylan

After my experiences in Chile under Allende, I knew in my gut as well as my head that after July 19, 1979, the day the Sandinista Front marched into Managua, there would be no peace with the Colossus of the North. It would orchestrate a counterrevolution mobilizing all the necessary military, economic and political assets necessary to topple the revolutionary government. This is why I decided to collaborate with the Sandinista front and the government to the fullest extent possible, undertaking a multitude of tasks, some of which made me the "agent of a foreign government" in the eyes of the US state.

The 11 months spanning from March 1980 to February 1981 were among the most intense, emotional and eventful in my life. The period began with a month-long trip to Nicaragua and El Salvador in March and early April and ended with the birth of my son on February 3, 1981. During that interval I co-authored a report for NACLA on the early months of the Sandinista revolution in power, married Patricia Flynn, started working as an intelligence analyst for the Sandinista foreign policy office, had a torrid affair with Vanessa Parks, signed a contract for my first book, witnessed and reported on the horrific killings by the death squads in El Salvador, and founded the Center for the Study of the Americas.

On the hemispheric level, these months were also eventful, marked by the assassination of Archbishop Romero of El Salvador, the defeat in the presidential elections of Jimmy Carter who tried to co-opt the

Sandinista government, the launching of the "final offensive" by the Salvadoran guerillas, and the assumption of the presidency by Ronald Reagan on January 20, 1981, who immediately began to fund the counterrevolutionary forces in Central America and to wage war against the Sandinistas.

In March 1980, the month after the release of my *Monthly Review* article contesting James Petras' thesis of the Sandinista revolution as "bourgeois reformist," I returned to Nicaragua for a second round of research and interviews for a forthcoming NACLA Report. Now I was more determined than ever to integrate myself into the Nicaraguan process. One of my first meetings was with Julio Lopez, the head of the Department of International Relations (DRI) of the Sandinista Front that provided regular reports to the nine-member National Directorate, the real decision-making body of the revolution. The DRI is analogous to the National Security Council of the United States, having direct access to the US president. It also had close ties to Cuban intelligence.

Even with the help of the Cubans in building up its infrastructure, the DRI after nine months was still woefully understaffed and lacking in training. They had a limited capacity to interpret and deal with the nuances of US policy, particularly in the last year of the Carter administration when there were divisions within the US foreign policy establishment over how best to counter the challenge of the Sandinista revolution.

With Julio Lopez I had several wide-ranging conversations on US policy, and one day he asked me if I would "conduct meetings, exchange information and present written 'informes' to key members of my staff?" Without hesitation I replied: "Of course, I'll do whatever I can to help the revolution by giving you as accurate an analysis as I can of what the United States is up to in Nicaragua." Thus began a decade-long relationship in which I basically worked as an intelligence operative for the DRI. I would enter the corridors of the State Department and the Pentagon in Washington, and converse with ambassadors and generals in Central America, writing up reports of what I found out for the DRI. Most of my work was open as I would write articles and give public talks on US policy in Managua and the United States. Along with talking to policy officials, I would research newspapers and foreign policy magazines, and analyze key speeches to understand what the corporate and government elites were up to.

Even if the CIA or FBI were tailing me, they would be hard-pressed to bring a case against me for working as an "agent of a foreign government." I was never paid a cent, and most of my writings and knowledge were made available to the public. But I do admit that in 1984 when I read in the newspapers that the US system of spy satellites was so sophisticated that "the National Security Agency could hear every toilet flush in Managua," I began to wonder what had been picked up in my conversations at the DRI and if the FBI would come knocking on my door.

In January 1980 before I left for Nicaragua, Vanessa Parks stopped off in New York on her way back to Central America after spending time with her boyfriend in London. On a pleasant winter night when a snowfall had painted New York a pristine white, she invited Pat and me for dinner at the house where she was staying in Manhattan. It was an enchanting evening, conversing with two elegant and classy women. Opposites in appearance—Pat with her darker Mediterranean complexion and Vanessa of Nordic descent with her blonde hair and blue eyes— they were quite similar in their social and political orientations. Both had been educated in private schools, Pat as part of the nouveau riche and Vanessa as a descendant of the English aristocracy. But they had freed themselves from their heritages and were liberated women, committed to participation in left politics and helping construct a new world.

Vanessa had told me about her boyfriend Jeffrey the previous October when we had had our first walk on the beach in Nicaragua. He struck me as a British version of Pat's ex-companion, Leon. Another bohemian of Jewish descent, he was completely dedicated to being a documentary film maker of mainly esoteric, albeit beautiful, works of art with complex socio-political themes.

After the dinner in New York, I looked up Vanessa when I went to Managua two months later in March. On a Saturday afternoon, we drove to the Pochomil beach about noon, played in the waves and on the beach in the afternoon, bought a fresh fish from a local fisherman as the sun began its descent, and barbecued it in front of the small cottage we rented on the beach. After long conversations about life, love and the revolution over an evening dinner, we retired to our hut and consummated our relationship, hoping that the sounds of our lovemaking would not travel too far beyond the thin adobe walls and the thatched roof.

The "Summer of Love" in 1967 in San Francisco is world renowned for its sexual freedom and its festival of peace and music. It pales in comparison to what happened in Nicaragua. The revolutionary struggle and the victory marked the start of a decade of tumultuous lovemaking as old relationships ended, and new lovers, often more than one at a time, were taken on. The subtitle of Nicaraguan Gioconda Belli's widely acclaimed book, "*A Memoir of Love and War*," rather than the title, "*The Country Under My Skin*," captures the sexual liberation that went hand-in-hand with the social revolution taking place in the country. Belli, ending her marriage to her first husband with whom she had two daughters before joining the clandestine struggle in the late 1970s, became involved in a second major relationship with a Brazilian with whom she had a year-old son by the time the Sandinistas took Managua. But she was now the lover of Henry Ruiz "Modesto," one of the nine commanders who led the revolution. When they entered Managua with the triumphant revolutionary forces, she relates that they made love in Somoza's abandoned bunker under his conference table.

As Belli points out, many of the male commanders often treated women in a machista fashion, although with the revolution there were "signs of a new era for the women in my country." Nicaragua's sexual revolution affected all classes, with even some peasant and working-class women tossing out their mates and taking on new lovers while others were content to simply be with their children after ridding themselves of their spouses. As in many third world countries, the Nicaraguan woman is often the one who puts the food on the table while the man is off spending what money he can get on his own needs and pleasures.

Given this amorous ambiance in Managua, my relationship with Vanessa, while still in love with Pat, gave me few qualms. And I almost felt like an innocent when I found out about Orlando Nunez's love life. During my trip to Managua in October 1979 he was living with an enchanting young French woman, Syta, who was about four months pregnant with his child. Moreover, unlike me, he had scattered his seed to the wind during his global travels the decade before. It was rumored that he had two daughters in Spain from his earlier life there, and then he met Ursula, a German woman living in Paris, with whom he had a son several years before the Nicaraguan revolution. Still in love with Orlando, Ursula would often appear in Managua to try to lure him back, but to no avail. Women would fall all over Orlando during the years I knew him and he had many clandestine affairs. But in the long term, he proved more "committed" to his primary mate than me, remaining with Syta to this day with whom he has two sons and a daughter.

After the March-April trip to Nicaragua I returned to New York to begin writing up the NACLA Report. When I was in the city I was often a guest at the weekly meetings at *Monthly Review* under the direction of its two editors and "wise men," Paul Sweezy and Harry Magdoff. They were quite a pair, predating in age the New Left of the sixties, with their friendly, yet paternalistic ways. At the meetings, virtually everyone would wait with bated breath for them to drop their pearls of wisdom. I befriended one of *Monthly Review*'s book editors, Karen Judd, who was not taken in by their political platitudes, often cracking a sarcastic joke about

Harry's and Paul's mannerisms and pontifications. I laughed with her, but developed a deep admiration for Harry and Paul. They treated me with respect and warmth, and I even began to fantasize that they might be grooming me for some editorial role with the *Monthly Review* magazine. They were after all well into their sixties and desperately in need of new blood for the organization.

In early 1980, *Monthly Review* decided to publish the manuscript I wrote with Pat, "Agribusiness in the Americas" with Karen Judd as our editor. It was a delightful experience working with Karen. As with most of my projects, I brought in others to help out: Hank Frundt, a friend I had collaborated with since the start of my work on agribusiness back in 1974; and Marc Herold, an old associate from NACLA on the West Coast, who after receiving his doctorate in economics from UC Berkeley, took a professorial posting at the University of New Hampshire. Marc had done his dissertation on the global subsidiaries of US multinational corporations, and I worked with him to assemble an appendix at the end of the book that listed the subsidiaries of all the agribusiness multinational corporations in Latin America.

My love life with Pat resumed upon my return from Nicaragua in April 1980 with as much passion as ever. I never thought of telling her about Vanessa. From the start of our relationship in the Bay Area, we had never agreed to practice monogamy. In fact, after our relationship began, she was the first to take on another lover when she traveled to Cuba on a Venceremos Brigade in 1977. I was hurt by it, but could accuse Pat of no wrong doing, and simply redoubled my efforts to woo her.

In New York in the spring of 1980 Pat stopped using birth control and became pregnant almost immediately. This time we both decided we wanted to have a child, although I was still terrified by the idea of parenthood. Tim Draimin stayed with us at about that time to work on the final drafts of the NACLA Report and I would occasionally joke that the child was really his, although I knew that he was the last person in the world who would take up with another man's woman, especially a close friend.

Our Report, "Nicaragua's Revolution," was released in May 1980. Tim and I in the opening pages wrote: "The new mood is everywhere. For a visitor it starts at the airport: 'Welcome to Free Nicaragua,' the gigantic banner reads. Fresh new murals and graffiti lauding the revolution adorn walls throughout the country. Even the Catholic Cathedral, which faces Managua's new Plaza of the Revolution, is graced with a three-story high portrait of Nicaragua's national hero, Cesar Augusto Sandino."

We found the entire country intense with activity. Throughout the cities, crews on government-sponsored public works projects repaired the enormous destruction caused by the Somoza regime. On weekends, thousands of volunteers headed into the countryside on buses and trucks to work on state-owned farms and plantations. Neighborhood mobilizations and massive demonstrations were commonplace: The reasons were domestic, such as the launching of the literacy campaign, or international, as happened with the huge assembly in the Revolutionary Plaza with the assassination of Archbishop Romero in neighboring El Salvador.

The rapid advance of political- and class-consciousness was astounding. One worker told me, "We are a poor country with many problems, but there can be only one solution for us—socialism." This was echoed by a rural organizer for the Association of Rural Workers (ATC), who declared, "Our real enemies are all the bourgeois elements, those who own lands and factories, and those who are still in the church and the government."

In the section of the Report titled, "Enemy at the Door," we discussed the gathering storm due to US efforts to stop the advance of the revolutionary upheaval in Central America. While the Carter administration had extended an aid package to Nicaragua in an effort to co-opt the revolution, the CIA was beginning to meet with the former Somocistas, particularly in Honduras where many officers and soldiers had fled.

The United States also opened the aid spigots to fund a major military campaign to destroy the revolutionary movements in El Salvador, led by the FMLN, the Farabundo Marti National Liberation Front. I stopped off in El Salvador in early April 1980 on my way back to New York from Nicaragua. Archbishop Romero -- who had openly denounced the Salvadoran armed forces from the pulpit for sponsoring the death squads that slaughtered thousands -- had just been assassinated on March 24. I immediately met with Guillermo Galvan, whom I had befriended on an earlier visit to El Salvdor in 1978. An advisor to Romero, as well as a militant in the revolutionary movement, Guillermo told me: "The war is claiming 300 lives a month, with cadavers clogging the streams, and tortured bodies thrown in garbage dumps and the streets of the capital weekly. The United States is backing this war with military aid and advisers. As the US ambassador to El Salvador, Robert White, has told Salvadorans privately, 'The United States will intervene militarily to prevent the Left from achieving victory.'"

After my talk with Guillermo about the dire situation in the country, I headed for the heavily fortified US embassy in the middle of San Salvador, presenting myself as a journalist and an academic interested in Central America. I managed to secure an interview with the political attaché, who while certainly not revealing any state secrets, declared, "The communist guerillas have to be stopped at all costs, it is unacceptable for the United States to have 'another Nicaragua' allied to Cuba in the heart of Central America."

I filed a report on this visit to the embassy with Julio Lopez, head of the Sandinista Directorate of International Relations. I'm sure that it was of marginal utility to the Sandinistas, given their intensive collaboration with the Salvadoran guerrilla movement. Nonetheless, every bit of information was useful as the revolutionary movements strategized over how best to resist the growing US presence in El Salvador. Orlando depicted the position of the Sandinista leadership when he said: "Nicaragua is a small country with less than 3 million people. To consolidate the revolution in Central America a victory in El Salvador is critical."

This geo-political perspective was somewhat analogous to Leon Trotsky's position after the Bolshevik revolution — that socialism could not survive and mature in just one country, the Soviet Union. The United States was determined to prevent a regional revolution at all costs and the Sandinistas were just as determined to see it advance. As Tomas Borge, one of the nine leaders of the Sandinista Front declared, "If the United States commits the adventure of intervening in El Salvador, we are going to consider it an aggression on our own soil." To that, Miguel D'Escoto, the Minister of Foreign Relations and a Maryknoll priest, added, "The result would be the Vietnamization of Central America."

26. An Unsung Marriage in Toronto

After the May Report, Pat and I, in spite of the appeals of the New York staff, decided that we would leave NACLA and move back to California in July. The experience in the Big Apple had been exhilarating, we had made many friends and we had accomplished a great deal. But I could never get used to the intensity of New York and its sharp and confrontational inhabitants. I had claustrophobic nightmares that I was trapped in a city of endless asphalt and high-rises as I tried to escape to the countryside.

Our pregnancy also played a role in the decision; as Pat said, "The Bay Area would be a better place to have a baby and raise a child." Hovering over our relationship was the question of marriage. I agreed with Marx's denunciation in the Communist Manifesto of "bourgeois marriage" as an institution designed to perpetuate the exploitation of women, children and men for the reproduction of capitalism. More importantly, I grew up in a dysfunctional unhappy union of my parents and swore I would never get married.

But I knew these were not Pat's thoughts and I actually first brought up the topic of matrimony one night, saying very hesitantly, "Perhaps we should talk about getting married," intending to have a sociological discussion of the values of wedlock. I immediately found myself losing control of the conversation with Pat taking it as a given that we would get married. After a lengthy discussion we agreed to drive back via Toronto, Canada, where Tim Draimin and his girlfriend Beth would arrange a brief wedding ceremony. As an event in a foreign country with no family or a big celebration, just two friends as required witnesses, I felt our marriage ceremony would leave a minimal imprint on society.

We left New York on July 2 and arrived in Toronto the next day. As fate would have it, the ceremony was set for July 4, US Independence day. Adding an unusual touch to the ceremony, the only person Tim could find to officiate on such short notice was an "old Catholic" priest who belonged to a small Catholic sect that had broken with the Vatican in the 19th century over the Pope's infallibility, claiming that this doctrine violated the "ancient Catholic faith."

I had schoolboy giggles and got stoned as the hour of the ceremony approached at sunset in Toronto, even trying to figure out at the last moment how to get out of it. The priest had no church to practice his faith in and the ceremony was held in his house. It was a surreal experience as I grinned in an idiotic manner and said "I do" to Pat in front of Tim and Beth.

We had dinner together at a great Indian restaurant, and I quickly accepted the reality of being Pat's married mate. We retired to our hotel room, and I will remember to the end of my days our spectacular lovemaking that night. Pat, now three months pregnant, was stunningly beautiful, a siren out of Greek mythology enchanting me with her charms and eroticism.

After leaving Canada, Pat and I drove to Wisconsin. Totally caught off guard by our marriage, no family gathering awaited us as we simply told my mother and father of Pat's pregnancy and our matrimony in separate conversations. There wasn't even a spontaneous outburst of joy, reflecting my family's Catholic Germanic culture. Marriages are supposed to be planned months, if not years in advance. Even my mother, who I knew to be very excited by her first grandchild, responded simply, "Oh really. That's good news."

Coincidentally, Orlando Nunez appeared in Madison as part of his Managua research center's collaboration with the Land Tenure Center at the University of Wisconsin in Madison. I met with him and broached the idea of possibly moving to Nicaragua during the next year to work with his center. He was open to it and said, "Let's discuss it on your next trip to Managua."

Then it was on to California. Pat and I had agreed to live at my place in Annapolis, a welcome respite in the countryside after our ultimate intense urban experience in New York. The long quiet summer days were perfect, as we took trips to the beach while finishing up projects that had begun in New York. Pat was working on a NACLA report on women and we both had to go over the *Monthly Review* galleys for our book, *Agribusiness in the Americas*. I continued my research on US policy in

Central America and began outlining a new book on the growing conflagration in the region.

In October we moved into Pat's house in Berkeley that she had sublet while we were in New York. It was a cozy place, just three blocks from the hospital where we would have the baby. Having settled in and waiting for the birth of our son in February, I flew off to Nicaragua in November.

27. Reagan Ascendancy, Clouds of War in Central America

US policy towards Central America was in a transitional period. In May 1980 Carter signed legislation authorizing 75 million dollars in aid for Nicaragua. Much of it was for the private sector and its clear intent was to co-opt the revolution, to provide an alternative to the Cuban and Soviet assistance that was already flowing to Nicaragua. The legislation authorizing the aid required Carter to provide letters of certification to Congress every few months, mainly to report that the Sandinistas were not actively supporting revolutionary movements in El Salvador or anywhere else in Central America. This he did in September 1980.

In El Salvador, US policy was a different story. A reformist junta comprised of military colonels and civilians had overthrown the government lead by General Carlos Humberto Romero in October 1979. But shortly after the assassination of Archbishop Romero (no relation to the general) in March 1980 the US Congress, at the request of Carter, voted to send economic and "non-lethal" military aid to El Salvador. The composition of the junta in January had shifted to the right as centrist civilians were replaced and then in May, the reform-minded Colonel Adolfo Majano was relieved as commander-in-chief of the army, rendering him virtually powerless in the junta. In spite of these changes, the Carter administration insisted that the "center" had to be supported in the government even though the military murdered centrist political figures as well as many on the left.

As the 1980 US presidential contest unfolded between Jimmy Carter and Ronald Reagan, the campaign centered around the loss of US power and prestige around the world, particularly with the seizure of hostages at the US embassy in Iran in late 1979. In Central America, Reagan and one of his chief Latin America advisers, Jeane Kirkpatrick, argued that it was better to support authoritarian regimes over totalitarian communist governments because the former were more malleable to change while the communists remained in power indefinitely. Unlike Jimmy Carter, they saw Nicaragua and even the revolution on the tiny Caribbean island of Grenada in 1979 as part of the expansion of the Soviet Union that had to be stopped. In a campaign speech, Reagan declared: "The Caribbean is rapidly becoming a Communist lake in what should be an American pond and the United States resembles a giant afraid to move." The Republican Party demanded the termination of all aid to the Nicaraguan government and a beefing up of military assistance to the Salvadoran government.

I arrived in Nicaragua just after Ronald Reagan won the elections. Orlando met me at the airport. Our conversation immediately turned to the implications of Reagan's victory and we drove to see Julio Lopez, the head of the Sandinista Department of International Relations (DRI), to discuss US policy. While Nicaragua had openly supported the Salvadoran revolutionary opposition, they had taken great care in the previous months to covertly deliver aid to the guerrillas, not wanting to antagonize the Carter administration.

With the election of Reagan, this policy was up for review, and intensive discussions took place at the DRI as well as within the Sandinista National Directorate. The question was whether Reagan's campaign statements on Nicaragua were largely rhetorical or if he would take a militaristic stance against Nicaragua. I made the case that the interventionist thrust of the Reagan team "runs far deeper than the influence of Jeane Kirkpatrick. The right wing is definitely taking control of US foreign policy."

I pointed out that in 1976, in response to the reformist Trilateral Commission founded two years earlier, the right wing set up the Committee on the Present Danger led by figures like Paul Nitze, Richard Pipes and Eugene Rostow. Its ideology and members dominated the Reagan administration's thinking and would soon morph into the core of the neoconservative coterie that would drive US foreign policy for decades to come. In my conversations with the DRI and Julio I asserted that "these policy makers are bent on nothing less than the destruction of the Sandinista revolution and all opposition in Central America and the Caribbean."

I doubt if my analysis of US policy had a major impact on the internal discussions among the Sandinistas although it certainly reinforced the public statements of Sandinista leaders that they intended to confront US intervention in the region, whatever form it took. In late 1980 the Sandinista National Directorate substantially stepped up arms assistance to the Salvadoran guerrillas who in November had united under the banner of the Farabundo Marti National Liberation Front—the FMLN. Aside from the escalating flow of military aid, training camps for the FMLN were set up on the outskirts of Managua and much of the Salvadoran leadership began to use Nicaragua as a planning and coordinating center for the war in El Salvador.

My other major conversations with Orlando took place over my possible role in CIERA, the Center for Research and Studies of Agrarian Reform, the new think tank of the Ministry of Agriculture and Agrarian Reform. Amazingly $1 million of the $75 million in US Aid to Nicaragua went to CIERA, primarily through the Land Tenure Center of the University of Wisconsin. As part of the aid package, the US Agency for International Development was authorized to pick an American as an assistant to Orlando and it settled on a classic liberal, anti-communist candidate whose name I forget. Orlando nominated Peter Marchetti who had close ties to the Land Tenure Center and backed by the Center, refused to accept anyone but Marchetti, and he carried the day. A radical staff was assembled at CIERA and it became a center of left thinking not only on agrarian reform but on the broader political strategies of the Sandinista revolution.

Aside from Marchetti, several other Americans and Western Europeans were at CIERA. It was certainly an appealing and creative intellectual environment for me. But Orlando suggested "it might be useful to set up a parallel center in the United States to collaborate with CIERA. We need a window on US agrarian reform policy and on its counterrevolutionary thrust in Central and Latin America." With the publication of *Agribusiness in the Americas*, I also had a base of knowledge and access to researchers in the United States that I could draw on to compliment the work and analysis of CIERA from abroad.

Moreover, the formation of a left research center in the United States had the endorsement of the DRI, which wanted a listening post in the United States to help decipher Reagan's policies. And Xabier Gorostiaga had already jumped into the fray on my earlier visit, stating, "Roger, you can help us build an international network to devise an alternative to US interventionist policies in Central America and the Caribbean."

I agreed with their perspective and quickly took up the idea of founding a new organization. I told Orlando, "It would be great to facilitate relations between the Sandinistas in Nicaragua and leftist thinkers and activists in the United States, particularly if I work out of Berkeley where we can build on the strength of the anti-war movement and the New Left in the 1960s." I had been prevented from continuing the NACLA West office due to the antagonism of the League for Proletarian Socialism in 1978, but now a new organization would emerge that could fill the void left by NACLA's closure.

It was agreed that the Sandinistas would help find seed money for the new organization. A couple of months later, Orlando was invited to speak and lecture in Spain and he persuaded a solidarity organization in Spain to provide $10,000 to what would become the Center for the Study of the Americas (CENSA). Even though the source of money was legitimate, to be on the safe side it was sent to UNRISD, the United Nations Research Institute for Social Development based in Geneva, Switzerland. It was headed by Solon Baraclough who supported the Sandinista Revolution and had been a major figure in Chile's agrarian reform program under Salvador Allende. Sometime in mid-1980, after a flurry of papers crisscrossed the Atlantic, $10,000 was deposited in the new CENSA bank account. At about the same time, CENSA was officially registered as a nonprofit research organization based in Berkeley.

Vanessa was in Managua when I visited in November 1980 and our relationship resumed. Objectively I was a cad, sleeping with her while Pat was pregnant with our child. But I did not see it that way. What did I prove by remaining faithful to her? I loved Pat and that was not in doubt. With Vanessa, like Pat, I had an intellectual rapport—it extended to politics and philosophy with a constant discussion of the unfolding revolution in Nicaragua. There is no deeper relationship and intimacy between human beings than one that merges the mental and the physical. To stop seeing Vanessa would have limited our growth as political and social beings.

Because of the growing intensity of the war in El Salvador and the increased bonds between the Sandinistas and the FMLN, I flew to San Salvador on my way back to California. The Salvadoran left was growing rapidly, attracting the very centrist forces that the Carter administration claimed it was trying to draw into the increasingly repressive junta. After the death of Archbishop Romero in March 1980 the Democratic Revolutionary Movement (FDR) was formed. It was a broad coalition backed by the popular movements, as well as by several of the guerrilla organizations. Among its leaders were Guillermo Ungo of El Salvador's social democratic party and Hector Dada, who had been a member of the first junta that was formed when General Romero was overthrown in

1979. Enrique Alvarez Cordova—a middle aged, disloyal scion of the notorious "Fourteen Families" that dominated the Salvadoran economy—became president of the FDR. He had served in three previous governments, most notably as Minister of Agriculture in the early months of the junta. Upon joining the FDR, he declared that "a change at the very center of power was necessary." The FDR's platform was "anti-oligarchic and anti-imperialist," espousing respect for human rights, political pluralism and popular participation in a revolutionary government.

28. Killing Fields and Birth

"No soldier is obliged to obey an order contrary to the law of God.... In the name of God, in the name of our tormented people who have suffered so much and whose laments cry out to heaven, I beseech you, I beg you, I order you in the name of God, stop the repression!"
–Archbishop Oscar Romero of San Salvador,
March 23, 1980 (the day before his assassination).

When I arrived in San Salvador in the third week of November 1980 death and repression were everywhere. I had previously met with many of the leaders of the popular organizations of the left at the national university but in June 1980 it had been closed and occupied by the military. Guillermo Galvan, who had helped me set up meetings with leaders on the left and organizers in my previous trips to El Salvador, had fled to Costa Rica with his family after he was denounced on TV as a revolutionary and his house machine-gunned by a military terrorist squad.

Now my main contacts were Ricardo Stein at the Jesuit-run University of Central America and Rafael Moreno who served as a parish priest in a community on the outskirts of San Salvador. Stein ran a research center at the university that was under heavy surveillance by the military as I readily ascertained at the entrance where two SUV vehicles, with tinted non-transparent windows and without license plates, were parked. A meticulous researcher, Stein told me that based on his examination of newspapers, press releases and funeral notices, "more than 600 people are being killed every month by the death squads; and this doesn't include rural massacres, such as the 147 refugees including 44 children who were slaughtered last month trying to cross the Lempa River into Honduras." He also helped me set up clandestine meetings with underground leaders, all of whom used *noms de guerre* when I talked with them. I met one militant, "Morenito," who said: "The number of recruits joining our struggle is growing by leaps and bounds, and we are stronger than ever in the cities and even more so in the countryside. But the death squads run rampant, going into the poor barrios at night and killing more and more people at random, dumping their bodies on the streets and rivers to terrify the people."

From June to November 1980, FDR delegations had traveled to Europe, Latin America and even the United States, meeting with international organizations and presidents, winning increasing support in their drive against US policy as the brutal repression in El Salvador shook even the minds and hearts of moderate, anti-communist leaders. Many of the FDR representatives, including Rafael Moreno, went to New York in October at the invitation of the United Nations assembly to talk about the plight of El Salvador. The Mexican government under President Lopez Portillo allowed FDR representatives to set up a public office in Mexico City, from which they traveled freely, raising funds to support the Salvadoran struggle.

By late October the repression had become so intense in El Salvador that the FDR leaders, most of whom were still abroad, decided to return home to publicly denounce the military's coordination of the death squads and to help rally public opposition. They hoped that their newly won international prestige would render them immune to the death squads.

On November 27, 1981, while I was in San Salvador, the leadership of the FDR held a press conference at the Jesuit high school, just three blocks from the US embassy. I did not hear about the meeting until minutes before it was to begin. As the conference was opening, some 20 heavily armed men dressed in civilian clothes stormed the school and forced everyone to lie face down on the floor. Then several dozen people, including the FDR leaders, were hauled away in full view of a contingent of Salvadoran soldiers standing outside. I approached the school after the assault, saw the turmoil and consternation of people at the entrance, and decided there was little I could do by getting closer.

The next day, five bodies were found at a lake near the city, including that of Enrique Alvarez and four other FDR leaders. Alvarez had been brutally tortured and his left arm missing, while the 28-year-old leader of the largest popular organization, Juan Chacon, was found with three bullet holes in his face, his left fist clenched in a final defiant salute raised above his head on the blood-spattered ground.

The news spread rapidly around the world. I felt overwhelmed but contacted whomever I could in San Salvador to see if I could help in any way. I called Vanessa in Managua and she decided to fly in the next day. She had been doing writing and photojournalism for alternative organizations and publications in Great Britain and could send stories from San Salvador.

I met her at the Salvadoran International Airport at seven at night. It was a new airport, a good hour's ride from San Salvador on a long lonely paved road with little around save pasture and farmland. Death squads had been known to toss mutilated bodies along the roadside. We took a taxi and were stopped at one checkpoint by uniformed guards, searched and waved on. Then we saw a body lying on the road. The taxi driver didn't even slow down, swerving around it and driving rapidly on. We went to stay with Alma Guerrmoprieto who was filing stories on the war in El Salvador for the Guardian of London.

The funeral for the dead leaders of the FDR was held the next day at the same cathedral where Archbishop Romero had been assassinated in March. A public rally in the plaza in front of the Cathedral was called at the same time to announce the new leadership of the FDR. Most people were fearful to attend because the plaza had been machine-gunned during Romero's funeral at the same location in March, killing at least 26 and leaving hundreds wounded.

Vanessa and I didn't even discuss the dangers, simply knowing that we had to be there. On that day, perhaps more than any other in my life, I was gripped by a death wish. I was torn by fears of fatherhood and thought that if I was felled by the death squads my son would know me as a martyr, not as a dysfunctional father. Also I felt that if I died, my death as an American would at least provoke an outcry that would help cut off US aid to the junta.

It was a sunny day as Vanessa and I walked among the sparse crowd in the plaza and the cathedral. We went into the church and as she was taking pictures of one of the FDR leaders whose face was visible through the glass panel in the casket, a bomb went off in the far corner of the plaza. We ran out to see people scattering, with no apparent injuries. Fortunately there was no more violence. Vanessa and I remained for another hour or so at the cathedral before returning to Alma's apartment.

The next morning we awoke to the stunning news that three American nuns and a lay missionary worker had been murdered the night before on the road between the airport and the city. The two nuns who were picked up by their fellow missionaries had arrived on the same flight that Vanessa had taken from Managua the night before. Death was all around us. Vanessa and I made love with more fervor than ever on our nights together in San Salvador. Years later she would tell me, "These were the most intense, passionate moments I ever experienced with you." We were seizing the passion for life in the midst of the killing fields.

Several days after the murder of the missionaries I flew out to San Francisco. To build the research center I had discussed with the Sandinistas in Managua, I called together a dozen potential collaborators at the end of December. By mid-January 1981 we had rented an office on Fulton Street at the base of the UC Berkeley campus, where CENSA remained until 2012. The first board of directors was comprised of me and four women, including Pat Flynn and Elizabeth Farnsworth, who was my mentor in the early days of NACLA.

When I left Managua, I was told that a major guerrilla insurrection was being planned in El Salvador to present Reagan with a fait accompli when he took office on January 20. During the month of December, the FMLN occupied 42 towns. Then on January 10 they launched a general offensive, coordinating guerrilla attacks on military targets throughout the country. Four days later the Carter administration restored US military aid which had been cut off after the American missionaries were killed.

The world around me was in upheaval as Pat entered the final weeks of her pregnancy. We had attended birth classes together that taught the Lamaze technique, a system of physical and breathing exercises with coaching by the father to help manage the pain and anxiety of the mother's birthing process. We eagerly looked forward to our first child, wondering what he would be like as he came into the world.

On the early morning of February 3 Pat began to have regular contractions and we went to the hospital three short blocks away, expecting a completely normal birth. To our dismay, by early afternoon she had not dilated beyond five centimeters. The doctor came to talk to us about a Cesarean section, and I more than Pat resisted the idea, saying "how could this happen, Pat is in perfect physical condition and we did everything right to prepare for the birth." But she was taken away from me to the surgical ward for what seemed like an eternity. Several hours later she was brought back to the hospital room where I waited and our newborn son wrapped in a white blanket was placed in my arms. He was so precious and peaceful looking. I immediately fell in love with him.

We named him Matthew Salvador, after Pat's father Matthew Flynn and my grandfather Mathais Burbach. The middle name reflected two Latin America political icons: Salvador Allende of Chile and Salvador Cayatano Carpio, the Salvadoran guerrilla leader who was fast becoming known as the Ho Chi Minh of Central America. The name Salvador also referred to the guerrilla offensive that was going on in El Salvador as he was born. The birth and this historic battle profoundly shaped the course of my life in different ways for the next decade.

29. Political Assassination in Managua

After the birth of our son, Pat and I moved from her rental in Berkeley into the house she had bought before we left for New York, not far from Lake Merritt and the historic Grand Lake Theater in Oakland. A bright house with bay windows set on a quiet street, it was two blocks from bustling Grand Avenue where we'd do our shopping and stop by the local newspaper vendor, an elderly Jewish gentleman who was a living historic landmark in the neighborhood.

Pat and I turned out to have good parental instincts, not spoiling Matt, setting boundaries for his behavior while loving him deeply. He was a quiet and pensive child, not given to much crying or tantrums. I helped out as much as possible, going to doctor's appointments, taking him on stroller rides to Grand Avenue and Lake Merritt, and providing a lot of care and attention at home, given the limitation that I could not nurse Matt in the middle of the night. But Pat would occasionally complain, "You're not pulling your share of the household duties." I admit my standards for maintaining the house were not as good as they should have been.

Pat did not object when I flew off to Managua in September, 1981, mainly to work with Orlando. We were becoming close collaborators because of similar political philosophies and our commitment to rethinking Marxism in light of the Sandinista revolution. While Orlando's research center focused on agrarian issues, he was also a major political theorist of the revolution and an adviser to the National Directorate of the Sandinista Front.

I would often go to Orlando and his companion Syta's simple white stucco house for dinner in the evenings, discussing the course of the Sandinista revolution as well as what was taking place in Latin America and the United States. These conversations were very useful to both of us, as it enabled Orlando to tie into the latest thinking on the left in the Northern world while I took back to the United States a better understanding about how the Nicaraguan revolution fit into the broader global struggle. Together we would go on to participate in international seminars, write articles and jointly pen a book that became the informal manifesto of the Sandinista revolution.

Vanessa was in Managua in September 1981 having arrived several days before I did. We stayed together at the home of a Nicaraguan and American couple on the outskirts of Managua. She had been spending more time in London as she and Jeffrey were trying to have children together. As it turned out, she was in the early stages of pregnancy, missing her second period while we were together. Some of the intensity was gone from our relationship but we felt like old friends who, having accumulated a common history in Central America, couldn't stop being together when we were in Managua.

On this trip I began work on a book of interviews with key revolutionary leaders from Nicaragua, El Salvador and Guatemala. In Nicaragua, I chose Orlando's boss, Jaime Wheelock, the Minister of Agriculture and Agrarian Reform and a member of the National Directorate. Wheelock proved difficult to deal with. His interview was largely uninformative as he was evasive and abstract in his answers. I interpreted his lack of openness to his believing that I was a meddlesome gringo who did not merit any insights into the Nicaraguan revolution. But I found this was not the case. Wheelock's general disposition was one of aloofness and disdain, a "*commandante*" of the revolution who could act as he pleased with his subordinates and underlings. His elitist perspective was reflected in his approach to agrarian reform. While Orlando and he worked together throughout the Sandinista years in power, they had major policy differences. Wheelock emphasized state-owned agricultural farms and agro-complexes run by the ministry while Orlando advocated an agrarian reform that focused on giving land directly to the peasants and to locally run cooperatives.

Wheelock's policy turned out to be a disaster, as many peasants who remained landless or had small plots never really came to identify with the revolution. Moreover, the state fixed the prices for food staples, forcing small producers to sell at low prices or to turn to the black market. By the late 1980s the failure of Wheelock's policies were finally recognized and the Sandinista government began distributing land directly to the peasants. But it was too late to turn the tide of the US war in the north where many peasants now sided with the Contras.

The revolutionary leader I most wanted to interview was Salvador Cayetano Carpio from El Salvador, known as "Marcial." In the 1930s, at a very young age, he began working as a baker, joining the Communist party-led Protective Bakers Union. By the 1960s he had become the secretary general of the party. But he left the post over internal disputes and founded a guerrilla movement, the Popular Liberation Forces Farabundo Marti (FPL), in the early 1970s when he was over 50 years old. The genius of the FPL under his leadership was that it moved beyond organizing guerrilla cells, building allied popular organizations, particularly among peasants, urban workers and students. When the five Salvadoran guerrilla organizations finally merged in 1980, the FPL was by far the largest.

I put out the word to my Salvadoran contacts in Managua of my interest in talking to Marcial. I was not hopeful as he shunned the limelight and gave few interviews. He spent most of his time with the FPL guerrillas in the stronghold of Chalatenango, coming occasionally to Managua to coordinate strategy and logistics with the Sandinistas. But to my astonishment I received a call one evening while I was with Vanessa. My contact told me to be ready in an hour to be picked up to see Marcial at a "safe house."

As I walked in the door I immediately found Marcial to be a warm, thoughtful and engaging figure, the opposite of Wheelock. Mestizo-looking and of a slight build with spectacles and a sparse mustache, he had a capacity to directly connect with you, speaking with emotion and from his personal experiences. We talked ardently for several hours about the current struggle in El Salvador and US intervention. "Listen companero," he told me (I used these words as the title for the book of interviews), "I have seen children of four, six, eight years old, shot down by bullets from helicopters with US advisors in them." He added, "The North American people do not deserve this image.... [They] "have a deep moral character and a tradition of fighting for liberty going back to before the French revolution.... It cost the North America people great sacrifices to reach a certain democratic development."

He said that in the war, "the suffering inflicted on our people is of another dimension—it is real genocide," noting that "helicopters are the guts of this kind of war. This explains why Reagan is constantly asking for the US to send more helicopters."

I woke Vanessa when I returned to the house where we were staying. Exhilarated by my encounter with Marcial, we talked until dawn about the greatest living revolutionary in Central America.

Over a year-and-a-half later, in April, 1983, when I was in California going over the final proofs of the book for publication, the news broke that Marcial had died in Managua. The initial story claimed he had committed suicide after ordering the assassination of the second-in-command of the FPL, Anna Maria (the nom de guerre of Mélida Anaya Montes) because of disagreements over political strategy. I refused to believe it. To this day, exactly what happened is disputed. But the story I find most convincing is that it was the head of the FPL internal security, Marcelo, who with collaborators of Anna Maria's own security entourage, carried out the assassination. Marcial did not order it, but there definitely were deep divisions between him and Anna Maria that were jeopardizing his leadership of the FPL. It was the deep sense of loyalty that Carpio elicited within the FPL that led Marcelo and others to assassinate Anna Maria.

Marcial was abroad at the time of the assassination but came to Managua a few days later, as had been previously planned. Tomas Borge, the Sandinista Minister of Interior called Marcial to his office. They were long time comrades, as they both held similar political positions, believing that guerrilla wars were "*guerras popular prolongadas*" (prolonged people's wars). Borge told him that there would be a trial of those in the FPL implicated in the assassination and that it would include Marcial himself.

Marical returned to the compound where he was staying and retired to his private room. There he shot himself, leaving behind a final testament, stating: "What wounds me and what I find unbearable is that my revolutionary brothers accept this slander as true.... To accept it not only destroys my revolutionary image, but harms the organization I care about so deeply.... I can find no way to accept this terrible event... the terrible loss of our companera, Anna Maria."

In the subsequent investigation of those involved in her assassination, none of them ever stated that they had been ordered to do so by Marcial. Even if Marcial had been involved, Anna Maria's assassination reflects the general failing of guerrilla movements guided by "democratic centralism," a belief that the leaders of the organization are justified in taking all steps necessary to ensure the "correct political line" is imposed, even if it involves the murder of other leaders. Moreover, the Salvadoran left has a particularly intense history of internecine politics and assassinations: Joaquin Villalobos, the head of the People's Revolutionary Army (ERP), ordered the murder of Roque Dalton in 1975, a brilliant revolutionary poet and journalist who dared to disagree with Villalobos.

While wrapping up my stay in Managua in September 1981 I met with Julio Lopez of the Directorate of International Relations (DRI). The CIA was already active on the Honduras-Nicaragua border, fomenting discontent and uprisings among Miskito Indians on the Atlantic Coast.

We agreed that on my way back to the United States I would stop off in Honduras to find out what I could about the Reagan administration's initial efforts to organize the remnants of Somoza's National Guard into a counterinsurgency force against the Sandinistas.

I did not ask Julio and he did not offer any contacts with Sandinista intelligence operatives who I knew must be working in Honduras. I would develop my own independent sources, talking to Honduran critics about what was happening in their country. As the director of the newly-founded Center for the Study of the Americas in Berkeley and with a doctorate, I could venture into the US embassy stating benignly, "I want to get a better understanding of US foreign policy." For Julio and the DRI, I would provide a unique perspective on Honduras while simultaneously gathering information that would enable me to lecture and write in the United States about the new thrust of US intervention in that country.

As during other visits to Central American countries, Tim Draimin provided me with a key contact in Tegucigalpa—Victor Meza, who ran CEDOH, the Honduran Center for Documentation. Victor was close to the Sandinistas, but had somewhat of a falling out with them because of his more independent temperament. He was an outstanding political analyst and had contacts and sources in the Honduran government and the military. A tall dark-complexioned man with big glasses and a commanding personality, he provided me with critical insights into what was happening in Honduras.

At our meeting, Victor told me: "A special battalion commanded by General Gustavo Alvarez Martinez runs death squads and torture centers that are systematically eliminating domestic opponents of the regime. The battalion is being advised and trained by the CIA." He went on to note, "CIA activities are expanding to efforts to bring together and organize former members of Somoza's National Guard, and other Somoza loyalists, some of whom are now in Miami."

Jack Binns, Carter's ambassadorial appointment to Honduras, was still there at the time, but would soon be relieved by John Negroponte who became the point man for coordinating what became known as the Contra army. Before he left, Binns cabled the State Department that he was "deeply concerned at increasing evidence of officially sponsored/sanctioned assassinations."

The department responded that he should use "back channels," meaning the CIA, for any further reports. With Negroponte's arrival in Tegucigalpa, the activities of the death squads intensified. Scores of unidentified bodies were found dumped in citrus groves and in a river near one of the major torture centers, about 16 miles outside of Tegucigalpa. It is documented that a CIA officer based in the embassy made frequent visits to this center.

At the US embassy, Cresencio Arcos, the press spokesperson, became my principal source of information. An appointee of the Carter administration with Hispanic roots in the US Southwest, he was very gregarious and an engaging personality. While not discussing the US role in the dirty war, he did admit that Alvarez ran death squads. More importantly, he told me: "There is a dramatic change in US policy in Honduras with the Reagan administration. It is determined to mount a campaign against the Sandinista government, which it perceives as a threat to the free world."

As the public spotlight on the US-backed war in Honduras intensified in subsequent months and years, I continued to meet with Arcos as he remained as press attache under Negroponte until 1985. The scuttlebutt among the press corps in Tegucigalpa was that Arcos managed to hold on to his posting so long because he had received CIA training before beginning his diplomatic postings and therefore, had a certain autonomy within the State Department. He was part of the post-Vietnam generation of agents who were not in tune with death squad activities. According to The Washington Post, in 1982 Arcos had the clout to go directly to Negroponte to demand the release of two detained victims held in one of the torture centers.

The September 1981 trip set the pace for my life for the next decade. I careened back and forth to Central America, averaging about three extended visits per year to the isthmus, gathering information, conversing with militants and leaders, talking to US embassy and military figures, and writing about the revolutionary struggles. Crisscrossing the United States, I gave lectures and attended meetings of solidarity organizations and research and policy centers in places as diverse as Santa Fe, Seattle, Austin, Hawaii, New York and Washington, D.C. When invited to Western Europe, particularly to Amsterdam and London, I acted as a spokesperson for the US opposition to Reagan's war policies.

I was driven by passion, politics and a commitment to supporting the revolutionary movements in Central America. When I returned to California in late September, I hung a black-and-white bloc print of Bertrand Russell in the new CENSA office. On it were etched words from Russell's autobiography that reflected my sentiments: "Three passions have governed my life: The longing for love, the search for knowledge and unbearable pity for the suffering of mankind." The poster hung in my office for three decades.

30. Contra War and the Nouveau International

It was a hot scorching day in Managua in June 1982 when Orlando picked me up at the Sandino International Airport. As soon as we got into his Toyota pickup truck he said: "A war has started. The CIA is sending ex-National Guard troops into Nicaraguan villages in the north, attacking and massacring innocent villagers. Two bridges were blown up back in March, the first major attack. New strikes are targeting peasants and villagers who support the revolution." As we drove into the city, I saw rag-tag Sandinista militia units marching in the streets, some of them preparing to go to the north to defend the bridges, roads and villages against the US-backed attacks.

That summer marked the start of a bloody war that would go on for the remainder of the decade. The CIA had set up base camps in Honduras to supply the counterrevolutionary forces, which would become known as the "Contras," to carry out military forays deep into Nicaragua. More than 300 villagers and their defenders would die between June and August of 1982 alone, with casualties escalating with each coming month.

The early covert CIA operations were not reported in the US press, but the Reagan administration left no doubt about its aggressive intentions towards Nicaragua. Assistant Secretary of State Thomas Enders was sent to Nicaragua in late 1981 to insist that the Sandinista army reduce its size to 15,000 soldiers (it already had 23,000) and that no assistance of any type be given to the Salvadoran guerrillas. In return Washington would pledge not to invade Nicaragua or intervene in its internal affairs. As Enders talked, the US began military exercises off the coast of Honduras. Given the long history of US invasions in Nicaragua and Central America, it is small wonder that Daniel Ortega told Enders "we fear attack" and "have decided to defend our revolution by force of arms, even if we are crushed, and to take the war to the whole of Central America if that is the consequence."

After the talks with Ortega and the Sandinistas collapsed due to US intransigence, Ronald Reagan signed a National Security Council document authorizing the CIA to fund and train forces from Somoza's former National Guard to launch attacks in Nicaragua, leading to the opening of the war with the blowing up of the bridges in March. US direct military assistance to the Honduran armed forces increased several fold and US troops began conducting joint exercises with the Honduran army in early 1982, particularly near the Nicaraguan border. The conflict began to engulf the entire region when Honduran troops with US advisers entered El Salvador's Morazon province in June to reinforce a US-trained Salvadoran battalion that was bogged down in fighting with the FMLN guerrillas.

On July 19, 1982, the third anniversary of the Sandinista revolution, Daniel Ortega declared: "We are undergoing a bloody and silent invasion and all of Central America is on the brink of war," adding that US intervention is why Nicaragua is "anti-imperialist." Pro-Contra elements also began infiltrating civic institutions like the Nicaraguan Red Cross. In early August, Lea Guido, the Minister of Health who would become my lover a few years later, wrote a letter to the International Red Cross asking for help in resolving the conflict between the workers and the pro-Contra leaders who were disrupting Red Cross medical assistance, particularly in the villages in the north.

I had come to Nicaragua this time at the invitation of INIES, the Nicaraguan Social Research and Studies Institute that Xabier Gorostiaga had set up the year before. Independently financed, mainly from abroad, the name of the institute obscures Xabier's grand vision of creating an international network of organizations and individuals in Central America and the Caribbean with organizational links to Canada, Europe and the United States.

This vision was rooted in the uniqueness of the Nicaraguan process. The program of the governing junta called for a "mixed economy." With the revolution, Somoza's vast holdings and the lands and businesses of his associates had been nationalized. This left the so-called "patriotic bourgeoisie" with control of about half of the "means of production," including two-thirds of the country's manufacturing assets. The state assumed the role of catalyst for overall socioeconomic development through its ownership of all the banks and financial institutions and its centralized control of foreign trade, dominating what is referred to as 'the commanding heights of the economy.'

This was viewed as a "transitional" economy, one that was necessary to reconstruct the country. But it was never clear when, or even if, this economy would become socialist. Many believed that Nicaragua, with less than 3 million people and one of the lowest per capita incomes in Latin America, was too underdeveloped to embark on a socialist path. Even Fidel Castro of Cuba advised the Sandinistas to go slow, to not expropriate all the private producers. Concurrently, a mixed economy enabled Nicaragua to capture the support of social democratic governments in Western Europe and Latin America that provided economic assistance during the early years of the revolution.

It was Xabier's genius to see the mixed economy as a viable "alternative" project that could be propagated in the rest of Central America and the Caribbean. He did not openly frame it as leading to socialism, but he did insist that the new economy should respond to "the logic of the majority," the needs of the workers, the peasants and the popular classes.

About three dozen participants attended the June conference from countries as diverse as Jamaica, Cuba, Mexico, El Salvador, Haiti and Grenada. It led to the establishment of CRIES, the Regional Coordinator of Socioeconomic Research. From the beginning, Xabier envisioned the centers he directed and collaborated with as a foundation for carrying out a broader campaign to influence public policy and diplomacy on the international front.

On the last Saturday evening of the conference we had a public banquet with high-ranking Sandinista leaders in attendance, including Bayardo Arce, one of the nine commanders of the National Directorate, reflecting the importance of Xabier's project from the government's perspective. In his address, Xabier declared: "We need an economic alternative for the region, one that obeys the logic of the majority. Our research and knowledge has to be directed at putting forth alternative policies internationally to counter the United States, which is trying to destroy the popular struggles in Central America and the Caribbean for a just social and economic order."

The next day, on Sunday afternoon, I went with Xabier, Tim Draimin and Richard Fagen to a small lake just outside of Managua. There on the beach, over a plate of fresh fish caught by the local fishermen, we discussed setting up North American organizations that would collaborate with INIES and CRIES, particularly in the United States and Canada. Fagen, even more than me, would labor for the next decade to carry out

Xabier's vision of creating a new policy alternative in the United States. He was a professor at Stanford University, in his late-forties, and our paths had crossed in Cuba in 1969 and then in Allende's Chile in 1972 and '73, where he directed the Ford Foundation's programs.

Over the years I had kept my distance from him, believing he was a classic liberal professor working for the establishment who eschewed radical analysis in his work. But starting with our meetings in 1982, we became supportive comrades and I came to admire him for his integrity. While our papers and books were cast in a very different style and language, we invariably came to similar conclusions in supporting profound social change from below and opposing US intervention. In our latter years we would become even closer as we consulted and commiserated with each other after we were both diagnosed with incurable blood cancers.

At our lakeside gathering, Fagen agreed to convene a conference at Stanford University in August 1982 that would bring together a half dozen US academics and former policy makers, along with Tim from Canada and a handful of Central American scholars. The fledgling organization I headed, CENSA, would also participate. Xabier, who had little experience in the United States, had taken the first strategic step in launching a scholarly and activist network that would even come to influence the debates over Nicaragua and Central America in the US presidential elections of 1984 and 1988.

When I returned to California, my dad picked me up at the San Francisco airport. A couple of months before, he had driven his car from Milwaukee to California after the failure of a strike at the metals plant where he worked. Never having flown in an airplane, he joked, "I'll go as high as you want me to as long as I can keep one foot on the ground."

He had been one of the organizers of the striking workers whose fundamental demand had been the recognition of their union and a better wage. I once called him during the strike to ask, "How's it going?" He responded, "Those damn foreigners are ruining us." Perplexed because I knew that he was not xenophobic or prejudiced I asked, "What do you mean?" He responded: "It's those scabs that Eisenhower brought over after the anti-communist uprising in the 1956. Now they are recruited by the employers in Milwaukee whenever they want to break a strike or a union."

When the strike failed he applied to go back to work but the plant refused to hire him. He was, however, able to file for unemployment benefits and with those funds he drove out to California for the first time in his life to visit his grandson and to see what I was up to, also hoping that he might find work. For the next decade, he lived partially in California, driving his car back to Wisconsin for extended stays of up to half-a-year or so.

Initially he stayed with Pat and me, doing remodeling work for her on the house. He and Pat never really hit it off, having frequent disputes over the work he was doing. While my Dad and I also had our differences, my relationship with him became closer than it had ever been. Our bond was solidified by the property I owned in Annapolis, California, a three hour drive up the northern coast from Oakland. He would often go there, and Matt and I would sometimes join him for extended weekends.

My Dad and I were still country boys at heart. The redwood trees and the solace of Annapolis gave me a certain sense of calm and stability throughout the 1980s as I returned from the wars in Central America or yet another conference somewhere in the world. Although I only owned two-and-a-half acres of land, not enough to grow any significant commercial crops, my Dad and I found plenty to do, including repairs on the house and starting in 1985, the construction of a second dwelling on the property. We also discovered that there was one very lucrative crop that could be cultivated in the foothills of California—marijuana.

Surprisingly, my relations with the rest of my family strengthened during this period, even as I dedicated more time to travel and political work. Matthew was the only grandchild on both sides of the family and Pat and I welcomed relatives and friends into our home who wanted to visit or even stay for an extended period of time. My sister Miriam, who had been laid off from her federal job in Utah in water management due to Reagan's budget cuts, came to live with us at the end of 1981 for a few months, and soon took up residence in the Bay Area.

We had a great Christmas dinner that year with Miriam, my mother and my sister Ann who flew in from Wisconsin, along with Pat's Mom and her only sister, Mary Frances, who came from Los Angeles. Pat, a great cook, made a splendid dinner of crab cioppino. Matt, now 10 months old, was, of course, the focus of attention as he crawled around on the floor engaging first one relative and then another. He seemed to take it all in stride, never acting like a self-centered child.

Unfortunately, Pat's and my relationship became more contentious, even as we began work on a new book in 1982, "The Politics of Intervention: The United States in Central America," (part of a new series published jointly by CENSA and Monthly Review Press). We both have strong personalities and argued more and more bitterly over issues big and small. I felt that Pat was a perfectionist, becoming more and more critical of my very persona that I found hard to take. Some of her criticisms of my behavior were reasonable, like I was flaky in keeping the house clean. But others cut more deeply, especially her critical comments of my comportment at gatherings with mutual friends, which I felt were not at all justified. Sometimes she became angry, lashing out at me. I would often react like my father, withdrawing and saying nothing.

But our relationship still had many moments of love and intimacy as when Xabier arrived in August 1982 and stayed in our home the day before the conference began at Stanford. The meeting brought together foreign policy critics of the Reagan administration, including William LeoGrande, a rising scholar on US-Cuba and Central American relations, and John Cavanaugh of the Institute for Policy Studies, based in Washington, D.C. Robert Armstrong, an ex-Peace Corps volunteer in El Salvador who filled my Central America position at NACLA after I left the New York office, also attended the meetings, along with a handful of Central Americans.

The conference decided to set up a US-based organization, Policy Alternatives for the Caribbean and Central America (PACCA). To my surprise, it was to be run out of the CENSA office and I was appointed the first director of PACCA. Xabier, given his charisma and fund-raising skills, secured funding for PACCA's first year during his brief trip to the Bay Area. He brought together a group of progressive donors, led by Melinda Rorick who came from a wealthy family back east and had recently moved to northern California. Our paths had crossed briefly back in 1971 when she had helped organize the May Day Tribe to shut down the Pentagon and Washington, D.C. Her family estate in Virginia had served as an organizing and training site for the anti-war demonstrators.

On the last night of the conference we held a banquet in San Francisco attended by Bay Area friends and supporters of the new PACCA project. Pat and I were there together and I sensed that we conveyed a certain magnetism, as a couple, as people conversed with us. I said to her, "We have worked together over the years and this gathering is part of what we have achieved. You contributed to this endeavor as much as me." For a brief moment in the San Francisco restaurant the world appeared to be in harmony as the lights flickered on the bay.

Due to this organizational work, along with my commitment to work with Orlando to create a new socialist perspective, I felt we were on the cutting edge of formulating a new utopian vision for the left. We were constructing a "Nouveau Internationale" rooted in the Sandinista and Central American experiences that envisioned a new world driven by revolutionary politics.

After Xabier's departure, PACCA hired an executive secretary to help me in building a national network. Our goal was to construct a policy alternative by working with liberal and progressive think tanks, particularly in Washington, D.C. I was assisted by a committee comprised of Richard Fagen and Saul Landau of IPS that met about once a month. Bob Stark, a parish priest from Chicago who had worked with Jesse Jackson and become involved in solidarity politics, had moved to the Jesuit house in Managua. He worked as Xabier's designated "trouble shooter" with PACCA, periodically taking extended trips to California and Washington to make sure its agenda was being advanced.

I began traveling to Washington to meet with people who were participating in the shaping of the new policy alternative, including Bob Borasage and John Cavanaugh of IPS. Bill Goodfellow and his sidekick Jim Morrell of the Center for International Policy also participated in PACCA. Relations with the International Center for Development Policy also developed, especially after Melinda Rorick moved to Washington and began building up the center, particularly by bringing in Robert E. White, the former US ambassador to El Salvador, who became a leading critic of Reagan's Central American policy.

During my trips to Washington I began interviewing officials in the Defense and State Departments who were involved in Central American policy. Once again, I used the cover story that I was doing policy research and now I even had a professional card to hand out saying I had a Ph.D. in Economic History and served as the "Director of CENSA, the Center for the Study of the Americas." The age of the Internet had not yet arrived and no one used the information on my card to conduct an investigation of CENSA and its activities. I found the State Department officials, usually desk officers on Nicaragua or El Salvador, to be uninformative bureaucratic hacks. But at the Defense Department it was a different story. Those in charge of Central American affairs were generally more perceptive and even more informative, perhaps because the press talked to them so little. Even the ambiance was different in the Pentagon, as unlike the staid corridors of the State Department, it had TV monitors in the halls carrying 24-hour news broadcasts of Ted Turner's recently founded CNN.

In my first Pentagon interview I met Colonel Larry Tracy who worked with the Defense Intelligence Agency's Briefing Team. He took pleasure in talking to people and believed he had a talent to change people's minds. This seemed to be the reason he talked to me at length, thinking that someone coming from Berkeley had to be some sort of liberal who he might be able to change. In our first conversation in 1983, he said: "Make no mistake the Reagan people are going to squeeze the Sandinistas until they cry 'Uncle.' You must be reasonable, you know there is no way the Nicaraguans are going to stop the United States." His communication skills and upfront language soon won him a position working with Otto Reich, who headed up the Office of Public Diplomacy. For the next three years I would talk to Tracy in Washington, garnering from him the latest insights into the Reagan administration's strategies in Nicaragua and Central America.

Much more moderate than Reich, Tracy left the Office of Public Diplomacy in 1986, just months before the Iran-Contra scandal broke. In our last meeting near the White House, where Tracy now worked much of the time, he invited me to a cafe where he introduced me to "a great microbrewed beer," Samuel Adams. After a few bottles we were both a bit inebriated and Tracy declared, "I know you are engaged in political activities against Reagan's policies." Taken aback, an adrenaline rush sobered me up as I expected him to drop the other shoe and say he had uncovered my political intelligence work with the Sandinistas. My mind even flashed on a detail of the FBI waiting at the door of the restaurant to arrest me for espionage.

But nothing of the sort happened. Tracy went on to say: "I hear that you are involved with William LeoGrande of American University who is a critic of Reagan's policy in Central America." I admitted working with him, saying, "I am interested in pursuing different policy options." To this day I am amazed that after three years of meetings with a military officer involved in White House planning with the Contras, all he had uncovered on me was the fact that I collaborated with LeoGrande, a respected liberal academician in Washington.

After leaving the military, Tracy became a private consultant. Years later, I looked him up on the Internet and found that he had joined the "GuruMaker: School of Professional Speaking." Based in Colorado, he worked at teaching others "in advanced presentation skills coaching, speaker development, and media training." His profile for the GuruMaker notes that Ronald Regan described him as "an extraordinarily effective speaker." The profile goes on to state: "Larry has a rare skill. He can train speakers and presenters to convert an audience that has already made up its mind. He is the embodiment of the GuruMaker philosophy."

31. Pope in Nicaragua, Specter of US Invasion

Late February 1983 found me flying into Managua again. The situation was much more somber than when I had left in June the year before as the contra attacks had become more frequent. Ronald Reagan and his cabal of neo-conservatives had fixated on Nicaragua, turning it into a major battleground in an effort to restore the imperium to its pre-Vietnam War days.

As I arrived in Nicaragua, the US military was conducting military maneuvers in Honduras, using these missions to leave weaponry and munitions behind for the Contras, and to menace the Sandinistas with the threat of an all-out US invasion. To meet this peril, the Sandinistas mobilized a poor country with less than three million people. A classic battle of David versus Goliath, it would last the remainder of the decade.

I came to Nicaragua with an assignment to write an article for Mother Jones magazine on the war, and immediately arranged an interview with Lenin Cerna, who as head of the Sandinista security forces was in charge of surveillance and infiltration of the Contras. A tall, foreboding, dark complected character, I admit I would never want to encounter him on a dark street. He was known for his harsh treatment of captured prisoners. The entire conversation was somber, not a bit of humor or even sarcasm as he described the evolving Contra strategies.

About a week after talking to Cerna, I went to the airport to see Pope John Paul II arrive. Elevated to the papacy four-and-a-half years before, his deep-seated conservatism was still not fully apparent. The Sandinista leadership hoped that he would call for an end to the war and a cessation of the brutal attacks on civilians in the north. A very Catholic country, the government spent $3 million on his visit, bringing in thousands of peasants from the countryside who wanted to see the Pope.

The Sandinistas were rudely disappointed. As the Pope walked out of the terminal, Father Ernesto Cardenal, the minister of culture and one of Nicaragua's leading poets, knelt to kiss the pontiff's hand. I could not hear the Pope's words, but it was clear from his demeanor that he was chastising Ernesto and his brother Fernando, a Jesuit priest and the minister of education, along with several other priests who held high-level positions, to end their participation in the Sandinista government. Fr. Xabier Gorostiaga escaped the Pope's direct condemnation because his research center, INIES, was nominally independent of the government. But he was on the receiving end of a broader Papal censure of those who preached the theology of liberation and thereby "divided the church" in Nicaragua against the hierarchy led by the reactionary Archbishop Miguel Obando y Bravo who was supported by the Contras.

The biggest uproar during the pope's visit came when he said mass at the July 19th Plaza, better known as the Plaza of the Revolution. I managed to secure a spot on the edge of the plaza, sandwiched in among the throng that was backed up into the incoming streets. From the chants, I soon gathered that many of those in front and closest to the pope were stridently anti-Sandinista. But the overwhelming majority in the plaza were poorly-dressed people who identified with the revolution. Some of them, led by the Mothers and Heroes of the Martyrs (whose sons and daughters had been killed by Contras), presented the Pope with a petition asking him to say something about the war. They specifically called for "words of commemoration" for the burial the day before of 17 members of the Sandinista Youth Organization who had died in a bus that was bombed by the Contras.

But in his sermon the pope said nothing about them or the Contra's savage attacks on civilians. Afterwards, as he was preparing to give communion, most of the crowd began to chant *"poder popular,"* popular power, and *"queremos paz,"* we want peace. One of the petitioners of the mothers of the martyrs rose with a megaphone and shouted, "Holy Father, we beg you for a prayer for our loved ones who have been murdered." The people around her applauded and most of the multitude yelled their approval, but those in front who identified with the Contras hissed and booed, yelling *"callete,"* shut up. As the mass drew to a close, one of the last cries I heard from the people near me was, "because of Christ and His Gospels, we are revolutionaries."

The pope was angered by this outburst and became even more hostile to the Sandinistas. His visit was a setback for the government, especially because the international press picked up on the Pope's perspective. While the poor continued to identify with the revolution, the right wing and the Reagan administration were elated that John Paul II had turned a blind eye to the Contra war and US intervention.

Several days later I took a bus to the city of Choluteca, 90 kilometers south of Tegucigalpa, the center for coordinating the activities of the Contra base camps near the Nicaraguan border. I found no representatives of the main Contra army the Nicaraguan Democratic Force (Fuerza Democrática Nicaragüense, or FDN) who would help me get into a base camp, but Honduran troops were everywhere in Choluteca providing the Contras with logistical support. A colonel in the Honduran army told me, "We are here to help the Nicaraguans fighting the communists. If they dare to cross the Honduran border to come after our allies, we are ready for them."

When I returned to the United States, Reagan was campaigning to rally more support for the Contra war and the FDN. In an address to a joint session of Congress in April, 1983, he painted an apocalyptic view of what would happen if the United States did not back the counter-revolutionary forces in Central America: "We cannot expect to prevail elsewhere. Our credibility would collapse, our alliance would crumble, and the safety of our homeland would be put in jeopardy."

The administration continued to intensify the war but the Contras over the next six months were unable to gain any traction, never taking or holding large villages or urban centers. The CIA then took a more direct role, using its special operations forces to assault Port Corinto, Nicaragua's largest harbor. In early October, Sea Rider gunboats manned by commandos fired on eight fuel tankers in the port and set fire to petroleum storage tanks, forcing the town's 25,000 inhabitants to evacuate. The Nicaraguan government would later successfully argue before the World Court in the Hague that this was a case of naked US aggression.

Shortly after the assault, the world awoke on October 25 to the news that the United States had invaded the tiny Caribbean island of Grenada. Four-and-a-half years earlier, just months before the Sandinista victory, the New Jewel Movement led by Maurice Bishop had seized power in a rebellion against Eric Gairy, an eccentric dictator. Bishop and his movement installed a "Popular Revolutionary Government," carrying out a series of social reforms similar to Nicaragua's while welcoming Cuban medical and economic assistance.

In 1983, infighting broke out within the New Jewel Movement over the proper ideological direction for the country to follow. The dissidents, led by the deputy prime minister, placed Bishop under house arrest. Demonstrators in the streets secured his release but in the melee that followed, Bishop was rearrested by the military and executed. The Reagan administration, claiming that the lives of US medical students studying on the island were in danger, launched "Operation Urgent Fury," sending a naval invasion force of 2000 Marines and Army Rangers to seize control of the island.

Nicaragua was shocked by the attack, fearing a similar fate awaited them as the United States had two aircraft carrier battle groups conducting naval exercises off Nicaragua's Atlantic and Pacific coasts. Intent on preventing the United States from employing a similar ruse against Nicaragua, the Sandinista Minister of Interior Tomas Borge informed the US ambassador that in case of any emergency the Sandinistas had designated three hotels and several planes for evacuating any foreigners who wished to leave Nicaragua. But hostile rhetoric continued to emanate from Washington, with Reagan himself saying, "I haven't believed anything they've been saying since they got in charge."

From Berkeley, I called Carlos Fernando Chamorro at the offices of Barricada, the Sandinista daily newspaper, to get his take on the US threat. He told me "With the checkmating of the Contras, the threat of a US invasion has never been higher. Reagan may be preparing to ride the Grenadian victory to Managua. Honduran troops are massing on the border and US military maneuvers, at levels not seen before, are taking place in Choluteca and southern Honduras, as well as at sea."

I hastily packed my bags and caught a flight to Nicaragua. If the US invaded, I had to be there with my comrades. When I landed, I found a country mobilized for war. Defensive trenches and bomb shelters were being built across Managua and the 100,000 strong militia forces had been fully activated. Anti-aircraft batteries ringed the outskirts of the city and Russian tanks were placed in defensive positions. In what was probably the first "shock and awe" strategy before Iraq, US planes flew overhead breaking the sound barrier, terrifying the populace with the fear that bombs might start falling at any minute.

After a couple of weeks I left as the tensions and the threat of an invasion subsided. But the Contra war only escalated in the coming months with no let-up in the bellicose rhetoric coming out of Washington. In May 1984 Reagan, in a nationally televised appeal for Contra aid, called Sandinista rule "a Communist reign of terror," adding, "we have seen it rolled back... in Grenada.... All it takes is the will and resources to get the job done."

32. Shared Utopia with International Solidarity Movement

"The Sandinista revolution was a shared utopia. Just as it marked a generation of Nicaraguans that made it possible and sustained it with arms, there was also a generation around the world that found in it a reason to live and believe."

Sergio Ramirez, vice president of Nicaragua, 1984-90
Adios Muchachos, A Memoir of the Sandinista Revolution

As Nicaragua defied the wrath of the US imperium, people from many continents rallied to its support. In a manner reminiscent of the Spanish Civil War half-a-century before, the Sandinista revolution became a shared utopia, a beacon of hope and struggle that ruptured national frontiers.

The international movement campaigned on many fronts, forming solidarity committees, signing petitions, organizing demonstrations, pressuring congresses and parliaments, writing in newspapers, collecting medicines, school supplies and agricultural implements for the struggling country. Many traveled to Nicaragua from North America, Western Europe and Latin America to work for the revolution. They helped build schools, harvested crops, worked in clinics and hospitals, served as advisers and technical experts in government ministries and joined the militias.

The Sandinista revolution altered the parameters of international relations in the midst of the cold war as the old East vs. West paradigm began to break down. Cuba and the Soviet bloc did provide substantial material and military assistance to Nicaragua. But this was complemented by economic and diplomatic support from countries as disparate as France, Mexico, Venezuela, Panama, Costa Rica, the Netherlands and the Scandinavian countries. This shift in international relations reflected and responded to the broad popular movement that mobilized around the world as it developed new forms of people-to-people assistance and collaboration.

US activists marshaled the largest grassroots movement in the world. Many of us who militated in the fight against the Reagan administration's intervention in Nicaragua saw in our efforts a revival of the Vietnam anti-war movement and the extension of the solidarity work in the aftermath of the brutal US-backed military coup led by General Pinochet that toppled the Allende government in 1973. We came to identify with the Nicaraguan struggle because we did not want the United States to promote more coups and wars in the world, especially on the pretext of "fighting communism."

An estimated 100,000 Americans visited Nicaragua in the 1980s, many as simple political tourists. Some came as part of delegations but most came on their own. It was an experience totally different from that of Cuba where the prohibition of US travel to the island meant that only organized delegations arrived via Mexico or Canada with assigned accommodations and structured tours. But it was not just the travel arrangements that were different. Those going to Nicaragua found an "open door" society: They could talk with anyone, travel to the countryside and stay where they pleased with no interference from the government. The established US media began to disparagingly call them "Sandalistas," claiming they were naïve Americans in Birkenstock sandals. This was not true. Most of the Americans I met in Nicaragua came in search of a better world and more often than not they saw in the transformations promoted by the Sandinistas the historic realization of their own dreams of a more just and humane society.

This hope became a deep certainty among those who stayed or returned to participate in the revolution, helping build schools or health centers, working alongside peasants picking coffee in the mountains or cotton in the hot flatlands. These experiences infused them with the enthusiasm to convince their compatriots back home that the task was more than just that of stopping military intervention. It was also to defend the viability of a new society.

The Nicaragua Solidarity Network in Washington, D.C. was only one among a plethora of diverse and multifaceted organizations that emerged to take up the non-intervention banner and provide assistance to the revolution. Church groups, sister-to-sister city projects, academic committees, human and health rights groups, and alternative technology organizations projected their efforts and causes into Central America.

Impressive on a smaller scale was the New World Agricultural Group (NWAG) and two of its leaders from the University of Michigan, Peter Rosset and Katharine Yih. I would often visit them in the evenings for dinner or just to have a beer. They would talk about the experiences of NWAG recruits—graduate students and professors—who came to promote alternative agriculture techniques, to teach at the agronomy university and to consult with the Ministry of Agriculture and Agrarian Reform.

The Bay Area became a flourishing hub of international networks with Nicaragua, spawning organizations like Tecnica, Bikes Not Bombs and the Elders, which was founded by members of the Abraham Lincoln Brigade that had fought in the Spanish Civil War. CENSA was enriched by this milieu as members and volunteers of these organizations dropped by our Berkeley office and even took on specific projects that we needed help with, such as setting up our first PC computers, adopting new printing and publishing techniques and dealing with the accounting system.

Our most extensive relations were with members of Tecnica, founded in 1983. I would occasionally stop by its Managua office and run into some of the twenty-odd volunteers that came down each month. They were librarians, computer programmers, engineers, mechanics and many other skilled professionals who often accomplished significant tasks in a short period of time. As one recruit said, "Tecnica hooks us up with a specific job and deals with the bureaucracy, the lodging and transportation, so we can get right into the work." One of them talked about being assigned to repair electrical pylons the Contras had blown up. Another used his engineering and design skills to construct a much-needed part for a state-owned cooking oil factory that was grinding to a halt because it had no dollars to import spare parts. As a computer scientist told me as he prepared to leave for the United States, "You feel for the first time you are accomplishing something that helps everybody. You feel wanted and useful."

Ben Linder became Tecnica's most famous collaborator in Nicaragua. I met him once in Managua on a Sunday afternoon when he was performing as a clown on a unicycle, his favorite hobby. He had found his way down to Nicaragua in 1983 on his own after graduating as an engineer from the University of Washington in Seattle and got Tecnica to help fund his work on electrical projects.

Ben was killed by Contras in April 1987 while working on a small-scale hydroelectric dam in northern Nicaragua where he had gone to live in an impoverished village in the war zone. Louis Proyect, the president of Tecnica, relates: "His death sent shock waves through the movement and drove home the risks of working in Nicaragua. As a sign that we would not be intimidated, volunteer applications doubled in the months following Ben's murder."

Ben was buried in Matagalpa, the main city near the village where he worked. The funeral procession was long, with several clowns juggling bowling pins among the many foreigners and Nicaraguans who came to lay Ben to rest. President Daniel Ortega, who served as one of the pallbearers, eulogized Linder over the open grave saying he "Was an American citizen who, full of love and joy, gave his life for the poor people of Nicaragua."

Shortly after the funeral, the FBI in the United States sprang into action against Tecnica. As Louis Proyect relates, "FBI agents went to the personnel offices at the workplace of 12 returned Tecnica volunteers and called them in for interviews in front of their bosses. They were told that Tecnica was at the center of an espionage ring that was running high technology out of Nicaragua to Cuba and the Soviet Union. Anybody who has ever been to Nicaragua would realize how ridiculous this charge is. There is only one elevator in the entire country."

In Berkeley, I half expected FBI agents to come knocking on CENSA's door. But nothing of the sort happened even though we were also engaged in an assistance program with Nicaragua. Four years before, about the time Ben Linder arrived in Nicaragua, Orlando Nunez and I had set up a project between CENSA and CIERA to begin searching for alternative markets in California for Nicaraguan agricultural exports. This was in part precipitated by my old corporate nemesis, Castle & Cooke, who I had locked horns with in my days at NACLA when I published reports on their payments of bribes to Honduran military officers for busting unions.

In October 1982 Castle & Cooke, through their subsidiary in Nicaragua, Standard Fruit Company, abruptly terminated their banana operations in Nicaragua, thus breaking a five-year contract they had signed the year before with the Sandinista government. It was supposed to lead to a gradual takeover of the company's assets by a Nicaraguan state-owned company. Castle & Cooke claimed that the decision to pull out was purely economic, that there was no market for Nicaraguan bananas.

I talked to Alejandro Martinez, the minister of foreign commerce, a few months later when he had already taken on the task of trying to commercialize the bananas in the United States with some limited success. He said: "Standard's decision to withdraw from Nicaragua at this juncture goes hand-in-hand with Reagan's hostile policies. The company is trying to destabilize Nicaragua while building up its plantations in Honduras and Costa Rica, which coincidently are the countries being used as US staging areas in the war against us."

When I returned to California, Eric Holt-Gimenez appeared at the doors of the CENSA office, offering to use his expertise to strengthen agricultural ties and exchanges between California and Nicaragua. I took Eric up on his offer and made him coordinator of the CENSA-CIERA project. About a decade younger than me, Eric was a recent graduate of the International Agricultural Development program at the University of California, Davis. He threw himself with enthusiasm into the work and soon secured a sizable grant for the project from the Presbyterian Hunger Fund in New York. Eric was the first person to ever call me "boss" when he showed up for work at the office. I was not sure how to take it, as a sign of respect, or if it meant I had passed into the ranks of the "elders" because of my advancing age.

1983 proved to be the year of work on "two, three many" projects for CENSA. Bob Stark, a priest with the Blessed Sacrament Fathers whom I had met the year before in Nicaragua, also appeared at the CENSA office to advance the work of PACCA, Xabier's organizational prodigy in the United States. A few years younger than me, Bob was strikingly hand-some with blonde hair and blue eyes and a real dynamo of energy. I never found out if he remained celibate or gave in to the women who must have thrown themselves at him.

I was delighted to have him involved in PACCA work as I was feeling increasingly disgruntled with spending time in Washington, D.C. work-ing on a blueprint for peace. Bob managed to bridge the work between the solidarity and grassroots organizations, which I favored, and that of the liberal policy activists in Washington who wanted to focus more on changing minds in the Democratic Party and Congress. He modestly argued, "I am not an intellectual. I don't know how to research and write policy statements." But he was not averse to knocking heads with the pol-icy wonks in PACCA to get them to work out their differences in draft-ing what became known as the Blueprint for Peace in Central America.

Bob took one of the early drafts on the road in 1983 as a booklet, getting labor, solidarity and church organizations to sign on to the docu-ment. Over 80 bishops agreed to support the Blueprint for Peace. Having served as a priest in Chicago in the 1970s before going to Nicaragua, he had befriended Jesse Jackson and worked with his community organiza-tion, PUSH. Using his ties to Jackson, Bob almost single-handedly got the Rainbow Coalition to use the Blueprint for Peace as part of its foreign policy plank in Jackson's campaign for the presidency in 1984.

I also became involved in another of Xabier's grandiose projects in 1983—rallying the research institutions and social democratic parties of Western Europe to support the Nicaraguan revolution. It is often forgotten that during the early Reagan years, many European governments strongly opposed US policy in Nicaragua and Central America, believing it was counterproductive and would only serve to radicalize the revolution and drive Nicaragua into the Soviet camp. French Socialist President Francois Mitterand even agreed to send military aid to the Sandinistas in 1982, to the chagrin of US Secretary of State Alexander Haig who expressed "strong disappointment."

With the support of Social Democratic foundations in Europe, Xabier organized a three-week seminar in The Hague, Netherlands, in June 1983. Bringing together investigators from Central America and the Caribbean, including Cuba, the seminar's main task was to draft economic position papers for presentation to the European governments to help secure more economic assistance for Nicaragua and other countries in the region.

As the representatives of alternative policy centers in North America, Tim Draimin and I were also asked to participate. Although we attended the working sessions and helped draft position papers, I must admit it was one time I felt I was on an international junket, often having dinners with conference participants in open-air restaurants on the Hague beach as the northern sun set at around 10 PM. On some evenings, I would catch the local train to Amsterdam to enjoy the city's night life at the cafes with a glass of wine and a toke of marijuana.

At the end of the conference I took a train to Paris to meet Vanessa (and her year-old son) who drove over from London. As Tim saw me off at the train station, he asked, "Roger, what is it that causes you to have such tumultuous amorous relations?" I had no answer for him. But on the train I ruminated about how my political passion and romantic life were inseparable. My fear of death and the void drove me to seek diversity and intensity in my work and relationships. If my mind or body stood still for a moment, I felt a chasm opening up.

I sensed that my tumultuous life would end in disaster, believing I might die in an airplane crash or be killed by a bullet or bomb in the field of conflict. I could not imagine, and did not want to find out what old age would be like. Being 60 seemed inconceivable to me. I wanted to go up in flames before then, like Icarus of Greek mythology who flew too close to the sun and perished.

In Paris, Vanessa and I spent a day or so visiting the Louvre and other sites and then drove off to northern France visiting old ruins, monasteries and the city of Rouen. I think her son disapproved of the trip as he never seemed very happy. In hindsight, the trip turned out to be the swan song for Vanessa and me.

33. Soviet MiGs and Nicaraguan Democracy

"There is scarcely any passion without struggle."
–Albert Camus, The Myth of Sisyphus and Other Essays

It was a rainy tropical day in Managua, May 1984 when I got a call from Orlando Nunez at the office: "Roger, the US ambassador Tony Quainton has requested your presence at a reception later this afternoon." Startled, I had no idea why I was invited, as I had never attended a social or political function at the embassy. It was widely known that Quainton was being relieved of his post. Seven months before Henry Kissinger on a whirlwind visit to Nicaragua as head of a commission on Central American policy had found Quainton insufficiently "anti-Sandinista" and told Reagan to fire him. An exchange of cables released years later with the US ambassador to Honduras, John Negroponte, revealed Quainton's antipathy towards the Contra war. When the Honduran embassy sent out a message saying that Negroponte was dining with Adolfo Calero, the head of the Contras, Quainton fired back sarcastically, "Your hospitality is legendary and Calero's charm is irresistible, but I have my doubts about a dinner at the residence for a man who is in the business of overthrowing a neighboring government."

I arrived at the reception and mingled with a gathering comprised of embassy staff, foreign journalists, American residents in Managua and Nicaraguans, mainly from the opposition, about 35 people in all. We circled around and chatted as Quainton, making his rounds, finally got to me. After exchanging pleasantries, he said: "Can you stay for a few minutes when the others depart? I'd like to talk to you because I know you have the ear of the Sandinistas." About another hour later, as the rays of the setting sun broke through the rain clouds, I met Quainton on the terrace. He began, "As you know, it has been reported that Nicaragua is about to get MiG-21s from the Soviet Union. This would be intolerable for the United States and would lead to direct action by Reagan to stop their deployment." I was, of course, aware of the MiGs. In 1981, the Sandinista government had signed a secret accord with the Soviets for the delivery of a squadron of them. Seventy Nicaraguans had gone to the Soviet Union for pilot and technical training, while construction began immediately on an enormous runway and attending complex of buildings by Punta Huete on the shores of Lake Managua.

Nicaragua at that point had no air force of significance and the MiGs were viewed by the Sandinistas as a way to secure the country's defenses against any US-backed threats from other Central American countries, particularly Honduras, which had a fleet of advanced US fighter jets. With the Contra war, the MiGs would also give the Sandinistas an ability to knock down US supply planes for the Contras that were being flown from air bases in Honduras and Costa Rica. I told Quainton of this rationale for the MiGs, and he responded, "This is why the Reagan administration will not tolerate the MiGs. They are seen as tilting the balance of military power towards the Sandinistas. Make no mistake, there will be a US military intervention if the MiGs arrive." Quainton had undoubtedly told the Sandinistas this via more direct and formal exchanges. With me he was simply hoping to find yet another channel to stave off what he saw as a clash over the MiGs that would mean only more destruction and death for the Nicaraguans.

I told Quainton I would relay his words and said what seemed to me to be more important at the moment were the Nicaraguan elections scheduled for November 4, 1984, two days before Reagan stood for re-election in the United States. Quainton appeared to wince when I mentioned that the Kissinger Report released in early January had already expressed a "lack of confidence" in the Nicaraguan elections, even though preparations had hardly begun.

As the elections unfolded, Orlando and I began drafting a manuscript on the role of democracy in the revolution. Nicaragua's turn to the ballot box represented a break in third world revolutionary politics, particularly the trajectory of the post World War II national liberation movements ranging from Vietnam and Cuba to Mozambique. Nicaragua's was not a revolution led by a dictatorship of the proletariat, nor was it formally socialist. It was officially designated "a popular, democratic and anti-imperialist revolution." Radicalized social democrats, priests and political independents, as well as Marxists and Marxist-Leninists served as cabinet ministers of the Sandinista government. Images of Augusto Sandino, Karl Marx, Che Guevara, Christ, Lenin, Simon Bolivar and Carlos Fonseca, the martyred founder of the Sandinista movement, often hung side-by-side in the cities and towns of Nicaragua.

While the National Directorate of the Sandinista National Liberation Front exerted leadership over the revolutionary process, it was not headed by a single strongman but by nine individuals who reached consensual decisions with input from popular organizations and leading participants in the government and the revolutionary process. The Nicaraguan revolution responded to internal and external challenges not by declaring a dictatorship as other revolutions had done, but by deepening its democratic and participatory content.

In 1980, the year after the revolutionary victory, the Sandinistas announced that elections would be held in five years. But they were advanced a year to 1984 in order to undermine the Contras and to demonstrate to the international community, particularly the countries of Western Europe, that Nicaragua was committed to a pluralistic democracy. The hard core right-wing parties that were sympathetic to the Contras formed the Coordinadora, an umbrella political organization for the elections. Arturo Cruz, who had earlier been a member of the Sandinista governing junta, left his post in the Inter-American Development Bank in mid-1984 to run as a presidential candidate of the Coordinadora.

Widely viewed as the Reagan administration's contender, Cruz was poorly received when he returned to Managua. Trying to tap into the shortages and the economic problems of the country, one of the slogans heard at his campaign rallies was: "With Arturo as president, we'll have toothpaste again." His campaign went nowhere with polls indicating he would lose decisively to Daniel Ortega. At Washington's urging, he withdrew. Several months later, US officials told The New York Times that the White House "never contemplated letting Cruz stay in the race" because a "legitimate" election would have undermined the Contra war.

As the campaign formally began with the participation of six other political parties, the United States stepped up its military aggression, hoping to disrupt the elections. On August 8 the battleship USS Iowa dropped anchor off the Pacific Coast of Central America with 1,200 Marines on board. The captain of the ship proclaimed, "If my country orders me to intervene in any Central American country, I have the capacity to do it." About 9,000 Contras began to regroup and mass on the Honduran border. The Reagan administration started circulating reports that the MiGs were about to arrive in Nicaragua and that they had to be stopped. In October, Daniel Ortega at the United Nations raised the specter of a US "landing and direct incursion of Nicaragua," like that of Grenada the year before.

Contra actions intensified in the immediate days leading up to the elections with scores of Nicaraguans dying, including nine electoral workers. On October 31 terrifying explosions erupted in the sky caused by the over-flight of the sophisticated black SR-71 spy plane, dubbed the "pajaro negro," or the black bird. For the next week-and-a-half it would cross the country from the Atlantic Coast to the Pacific Ocean, intentionally producing window-rattling sonic booms as it flew over Managua.

With the threat of all-out war looming, about three quarters of Nicaragua's registered voters trooped to the polls on Sunday, November 4 to elect Daniel Ortega president with 63 percent of the vote. Reagan, re-elected two days later, denounced the Nicaraguan elections as a sham, insisting that Nicaragua was run by a "totalitarian Marxist-Leninist" regime. The United States announced that it would take "all necessary measures" to stop the off-loading of MiGs from a Soviet ship headed for Puerto Corinto. Several US divisions were mobilized, including the 82nd airborne, which had invaded Grenada. Ortega declared a state of emergency, placing the armed forces and the civil defense units on full alert. Twenty thousand student volunteers who were about to leave to pick coffee in the mountains were told to stay in Managua to defend the capital with arms they were given.

The MiGs never did arrive. In fact, the hoopla over the MiGs served to obscure the arrival of the Mi-25 helicopter used by the Soviets in Afghanistan that proved invaluable to the Sandinistas in the war against the Contras. Nicaragua and the Soviet Union, under the astute and determined advice of Fidel Castro, had decided to replace the MiGs with the helicopters. Perhaps US ambassador Quainton's constant cajoling about the MiGs in Managua also played a role. In any case, the events of 1984 marked the closest that Nicaragua and the US came to a direct invasion during the Sandinista years.

I headed for El Salvador shortly after the elections, on my way back to California. There I found official US circles optimistic that the Salvadoran military had seized the initiative in the five-year-old war against the guerrillas. As Col. James Steele, the head of the US military group in San Salvador, told me in an interview: "We are on the brink of turning the corner in this war, and the trend line is definitely upward." With $10 million in US approved funding, El Salvador had held its presidential elections in May in which US-backed Christian Democrat Jose Napoleon Duarte succeeded in defeating Roberto D'Aubuisson, who was linked to the death squads. Now the US had a cleaner image to pursue the war, even though Duarte was largely a figurehead with the Salvadoran military and the death squads doing pretty much as they wanted to. The army launched repeated offensives into the heart of insurgent territory even though the FMLN had not mounted a major attack in almost half a year.

My conversations with guerrilla representatives indicated that it was overly optimistic: The FMLN had not suffered a single major military defeat over the past year, and it continued to field and supply a revolutionary army of 12,000, the largest and best armed insurgency force that had ever been assembled in modern Latin American history, with the possible exception of the FARC, Colombia's guerrilla movement. It had by no means lost the ability to undertake new initiatives on the military battlefield or the political front as the coming years would reveal.

The key to ending the wars in El Salvador and Nicaragua lay in stopping US aggression. However, I found the political situation to be particularly bleak when I arrived back in the United States. PACCA had failed in its mission of trying to galvanize public opinion sufficiently to influence the course of the US elections. In a new publication CENSA had just launched, *The Strategic Report*, I wrote an editorial titled "The Winter of our Discontent," in which I said: "The defeat of the Mondale-Ferraro ticket compels us to critically assess the anti-intervention movement. The fact that Ronald Reagan was able to win overwhelmingly on a right-wing platform means that the task of those opposed to intervention in Central America is increasingly difficult."

"What is to be done?" I asked. "First of all, we must remind ourselves that the emergence of the movements against nuclear arms and against intervention in Central America represent real alternatives for progressive forces. It is especially significant that both movements challenge fundamental assumptions that have dominated US policy for years, and that they have burgeoned in the last four years, at the very time the right-wing was solidifying its control of the US government."

The solidarity movement and the revolutionary forces did affect the course of history, even though we were not able to turn Central America into a permanent beacon of revolutionary transformation.

My relations with Pat deteriorated during these somber times. Neither of us was happy and we argued incessantly. We had several sessions with a marriage therapist but to no avail, and in early 1985 we agreed to separate. I moved out and found a place in a housing collective nearby so I could help take Matt back and forth to day care and pre-school. In the spring, I began to make plans to go to Nicaragua to work for several months with Orlando's research center. I purchased a new Yamaha motor cycle, planning to take it with me on a returning banana boat from Los Angeles to Puerto Corinto. I went on a test drive and as I was taking a sharp left turn onto the street that ran by the Berkeley downtown post office, I lost control, jumped the curb, and crashed the bike on my right knee. It was badly fractured and I needed surgery to pin it together. I spent a week in the hospital, followed by a couple of months of convalescence.

Pat graciously agreed to let me stay with her during my recovery. It was good for Matt, since we could spend a lot of time together. Then on a sunny May 1st, while I was lying in bed, President Reagan appeared on the television to announce, "The policies and actions of the Government of Nicaragua constitute an unusual and extraordinary threat to the national security and foreign policy of the United States and I declare a national emergency to deal with that threat."

To this day it bewilders me as to how the threat of a small impoverished country of less than 3 million people constituted a "national emergency." Existent trade, including Nicaragua's principal export to the United States, bananas, was severed and no ships from Nicaragua could dock in US ports. I would not be taking a trip on a banana boat to Puerto Corinto but I did go to Nicaragua several times over the next year, flying on US airlines, mainly to work with Orlando on our book on the Nicaraguan revolution and its significance for the Americas.

34. Chile, the Dream

In mid-June 1986 I looked out my airplane window as I flew southward towards Chile, down the long chain of majestic snow-capped Andean mountains. It had been almost 13 years since I left Chile the month after the military coup against Salvador Allende. Although I was intensely involved with the Nicaraguan revolution, I had always been preoccupied with Chile, following closely the news and reports on the repression and opposition to the Pinochet dictatorship.

Before I left the Bay Area I went to the La Pena Cultural Center in Berkeley, founded in 1975 by Americans and exiled Chileans, mainly from the Left Revolutionary Movement (MIR). I asked for contacts in Chile and offered to serve as a courier for any messages. The people I had befriended in Chile from 1971 to 1973 had left the country, died in the resistance or had moved to new residences that I had no phone numbers or addresses for. Paul Chin, the executive director of La Pena, said he would check with the Chileans and get back to me. A few days later he called, asking me if I could come to La Pena. When I got there he showed me an impressive looking cassette/CD boom box, bigger than anything I had had ever owned. Inside of it was a small state-of-the-art electronic device that could be used to pick up nearby conversations, including those of the police or military. Paul asked me if I could take it to Santiago to a designated house. I, of course, responded affirmatively.

Santiago's international airport seemed ominous as I arrived at about noon. Customs police and soldiers were everywhere. First, I had to pass through the visa line with my brand new passport. I had "lost" my previous one because of the innumerable stamps that I had from visiting Nicaragua. The visa official who squinted at me through the glass win-

232

dow between us asked if I had ever been in Chile before. I said no, correctly calculating that he would not have access to files or records of my flights in and out of Chile in the early 1970s.

He stamped my passport and passed me on to customs with my luggage. A stern-looking customs official asked me to open my suitcases and poked around in them for a minute or so, even opening my medicine bag. Then he asked to see the boom box that I was carrying in my hand. He took it and pushed the start button. He queried, "How come it doesn't work?" I responded, "As you can see in the battery slot, it has no batteries and I dropped it as I got off the plane, so it might be damaged." He glared at me suspiciously for a few seconds as my heart raced and then waved me on to the exit door.

Santiago looked gray and grim as I took a taxi from the airport on a cold wintry day. The address I had for delivering the radio was in a middle-class barrio on the other side from the airport. I knocked tepidly on the door and asked for Sergio, the name that had been given to me. A slight man in glasses, who appeared to be in his mid-30s, greeted me and asked me to come in. I quickly handed him the radio, he said thanks, and deposited it in the back room. His companion Mirian came into the living room and we sat down and had coffee together. Almost immediately he told me his real name, Fernando Zegers, and said he worked as a lawyer for CODEPU, the Corporation for the Promotion and Defense of the Peoples Rights, a nonprofit organization founded in 1980 that fought legal battles on behalf of people who were imprisoned, tortured or detained by the government. As I subsequently found out, most of the people who worked for CODEPU were from the MIR or the Communist party, Fernando being from the former. Given Fernando's last name, I thought he might be of recent European origin, but he explained that he came from an old Chilean family of Dutch descent via France and Spain. One of his ancestors, Juan Francisco Zegers, had migrated to Chile at the beginning of the 19th century and served as foreign minister in the government of the Chilean liberator Bernando O'Higgins. Of a quiet, reflective temperament, Fernando and I would become fast friends in the coming years as we both worked in different ways to help bring down the Pinochet regime and to push for transformations in the subsequent governments.

After departing from Fernando's at about four in the afternoon, I headed out to see Tonio Kadima, a Chilean whose address was also given to me at La Pena. He lived on the street Arturo Pratts, just south of the center of the city, in an old apartment house. He greeted me warmly as I introduced myself, throwing his arms around me in a big hug. About the same stature and age as me, he had a strong, assertive personality and a bohemian style of life as I would soon discover. An artist of many forms—painter, poet, actor and graffiti artist—he was deeply involved in cultural resistance to the regime and ran an organization called Taller Sol, the Sun Workshop. As he told me, "I and my companeros wage guerrilla cultural war through Taller Sol to inspire people to get involved and break from the oppression. It is as important as armed struggle." A dynamo of energy and constantly on the move, I don't know if I ever saw him sleep. He was apprehended five times during the 17 years of the dictatorship.

I spent several days at Tonio's place, crashing on a mattress on the floor. The first Sunday I was there I accompanied him to a plaza in the barrio Bandera, one of the poorer neighborhoods, or *"poblaciones"* of Santiago. There an amateur troop of actors assembled and began to put on a play that made fun of Pinochet, his wife and his government ministers. Lookouts were posted on the streets leading into the plaza, and at the first sign of approaching police or military, which occurred about mid-way through the play, the actors and the audience scattered.

On another day, Tonio and I boarded a bus, then at the next stop another person got on and they began to put on an anti-Pinochet skit that was joined by a third person at the next stop. The people riding on the bus began to laugh and converse among themselves about the skit. After about 10 minutes, all four of us hopped off the bus before any police or soldiers had a chance to intervene.

1986 was proclaimed *"el ano decisivo,"* the decisive year in the struggle to topple Pinochet. Opposition to the dictatorship had been building since 1983 when the first major demonstrations erupted as the country slipped into an economic crisis. By the time I arrived in June 1986 opposition in the *poblaciones* had reached a boiling point with spontaneous demonstrations occurring that brought in the military and armored vehicles, often leading to pitched battles and mass arrests.

Indeed, the entire country was in upheaval. In April the moderate political forces that were grouped together in the Democratic Alliance joined with the leftist organizations in the Popular Democratic Movement to form the Civic Assembly. Guerrilla actions in the countryside and the cities grew increasingly frequent, led by the MIR and particularly, by the recently formed Manuel Rodriquez Patriotic Front, affiliated with the Communist Party. The Civic Assembly drafted a platform calling for Pinochet's resignation and free and fair elections. The regime was given 30 days to respond to its demands, with a national shut down called for on July 2 and 3 if there was no favorable response.

Preparations for the shutdown were already well advanced when I arrived in mid-June. Pamphlets were passed out in the streets, public gatherings discussed the impending shutdown and even radio commentators talked about what might happen on July 2 and 3. On the morning of the second, demonstrations started out early and I went out to participate with Zegers and other recent acquaintances. Angry chants of all kinds had one common demand—the departure of Pinochet. My contingent was hit by tear gas and then the dreaded *huanacos* (mobile water cannons) arrived to knock us down with their powerful jets of water. The repression was brutal as the police and the military moved through the streets, beating and arresting people. I managed to escape up a side street, but seven people were killed during the two-day shutdown, including the photographer Rodrigo Rojas who was doused with gas and set on fire just blocks from where I had been demonstrating earlier in the day.

The shut-down in Santiago was complete and the opposition viewed the national mobilization as successful. Sectors of the military were even rumored to be talking with the opposition. Zegers explained to me that "the strategy of the militant left ever since the ignition of the first large-scale demonstrations of 1983 has been to build a broad coalition that would mobilize in the cities to increasingly isolate the dictatorship."

"Simultaneously," he said, "we will carry out armed actions that will augment in frequency and scale. Eventually, a massive popular insurrection will break the regime and the road will be open to establish a coalition government that will then conduct free and open elections in which the Left will be triumphant because it has served as the main force that toppled the regime." July marked a high point in the unfolding of this strategy. I left Chile a few days after the general mobilization, firmly believing that Pinochet's days were numbered and that the revolutionary forces would sweep away the regime, restoring President Allende's dream of a socialist democracy.

About two months later, when I was back in my office in Berkeley, I heard on the KPFA-FM evening news that the Manuel Rodriquez Patriotic Front (FPMR), an armed organization that had links to the Chilean Communist Party, had tried to assassinate Pinochet. As he was returning from his country estate south of Santiago on the afternoon of Sunday, September 7, with his armed caravan of five vehicles, the road was cut off in front and behind him. Some 20 FPMR operatives carried out the ambush, firing heavy machine guns and lobbing grenades at the caravan. With rocket launchers they fired at the heavily-plated Mercedes Benz that Pinochet rode in. One rocket struck the vehicle but failed to explode. After about five minutes of fighting, the guerrillas retreated. Five guards died, while Pinochet escaped with minor lesions on one of his hands.

The country was shocked by the assassination attempt and the discovery, a month before, of a huge armaments cache in northern Chile. The FPMR had hoped that a successful strike at Pinochet would set off a national insurrection. Instead, a state of siege was declared and another round of bloody repression was unleashed. Ricardo Lagos, who would one day become president, was arrested along with 43 others, none of whom were involved in the ambush. The day after the assassination attempt four prominent leftist professionals were taken from their homes by the security forces and brutally murdered, including Jose Carrasco, the international editor of the magazine *Analisis*, who I had met just two months before on my visit to Chile.

I had also talked to Juan Pablo Cardenas, the general editor and driving force behind *Analisis*. Cardenas is the most committed and principled journalist I have ever known. A very affable man with a wry smile and a gentle sense of humor, his mellow persona belied the iron will with which he faced the harassment and threats of the Pinochet regime. Founded in 1977, *Analisis* had been shut down a number of times, only to come back as an ever more powerful voice opposing Pinochet. Cardenas had already been imprisoned three times when I met him in July 1986.

After the attempted assassination of Pinochet in September, Cardenas might have suffered the same fate as Carrasco if he had not fled his home and gone to a safe house. Analisis was, of course, shut down and as Juan Pablo later told me, he faced one of his "darkest moments," especially with the death of his close colleague. But his tenacity and creativity came to the fore as he collaborated with West German solidarity organizations and trade unions to come out with the *Analisis* International edition. Written by Chileans who were temporarily accredited as "German journalists," *Analisis International* rolled off the German presses and was sent to Chile for distribution. As Juan Pablo said: "You can imagine the surprise of our subscribers when just several weeks after the regime had shut us down, they received a magazine printed on better quality paper with a more refined and attractive cover page." After five editions of the magazine and growing public ridicule, the Chilean military censors decided to allow *Analisis* to be published again in Chile.

The dramatic assassination attempt against Pinochet shook up the centrist political forces, including the Christian Democrats. They believed that continued confrontation with the regime would only radicalize the country further and undermine their political position. The

Reagan administration agreed, and fearing another Cuba or another Nicaragua, abruptly changed its position from one of total support for the Pinochet regime to one of pushing it to talk with the moderates in order to carry out a controlled transition.

THE GLOBAL UNRAVELING OF UTOPIA

35. The Pact with a Dictator

I did not return to Chile for a year-and-a-half, until January 1988. This time I almost wound up in Pinochet's prisons for all the wrong reasons.

As usual on my international flights I spent the day before in a mad rush packing my bags and getting my office and paperwork done. On this flight I was running very late in wrapping up the details in the office. My plane was due to depart at about 7 AM and at 5 AM I realized I would have no time to go home to fetch my bags. So I asked a friend to bring them into the office and we drove off to San Francisco airport. The gate was about to close as I reached the agent at the ticket counter. I hurriedly gave her my two suitcases without ever opening them, and dashed off to catch my flight on Continental Airlines, headed for a stopover in Miami.

I arrived at the Santiago airport early the next morning and picked up my bags as they came out on the conveyor belt. As on the prior trip I went first to get my passport stamped and then headed for customs. I then noticed that the reddish brown leather suitcase I had bought in Colombia years ago had a big gash in it, almost as if someone had slashed it with a knife. Instead of going to the regular customs check-out I went to the missing luggage claim office where I thought I might be able to file a claim for my damaged suitcase. While waiting in line I opened it up and to my utter shock I found myself looking at a black garbage bag with about a pound of untrimmed marijuana stems. I knew immediately that the bag had come from my place in the countryside where I grew marijuana with my father. Somehow, in my trips back and forth between my country home and the city, the marijuana had wound up in my suitcase. I was dumbfounded, but managed somehow to keep my composure. I quickly noticed that there was also an exit past the luggage office. So I waited for a moment until an irate customer with a lost suitcase had so upset the airline agent that she did not notice me as I nonchalantly sauntered out the exit door.

I cannot describe my mood as I walked out of the airport to catch a taxi. It had all happened so quickly. What puzzles me to this day is why did someone slash my suitcase? I can't believe it was accidental. Did a baggage or customs officer in San Francisco or at my transfer in Miami slash the bag in order to draw attention to it? But why wouldn't they just impound the bag and track down the owner, perhaps even before I left Miami?

In any case, there were a lot of happy people in Chile as a result of my carelessness and neglect. As it happened, I stayed this time in an apartment building with a young couple just out of college from the United States who were continuing their studies in Chile. They were delighted to get some of my sinsemilla herb, especially since the Chilean blend was terrible. Many Chileans, even during the Pinochet years, smoked the herb, but to this day they have not figured out how to grow quality marijuana.

Of course, the last thing the Chilean resistance was interested in was producing marijuana. The political situation in the country had changed dramatically since the year before. The reformist and centrist opposition had rejected the insurrectionary and mass mobilization strategy and instead opted to negotiate an accord with the military regime for a plebiscite on whether or not Pinochet would remain in office until 1997.

It was a weak challenge to the dictatorship. A "yes" vote would have enshrined Pinochet in power and even worse, implicit in the pact was an acceptance of the 1980 constitution and the political structures imposed on the country, as well as the neoliberal free-market economic system. A "no" vote didn't imply a return to a true democracy, much less a socialist one.

Organizations on the left rejected this approach. Seven political formations, including the MIR and the Communist party, joined together in mid-1987 to form the *Izquierda Unida,* the United Left. They denounced "the grotesque farce called the plebiscite" and endorsed a "nationalistic and popular" platform committed to "anti-imperialism, anti-monopolism" and the "construction of socialism in our country." The *poblaciones* continued to be a radical force, coming together in the *Comando Unitario de Pobladores,* the United Command of the *Pobladores.*

Its representative denounced the "illness of plebiscite."

Even the US ambassador to Chile, Harry Barnes, recognized the strength of the militant left. After visiting the *poblaciones* he proclaimed: "The country is in an insurrectional state."

Pinochet was not a popular figure and as a result, most of the centrist forces and even right of center organizations came together in the *Comando de No* to orchestrate a no vote against Pinochet. The plebiscite scheduled for October 5, 1988.

In January when I arrived it was already strikingly apparent that the United States under the direction of Ambassador Barnes was throwing its weight behind this political coalition with the intention of isolating the left, particularly the Communist party and the MIR. The National Endowment for Democracy, a US Congressional-funded foundation, provided extensive financing to an array of organizations, including political parties, trade unions and the media. New front organizations were set up specifically to work in the *poblaciones* to back the no campaign and marginalize the left.

When I met again on this trip with Juan Pablo Cardenas of *Analisis*, he told me of his personal experience with the manipulative efforts of Ambassador Barnes. The ambassador invited him and one of *Analisis* most prominent writers, Monica Gonzalez, to have breakfast with him. Barnes quickly came to the point of the meeting, to offer $1 million dollars, to *Analisis*. "This sum" said Cardenas, "would have enabled us to consolidate *Analisis* as a publication for years to come." But the offer of course came with strings attached: "The ambassador made it clear that we would have to exclude the Communist party and any radical columnists or writers who espoused the position of the Democratic Popular Movement. Cardenas, of course, rejected the offer but noted that many other publications and media organizations had succumbed to US offers, thereby undermining those who would not accept Barnes' agenda of "Pinchetismo without Pinochet".

When I met Cardenas he was serving a sentence of 541 nights in prison. A bizarre sentence, he was free to go about his work during the day at *Analisis*, but he had to return to prison at 10 PM every night and stay until 6 AM the following day. Fearful that he would be assassinated as he left or returned to prison, he was always accompanied by a detail of friends and supporters, including renowned international figures, such as Eduardo Galeano, Arthur Miller and Osvaldo Soriano. As Cardenas wrote years later, "An infinite number of politicians, writers, religious people and resistance fighters from the most diverse latitudes wrote about me... or appeared unannounced before my cell."

At the end of my trip I took a long night train from the Santiago Central Station to points southward. I had not visited the south of Chile for years, since 1972, when I rode my motorbike down the Pan American highway to Puerto Montt. I wanted to get out of Santiago to see and sense what people were up to in the provincial areas of Chile.

For the first hour or so I focused on looking out the window at the lingering sunset on a beautiful summer evening. Then as night set in I noticed an attractive woman sitting on the other side of the train aisle. We exchanged glances, I noticed that she had a tape player with head phones, and I asked her what she was listening to. "You can listen too if you want to move over," she said, beckoning to the empty seat next to her. She had an ensemble of New Age music and Bob Dylan. I was entranced by the New Age cut, which seemed to be of Greek origins, and then I caught a song of Dylan chanting, "Come in she said, I'll give you shelter from the storm."

For the rest of the night, until the summer dawn, we talked about our lives and politics with interludes dedicated to listening to music. It was sensational. We were enchanted with each other. Her name was Gabriela, a tall strikingly beautiful woman of 30 with bronze, Mediterranean-like skin. She was on her way to Temuco, where she was doing field work for her master's degree in anthropology on the Mapuche culture. She told me she was married to a Chilean of German ancestry who taught at the University of Chile in Santiago.

She got off the train at about eight in the morning, and I reluctantly continued on my way south to Puerto Varas, the final train stop. Before we parted ways, she gave me the address where she would be staying, about 5 km outside of Temuco, and we agreed I would stop by on my return trip in a few days.

In Puerto Varas, I caught a bus to Puerto Montt, 20 km away and spent a day in a rustic hotel next to the harbor. The array of sea food was exotic and delectable, particularly the *pico rojo*, a long seashell with an orangish-colored flesh that you pulled from the shell and ate raw with lemon juice. I then caught a two-hour ferry ride to Chilé a small, enchanting and mysterious island that is usually enshrouded in fog and has 16 churches made of native lumber that are World Heritage sights. In Santiago, I had gotten the names of a couple from the Socialist party but couldn't locate them at the address I was given. I then visited a couple of the historic churches but quickly found that boring, given my antipathy to religion, particularly Catholicism. I strolled on one of the beaches, picking up seashells and then, as the fog rolled in, I also found that boring. I admit I was obsessed with Gabriela.

After a day-and-a-half I headed back to Puerto Montt. This time I took a bus up to Temuco where I arrived at about midday. I caught a taxi out to Gabriela's address and knocked on the door of a quaint farm house with a large attached stable that was partially enclosed. Gabriela answered the door, we hugged and she introduced me to Mira, also a student who lived there for much of the year. After a quick lunch I headed out with Gabriela to meet some of the Mapuche she was working with. Her favorite friend Liclan was a shaman, an older woman steeped in the Mapuche spiritualism. We met at a small river and talked for several hours. Mapuche beliefs and even fortune-telling were part of our conversation, but politics also turned out to be an important theme, particularly the oppression experienced by the Mapuche under Pinochet. Not long after the coup in 1973 one of her uncles had been taken from his home by the army and "disappeared."

The Mapuche people are the largest ethnic group in Chile and constitute approximately 10 percent of the Chilean population. Half of them live in the south of Chile from the river Bío-Bío to the Chiloé Island. The other half is found in and around the capital, Santiago. Today, the situation of the Mapuche in Chile is still vulnerable. Chile is a strongly pronounced class society where the Mapuche belong to the lowest class. All through history, the State and the Church have carried on strategies to assimilate the Mapuche into Chilean society. During the Pinochet era, all Mapuche land was privatized and to a large extent, sold to wealthy landlords and foreigners. Pinochet also introduced new laws, which declared that there were "No indigenous people in Chile, only Chileans." The loss of a large quantity of their land resulted in migration to the big cities.

Conditions of the Mapuche have hardly improved under the subsequent Concertacion governments. Discrimination and migration continued as the huge Bio-Bio dam and electrification project in the south expelled thousands. However, the resistance and combativeness of the Mapuche has only intensified as they demonstrate in the cities and countryside and even carry out armed actions to defend their lands.

After conversing with Liclan, Gabriela and I picked up a few interesting pebbles from the river bed as mementos and then headed for her house at sunset. It had been a spectacular day. We briefly conversed with Mira, grabbed a hunk of cheese, bread and a bottle of wine and headed for the enclosed part of the stable. In a loft we talked, kissed, enjoyed our banquet, and gradually undressed. I am not sure as to what order it all happened. Finally, we lay down and began to make love. I asked her if we needed condoms and she said she was on the pill. Since neither of us was in the population cohorts linked to AIDS, I did not worry any more about birth control. We made the most exquisite love well into the night.

We woke up in the morning and once more made love before heading down to see Mira for breakfast. Mira almost immediately asked Gabriela how it went. "It all worked out well," she said. The response and tone of their voices made me feel as if there was some sort of a conspiracy between the two women.

We parted ways that afternoon. Gabriela had more fieldwork scheduled and would leave the next day, and I was intent on stopping in the Curicó region to see the new export production in grapes and fruit that had developed with the "free market" economy under Pinochet. This time I hitchhiked up the Pan American highway, once again with the idea of chatting with people. Rides were frequent and I made good time. I arrived in the small city of Curicó, took a hotel room and the next day made an appointment to visit one of the larger "*fundos*" (landed estates) where they were producing grapes for export to the United States.

The most striking aspect of the *fundo* was that its work force was virtually all women, in the fields as well as the processing sheds where they washed and packed the grapes. Moreover to avoid having to pay any benefits, the women were contracted from employment agencies. Wages were below the official minimum wage and two women I talked to complained about the long hours and miserable pay. They also said that some of the women suffered from the chemicals they were using in the fields and the sheds. The administrator, a man of course, who grudgingly agreed to talk to me, said: "This is the way things are, these women should be glad they have any job." Under Pinochet women were increasingly entering the workforce, but it was under the worst of conditions.

I left Curico the next day, this time catching the train to Santiago about 180 km away. When I arrived at the Central Station, I called Gabriela. She sounded distant, saying she was busy and didn't really have much time. I flew back to California two days later, perplexed about what had transpired between us.

36. Chile, Selling Out a Revolution

Early on the morning of October 6 I joined tens of thousands of demonstrators from all parts of Santiago who were marching towards the Casa de la Moneda, the presidential palace. The objective—to take the palace and throw out General Augusto Pinochet Ugarte who had usurped the presidency and the palace from Salvador Allende 15 years before. Just a few hours before, at 2 AM, a spokesman for the military regime had conceded that Pinochet had resoundingly lost the plebiscite to continue in office until 1997. He did not give up, however, without a last desperate maneuver. Earlier in the night he presented the other members of the military junta with a decree that the results of the plebiscite would be annulled and he would assume all powers. Lead by the head of the Air Force, General Fernando Matthei, the rest of the junta refused to accept the decree and the game was up for the dictator.

I had returned to Chile two weeks before the plebiscite. This time there were no difficulties at the airport. I did notice more bustle and a lot of well-dressed Americans and other foreigners coming into the country. Indeed Chile was being inundated by international election observers, reporters from around the world, political consultants and operatives, many of them from the National Democratic Institute and the National Republican Institute of the National Endowment for Democracy—US government funded organizations.

The entire country was in a state of ferment as the opposition and Pinochet's allies campaigned relentlessly on the air waves as well as the neighborhoods. The opposition was comprised of two tendencies. The grouping of parties in the Commando de No backed by the US wanted no confrontations with the regime or militant mobilizations, while the Communist Party along with the MIR and the leaders of the popular movement rejected this approach, encouraging mass mobilizations to stimulate participation in the plebiscite. As my friend Fernando Zegers, a member of the MIR and Codepu (Corporation for the Promotion and Defense of the Peoples Rights) told me: "Earlier this year the grassroots organizations, including the *poblaciones* came together forming ACUSO, the Accord of Social Organizations for a No Vote. It called the first mass rally of the plebiscite campaign on September 4 despite the reservations of the political parties in the Commando." It was a huge success with more than 300,000 people showing up. As ACUSO President Hector Moya noted, "The demonstration showed that we were many, that we weren't isolated. People lost their fear and began to believe they could rid the country of Pinochet."

The Commando de No on the other hand focused on ads in the media (usually prepared with international consultants) and ran a campaign under the slogan, *"Ya viene la alegria,"* meaning "happiness will arrive" if the no vote wins. At the end of September when I was there the Commando de No finally threw its weight behind a massive 10-day march of peoples from Arica in the north to Puerto Montt in the south. They converged on the capital in support of a No vote and in a nod to the Commando, it was called the "March of Happiness."

Before the plebiscite I met with Juan Pablo Cardenas who was still serving his sentence of 541 nights in jail. I was delighted to see that the Simon Bolivar press, a subsidiary of *Analisis*, had come out with a Chilean edition of *Democracia y Revolucion en las Americas,* which I had written with Orlando Nunez of Nicaragua. We had a festive party one evening to celebrate the book's release as well as the impending defeat of Pinochet. Juan Pablo, Fernando Zegers and I each brought a 5-liter carafe of wine that got just about everyone at the party well inebriated. I am not sure how Juan Pablo made it back to his jail cell that night. I know I didn't take him.

I also looked up Gabriela. I called her and she agreed to meet me at a cafe in the Plaza Nunoa around sunset. I was shocked when she arrived. She was very pregnant, looking as if she could give birth any day. She proclaimed, "Don't worry, it's not yours." We proceeded to make small talk while I haltingly tried to do the math in my head. Finally I concluded that it was possible that the child was mine, depending, of course, on exactly when the child was due. She didn't volunteer any dates, and I was too unnerved to query her on the issue. I did ask her about the letters I had sent her from California and why she only responded once.

She didn't directly answer my question, instead saying: "I have the letters safely hidden in a small box with a lock, along with the pebbles we picked up by the river in Temuco."

We soon parted ways. She said she was happy with her husband and made it clear that she did not intend to see me again. To this day, I am not sure what to think. It has crossed my mind that she may have had trouble getting pregnant, and when she spotted another man on the train of German ancestry like her husband, she may have decided to roll the reproductive dice with me. Also, it doesn't seem likely that she was using birth control pills as she told me. Even if she had stopped taking the pill immediately after she left me it is unlikely that she would have gotten pregnant so quickly with her husband. This is one of the mysteries of my life that I will never resolve. Perhaps even Gabriela is unsure of the paternity of her progeny.

On this trip I was commissioned by the Pacific News Service and the World Policy Journal to write on the plebiscite and the transition. Thus, the evening of the plebiscite found me hanging out with the press corps at a hotel next to the presidential palace in an enormous press room replete with phones, faxes and new computer word processors. I found the experience irksome; the press didn't know anything more than the official statements of opposition figures and the regime's declarations.

It was with relief that I left the press center in the early morning to join the thousands of Chileans who were massing in the streets celebrating Pinochet's defeat, many of them marching down the Alameda, the main avenue that leads to the presidential palace. The dictator appeared on television in full military regalia in an effort to assert his authority while the demonstrators called for his immediate ouster. The leaders of the leftist parties joined the spontaneous demonstrations, but the Christian Democrats and other parties in the Commando de No sought to contain the masses. I stood in front of Sergio Bitar, one of the moderate socialist leaders of the Commando, as he got up on a box and called on the demonstrators to "Go home, we have the situation under control." He was jeered at by the people around me who called him a *"cobarde"* (coward) and a *"vendepatria,"* (sellout). Bitar went on to become a major player in the Concertacion governments, serving as Senator in the Parliament, Minister of Education in the government of President Ricardo Lagos, and Minister of Public Works under President Michelle Bachelet.

While the more militant demonstrators tried to break through the military corridor around the presidential palace, it was business as usual for the regime. Four people were killed and scores wounded by the security forces in the post-plebiscite demonstrations. The decision of most of the political parties not to confront the regime or press for the immediate ouster of Pinochet established the framework for the transition period. There would be no revolution, the political and social institutions of the dictatorship would not be swept away. Disillusionment set in, especially among the popular organizations. A common expression was *"ya han vuelto las viejas caras,"* the old political faces have returned.

Over the next few days I began work on the article for the World Policy Journal, but didn't get very far. When I got back to the US I had writer's block, I couldn't finish the article. I had returned to Chile in 1986 believing that the left and the revolutionary forces would reclaim the democratic socialist legacy of Salvador Allende. Instead the centrist and conservative forces backed by the United States had formed a pact with the dictatorship to run the country. Pinochet would remain as head of the armed forces until 1998 and then he would become a Senator for Life. I simply couldn't write this up, I couldn't admit that the path to utopia had once again been obliterated in Chile.

The editor of the World Policy Journal, Sherle Schwenninger, indulged my mental anguish and inability to write. He paid my expenses to go back to Chile in early December to interview representatives of the two different positions on the transition. I selected Sergio Bitar and Juan Pablo Cardenas. I had actually talked to Bitar several days before the plebiscite, but he did not remember my participation in the unruly crowd that taunted him.

The basic difference between the two was their respective views of the transition and the new state that should be formed. Bitar called for a *"concertacion,"* basically a corporatist state that involved "a process of negotiating accords among workers, the state, and private entrepreneurs...." He also envisioned a special role for the military, saying "We cannot isolate the armed forces again ... we have to find ways of involving the military in development issues, and so forth."

Cardenas cut right to the core of the calamitous decisions made during the transitional period: "Chileans voted 'no' thinking that Pinochet's defeat would put an end to the military regime. In the days following the plebiscite, people took to the streets and demanded the immediate resignation of Pinochet. A tense period ensued in which the government forces were clearly thrown off balance. But the political leaders of the opposition parties were not willing to exert the pressure necessary to drive Pinochet from office. On the contrary, they were ready to continue working within the institutional framework set by Pinochet."

On a Sunday, the day before I left Chile in mid-December to return to California, I headed out on a bus to Vina del Mar on the coast and from there took another bus south to Isla Negra, the old residence of the Nobel Prize-winning poet, Pablo Neruda. A Communist and a supporter of Salvador Allende and the Popular Unity government, he died just days after the military coup in 1973. With my hopes dashed for a new Chile, I hoped to find solace in his legacy and the house that had been converted into a museum. Built like a ship with low hanging ceilings and numerous seafaring artifacts, it opens up to vistas of the sea with dramatic waves crashing down on the rocky shore. I found a bench outside and just sat for a long time, mesmerized as I took in the warm sun and the spectacular view.

All too soon I had to head out to catch my flight from Santiago. I hitchhiked back to Vina del Mar and made it to the main plaza several blocks from the terminal for the buses to Santiago. As I sprinted across the plaza I was accosted by a young gypsy woman. Chile has a Roma colony of about 15,000 to 20,000, many of whom ply the coastal cities, particularly Vina del Mar and Puerto Montt. Like many of her kin this woman was selling jewelry, scarfs and assorted trinkets. She also wanted to tell my fortune, grabbing my hand and pulling it close to her chest while looking at me intensely with her fiery brown eyes. For a moment I felt like Ulysses on his way home in the Odyssey as he tried to avoid being shipwrecked on the island where the Sirens were calling. I resisted her entreaties, saying, "I will be back another time, I have to catch the bus." She responded with the familiar Gypsy admonition that she was placing a curse on me: "Something terrible will happen to you soon. You can only lift this curse if you return here." I am not superstitious. But I did not go back and less than four months later I almost died in the same Pacific Ocean thousands of miles north of Vina del Mar.

37. A Christian Woman, Marijuana Bust and War

"Row, row, row your boat,
Quickly up the stream,
Merrily, merrily, merrily, merrily,
Life has many dreams."

I, by no means, abandoned my work in Nicaragua and Central America during the two years that I became involved with the Chilean resistance. During that time dramatic events shook the isthmus and echoed in the corridors of power in Washington. On October 5, 1986, a CIA contracted cargo plane loaded with arms and munitions for the Contras was shot down over southern Nicaragua. Two Americans and one Nicaraguan died in the plane crash but Eugene Hasenfus, a marine in the Vietnam war, managed to parachute out before it crashed and was captured a day later eating a wild squash while sitting in a hammock fashioned out of his parachute. A photo published in newspapers around the world taken shortly after his capture personified the war in Nicarauga: Hasenfus, an archetypal gringo, slightly corpulent, tall and blond, was led by a rope tied around his hands by 19-year-old Jose Fernandez Canales, bronze-skinned, slender, of obvious indigenous origins, wearing an olive green Sandinista army uniform with a cross hanging from a rosary draped around his neck.

I went to a brief press conference in Managua a day later, attended by a large number of international and Nicaraguan journalists. He simply declared: "My name is Eugene Hasenfus. I come from Marinette,

Wisconsin. I was captured yesterday in southern Nicaragua." I was surprised. Marinette is just 160 miles from Watertown, Wisconsin where I grew up. Three years older than me, he was part of the pool of Vietnam veterans who never turned against the war and became pawns in the ongoing anti-communist crusade waged by the Reagan administration in the Third World.

Five days later, Mike Wallace host of the CBS show "Sixty Minutes" conducted an interview with Hasenfus:

Wallace: Nicaragua's Foreign Minister, Miguel D'Escoto, who was in New York last week, told me that one of the first things you said when you were captured was, 'Hell, this isn't my war.'

Hasenfus: Yes, that's what I said.

Wallace: What did that mean?

Hasenfus: I was contracted.... I'm an American. This is a Nicaraguan war. I'm here working, not as a soldier. That's why it isn't my war. I don't believe that this is an American war....

Wallace: Yes, but you were making money, is that it?

Hasenfus: Yes, I was making money, that's true.

Wallace: Can I ask you how much, or shouldn't I go into that?

Hasenfus: I was making $3,000 a month.

Wallace: Right, that's how you came here to work. Doesn't that make you a freedom fighter like those that Reagan talks about?

Hasenfus: No, I'm not a freedom fighter. I'm not one of those soldiers of fortune or whatever. I was an individual who was asked if he wanted to work. It was something you do, a way to make money, and that's what we did.

Hasenfus was tried in November by a Nicaraguan People's Court and sentenced to 25 years, but the next month he was pardoned by President Daniel Ortega at the urging of Senator Christopher Dodd, a critic of Reagan's Central American policy who was visiting Managua. Over the years, I followed Hasenfus' life, particularly when I visited my home state. He led a rather dismal existence after his return. He tried to sue the company that owned the cargo plane he parachuted out of, found no steady employment, and divorced his wife. His life continued to unravel, as he was arrested three times for indecent public exposure, spending time in jail.

The Hasenfus affair in Nicaragua roiled Washington in late 1986, raising questions about the role of US funding and participation in the contra war. Twelve days after his capture, Ronald Reagan signed into law a bill authorizing $100 million in assistance to the Contras. This occurred two years after Congress had passed the Boland amendment that prohibited military assistance by the CIA and the Defense Department to the counterrevolutionary forces. Then in November 1986 the Iran-Contra scandal broke, revealing that the United States had secretly sold arms to Iran and diverted the proceeds to the Contra, thereby violating the Boland amendment.

In spite of the illegal covert assistance, the military situation in 1985-86 had unraveled for the Contra forces in Nicaragua. Humberto Ortega, the head of the Sandinista army, waged an efficacious military campaign, inflicting heavy casualties on the Contras, driving them back into their sanctuaries in Honduras. The new official $100 million in assistance, however, enabled the United States to assume a more direct role, training hundreds of Contra on US soil. CIA and Pentagon advisers in large numbers moved into the Honduran border area, reorganizing, advising and guiding the counterrevolutionaries.

The end of 1986 and 1987 was a very busy time for me and CENSA, the organization I directed. The book I wrote with Orlando Nunez, *Fire in the Americas: Forging a Revolutionary Agenda*, was published in the US after receiving the Carlos Fonseca award in Nicaragua for the best political treatise in Latin America on the Sandinista revolution and its influence throughout the Americas. In June 1987 the book served as an inspiration for a conference in Managua, "Crisis and Revolutionary Alternatives in the Americas" that brought together over 35 political activists and revolutionary figures from South America, the Caribbean (particularly Cuba), Central America and the United States.

Eric Holt-Gimenez, who headed up Censa's agricultural assistance project starting in 1984, decided to move to Nicaragua in July 1986 where he worked with CIERA, Orlando's agricultural research center, and UNAG, the Nicaraguan Farmers' and Cattlemen's Association. He also launched a *"campesino a campesino"* program that sent Nicaraguan peasants to Mexico where they received training in soil conservation from Mexican *campesinos*.

My personal life was as convoluted as ever during these years. In 1985 I broke up with Pat Flynn over "irreconcilable differences," meaning we argued with each other incessantly and couldn't agree on anything. Pat moved to El Paso, Texas with Matt where she worked on a PBS-funded program on Latino news. I visited her and Matt, thinking of a possible reconciliation. But that thought ended when we were on a drive through the nearby Organ Mountain National Recreation Park and began verbally abusing each other over some absurd point I can't remember. Matt, always a mellow kid, suddenly piped in from the back seat: "Will you stop it!" I realized that if Pat and I continued as a couple we would harm his emotional development more than we would by separating. A year later, I met Linda Sclater, a vivacious red head, two years younger than me. She worked at Citibank, just down the street in Berkeley where CENSA had its bank account. In addition to the account, I had $10,000 in funds for personal or political emergencies that I deposited in a safe deposit box in the bank's large vault.

Linda usually worked at the Customer Services desk, close to the entrance, and was responsible for taking customers into the vault. I became friendly with her and when my father was arrested for growing marijuana on my place in Annapolis, California, I had to withdraw the funds to bail him out. There are few things more erotic then to go into a bank vault with a captivating woman. Alone in a large chamber with untold fortunes and myriad secrets locked in the safety deposit boxes around us, she and I had separate keys that we both inserted to get into my box. We touched hands as we simultaneously turned the keys and her right breast brushed against me. I wanted to passionately kiss her, but refrained myself and asked her out, saying that it would be after I bailed my Dad out. We met five days later at a Cambodian restaurant. As fate would have it, I was care-taking the house of my lifelong friends Glenn and Marilyn Borchardt on Ocean View Drive in North Oakland, which has a view of the ocean from the third floor master bedroom. On a warm night we made love ravishingly and talked until the early morning hours.

Linda was a totally new experience for me. She had two daughters, aged 10 and 14, was a fundamentalist Christian, and had been married three times. Her last husband was a self-proclaimed preacher who would on occasion roam the woods of northern California in search of Christ. Linda told me she left him when the lumpy divide in the mattress between them became insurmountable because he was offering up his abstinence to Christ. She was working class, the opposite of the intellectual, political women I had usually been involved with. I viewed her as a challenge to see if as a good Marxist I could "convert" a working-class woman. I later realized that Linda had parallel and contradictory hopes, that she could convert me to Christianity. But this was all ignored as we continued to make love, whether it was her apartment in the community of Pinole, 20 miles north of Berkeley, at Ocean View Drive or in the redwoods at my place in Annapolis, California.

With the $10,000 I bailed out my dad being held at the Sonoma County jail in Santa Rosa. Arrested under Operation Camp (Campaign Against Marijuana Growing), replete with helicopters and a half-dozen sheriff vehicles that swooped down on my house in Annapolis, they made my dad sit on the front porch for several hours while they conducted a search of my property, which yielded a dozen immature pot plants. He refused to say anything and when they took photos of him on the porch he protested and held his hands in front of his face.

My dad was glad to see me in Santa Rosa but he protested that I shouldn't have put up the bail because "the food is good," and in any case the sheriff's office told him he would be released on his personal recognizance the next day. He was charged with cultivating marijuana by the US attorney's office in San Francisco. The prosecuting attorney almost immediately came after me as the "master mind" of the operation, and charged me with growing and possession of marijuana. Eventually the charges were dropped against my dad, but my case dragged on for over a year as a progressive lawyer who knew me from my political work in Central America took on my defense. We suspected that the US attorney's office came after me because of my political activities, but in our "discovery" filings, we were never able to uncover any specific evidence of personal surveillance or wiretapping of my phones. Such information, of course, would be top secret in the files of the FBI, or perhaps the CIA.

Eventually I came to an agreement with the attorney's office that I would plead guilty to a misdemeanor, pay a fine of $11,000 to retain my property, and enter a drug rehabilitation program. The fine was largely covered by the $10,000 I got back from my father's bail, and I had to enroll in a drug rehab course at Contra Costa community college near Linda's house. I found the course fascinating. It was comprised mainly of men and women who had problems with substance abuse and were repeat offenders. I wanted to write a story on the course and the participants for Pacific News Service in San Francisco but the Filipino-American woman who taught the course begged off from being interviewed for the article, fearing that she would get unwanted attention. I dropped the article, given that she was in charge of giving me a passing grade for the course, so I could end my "drug rehabilitation."

In spite of my violation of normative Christian values, Linda's passion for me did not attenuate and she often made love without using birth control. I prided myself on my ability to withdraw before ejaculating, a skill I had learned with my first lover two decades before. This worked for a while but Linda began to get furious when I withdrew. After a couple of months of this, I gave in to my primordial instincts, also rationalizing that Pat was taking away our now five-year-old son, Matthew. I thought, what the heck, I can have another child so I won't have to be a modern equivalent of King Solomon who called for dividing a child in half. In August, 1987, just one period after I stopped withdrawing, Linda became pregnant, most likely when we made love in the redwoods next to the new house I was building with my father in Annapolis.

Even though Linda had never traveled abroad, she recognized my frequent trips to Central America and Chile as an integral part of my work. She even accompanied me on a trip to Managua in November 1987. At this time the international scene had shifted perceptively in Nicaragua's favor. Earlier in August, four Latin American nations surrounding Central America—Mexico, Panama, Colombia and Venezuela—convened a conference with the Central American governments of Nicaragua, El Salvador, Honduras, Guatemala and Costa Rica. The region had grown tired of the war, viewing the Reagan administration as the primary obstacle to peace. The first three aforementioned Central American governments, which had insurgent forces within their borders of one type or another, agreed to negotiate without the presence of the United States, signing the Esquipulas accords that committed them to negotiating with the insurgent forces and ending external military assistance from non-regional powers, meaning principally the United States. The accords were greeted with euphoria by the Central American populace.

Ronald Reagan labeled the Esquipulas accords "fatally flawed" and called on Congress to approve more military aid for the Contras. My contact at the Pentagon told me: "So damn many things are now up in the air. The peace plan has unsettled everything. It doesn't deal with our US security concerns and the Sandinistas or the Salvadoran guerrillas could turn it all to their advantage."

In March and April 1988 I was commissioned by Pacific News Service and the San Francisco Chronicle to report on the conflict in Central America. I traveled to Panama, El Salvador, Honduras and Nicaragua, finding a region in turmoil. On February 29, the US Congress had terminated all military assistance to the Contras and they began moving back to their base camps in Honduras. The Sandinista army then launched a military offensive, turning the Contra retreat into a rout as they even attacked base camps in Honduras. To prevent the complete collapse of the Contras, Reagan used his executive powers to send 3,200 combat troops to Honduras on March 16, threatening to dispatch even more US forces. The Sandinista army pulled back from the border, thereby removing a pretext for a wider war with the United States.

Bloodied and demoralized, the Contra leadership met the Sandinistas at Sapoa, Nicaragua and signed an historic agreement on March 23 calling for an end to hostilities. The White House was stunned by the accords, with some conservative US officials even viewing Sapoa "as a betrayal" of the United States by the Contra leadership. I traveled overland from Managua to the border area of Honduras where I found middle and lower level Contra officials also opposed to the Sapoa Accords. "We were sold out" said Sergio Meza, a local Contra leader in San Marcos. "We are expected to lay down our arms and we get nothing for it. We'll never give up."

I also found a deteriorating situation in the Honduran capital, Tegucigalpa. There was growing public discontent with the presence of US troops and the prostration of the Honduran government to US interests. Then on April 5, 1988, a US Special Forces unit of 60 Cobras kidnapped Juan Ramon Matta, a reputed drug trafficker who owned an airline contracted by the CIA to fly supplies to Contra bases, and spirited him back to Miami to face trail. Matta enjoyed widespread support because of his dispersion of funds in the poorer barrios. Over a thousand demonstrators responded by setting fire to the US Agency for International Development annex to the embassy out of which the CIA operated. US Marine and Honduran private guards in the embassy fired on the crowd killing five people, including a young girl. The US embassy later claimed a unit of the Honduran riot police had done the shooting. On hindsight we see that the kidnapping of Mata marked the start of the US arresting foreign citizens in their own countries and trying them under guise of the war on drugs.

On April 7 I caught a Continental Airlines flight from Tegucigalpa to Miami, having wangled a first class seat for coach fare. To my astonishment I found myself sitting one row away from Adolfo Calero and Pedro Joaquin Chamorro, two of the top five Contra leaders. I introduced myself as a correspondent with the San Francisco Chronicle, and we talked freely after a few drinks. Pedro Joaquin was the brother of my friend Carlos Fernando Chamorro, who worked with the Sandinistas as the editor of the daily newspaper, Barricada. They were the inspiration for Stephen Kinzer's book on the war in Nicaragua, "Blood of Brothers."

Calero and Pedro Joaquin were skeptical of the Sapoa accord with the Sandinistas. Both said they had no alternative but to sign the agreement at Sapoa. "Congress cut off aid. That gave us few options," said Calero. "We could sign the agreement or go on fighting in a war that had bloody consequences."

And both said they would not live in the ceasefire zones that the accords established for the Contras inside Nicaragua, with Pedro Joaquin saying he might not even live in Managua if the opportunity came up. "I have four children. The schools in Nicaragua are no good. My children were going to the French school in Managua when I left three-and-a-half years ago. Even though it was private, it has deteriorated because of Sandinista rule." Calero, regarding the zones, said "I'll keep in close touch, but I won't live there. I have to be in communication with other parts of the world." He, as well as Pedro Joaquin, lived in Miami with their families.

I was surprised at Pedro Joaquin's shallowness compared to the commitment and agile mind of his brother. He and Calero demonstrated little enthusiasm for the Contra cause, and they would shortly be pushed aside as the US opted for a new strategy against the Sandinista government.

Just over a month after I returned, Linda gave birth to our daughter. She was born in the same hospital as my son, Alta Bates in Berkeley, and was a beautiful child with reddish blonde hair. I had picked out the name Alexandra after Alexandra Kollontai—the feminist of the Bolshevik revolution who outlived Stalin's purges—and Linda went along with it. It was one of the last significant decisions I would make regarding my daughter's life. A few hours after the birth, I brought into Linda's bedroom a large potted rose plant. Linda, as well as the nurses, laughed good naturedly at my unique offering. Linda has always been into flowers and gardening. To this day, whenever I drive by her house to pick up Alexandra, I marvel at her front yard with its stunning array of beautiful flowers.

Linda was a possessive mother. She took total control of our daughter, almost immediately naming her Allie, which obviously had little relation to the Russian revolutionary's name. After a few months, Linda reluctantly returned to work at Citibank and I would stay home and take care of Allie. Linda would always leave breast milk and a list of what baby foods Allie should eat. One day I was having refried beans and watermelon for lunch. Allie expressed an interest in my plate, so I gave her a taste of beans and watermelon. When Linda returned home, she asked me, "Did you give Allie the food I left for her?" I replied yes, of course. A couple of hours later Linda changed Allie's diaper and to her chagrin, she discovered a watermelon seed and bean shells. She yelled at me, "How could you do this, you are imperiling Allie's life." Of course, nothing happened to Allie. Years later I recounted this story to Allie as well as her mother, and we all had a good laugh. But at the time Linda was dead serious, and accentuated my feelings that I was a fifth wheel around her and Allie. I soon realized that Linda was a "super" traditional mom, believing that the father's sole responsibility is to bring home the bacon, while she would dote over her daughter and enjoy the pleasures of motherhood.

Linda also had another reason for being upset with me. I had promised to marry her after she became pregnant, and had used "Nolo's Essential Guide to Divorce in California" to get the forms and file for a divorce with Pat. She was aghast when I sent her the papers, refused to sign them, throwing them in a wastepaper basket. I continued to pursue the divorce but got nowhere. Pat bickered incessantly, and just as we couldn't agree about anything in our daily life when we were together, it was the same with the divorce. Linda huffed: "In America anyone can get a divorce." I said, "That's true, but you don't know Pat. She'll drown me in paper work, retain a lawyer and even haul my ass into court."

Linda grew increasingly angry with me. She couldn't accept my reasoning about the difficulties of divorcing Pat. And I became increasingly upset with her conservative social values and her determination to control Allie's life. Our relationship would not survive the physical trauma that struck me less than 10 months after Allie's birth.

38. Nirvana and the Woman of My Dreams

"It's better to burn out, than to fade away."
—Neil Young song quoted in Kurt Cobain's suicide note

I arrived at the Augusto Cesar Sandino International Airport in Managua in late December 1988. As I disembarked I was greeted by a banner proclaiming: *"Reagan se va, La Revolucion se queda,"* Reagan is leaving, the revolution stays. It was a time of elation in Nicaragua. During the course of the year, the Contra army had suffered a strategic setback on the battlefield, its leadership was forced to sue for peace, and Reagan was leaving office in less than a month, having lost the support of Congress and the American public in his eight-year war against the Sandinistas. The Sandinista leadership began to believe that, like Fidel Castro and Cuba, the Nicaraguan revolution would outlive a number of US presidents.

But there were ominous signs on the horizon. The Nicaraguan economy was a disaster, with inflation at over 20,000 percent in 1988. Speculation was the main economic activity. Little was invested in real production and there were shortages of just about every consumer commodity, with people waiting in lines to buy basic food staples. The country's exports collapsed and Nicaragua was completely dependent on subsidized imports for its survival, especially petroleum, from the Soviet bloc and Cuba. This was a dangerous position to be in, as the Soviet Union was undergoing its own economic crisis with the failure of Mikhail Gorbachev's reforms, known as Perestroika.

I came to Nicaragua to start working on a new book with Orlando, and to escape the ubiquitous Christmas drumbeat and the dreary winter days in the United States. I always dreaded late December, as it reminded me of my boyhood and the icy cold winter in Wisconsin, with the sun setting before 4:30 PM. So I escaped to Nicaragua and had a Latin Christmas, which is usually more festive and less Christian, not to mention temperatures that are usually in the upper 70 degrees F. I went to Orlando and his partner Syta's house where his mother and sisters gathered along with various offspring. No church services and no discussion of Christ, as Orlando, Syta and I were nonbelievers. And plenty of great food: tamales, black beans, roasted chicken and sweet plantains, and liquor to imbibe, including Nicaraguan rum. My only lament is that it is a Nicaraguan tradition in the barrios to see who can set off the loudest fire crackers and cherry bombs, starting on December 8, the Day of the Immaculate Conception, continuing on to Christmas Eve and New Year's Day.

Around the turn of the year, Orlando asked me if I would like to go to a party at Lea Guido's house. A few years younger than me and Orlando, she had served as the Minister of Social Welfare and then the Minister of Health in the Sandinista government. A militant in the Sandinista revolution against Somoza, she was the cofounder of the woman's association in 1977, one of the most repressive years of the dictatorship.

I walked into her house as the sun was setting. A tall, slender, shapely and exotic looking women of Italian, African and Indian descent, I was immediately smitten by her charm and elegance. We started talking and she related to me, "Roger, we met in New York while you were working at the NACLA office in 1980, and you wouldn't give me the time of day." I confessed, I had no memory whatsoever of our early encounter. It never ceases to amaze me that whether or not there is a mutual attraction depends on immediate circumstances and one's disposition. I don't believe that there is a perfect mate awaiting one in the world at large. Romance is a roll of the dice, anything and everything can happen.

Lea related to me that her former husband was Julio Lopez, the head of the Department of Foreign Relations of the Sandinista Front, who I had collaborated with in the early years of the Sandinista government in analyzing US foreign policy. She had studied in Switzerland and returned home in the mid-1970s and had married Julio. They had a son and separated amicably after the revolution, as did many Sandinista couples who were caught up in new explorations, political and amorous.

The party went on until very late and I enjoyed every moment of it. A number of my friends who I had met over the past decade were there. Lea had a Spanish style adobe house replete with palm trees in the backyard and a swimming pool. She told me it was built by her father, Armando Guido, who had been part of Somoza's entourage and had served as a deputy in the Somoza dominated Congress. Born to a mother of Italian origins and a mulatto father, Armando, impoverished and illiterate, moved from the provinces to Managua to seek his fortune. He ingratiated himself with the Somozas, undertaking several construction projects that were very lucrative. At the time of the revolution he had extensive real estate holdings, including the house Lea lived in. He fled to Miami along with the six children from his first marriage, leaving behind Lea's mother—a mestizo of humble origins who worked in Managua's central market—and Lea who was committed to the revolution. Lea became the de facto owner of the family's property, and she turned much of it over to the Sandinista Front for its use. One estate on the outskirts of Managua, where Julio and Lea had been married, became a training camp for the guerrillas from El Salvador.

As the clock struck midnight I found myself dancing with Lea. I was never a good dancer and Lea humorously told me, "You dance like a Cartesian," referring to the French philosopher Rene Descartes who is famously known for the phrase, "I think, therefore I am." In my case it meant, "I think, therefore I dance," as I used my mind to think out every awkward dance step instead of moving with the rhythm of the music.

Fortunately Lea didn't let my poor dance performance stand in the way of more romantic interests. By 1:30 most of the guests were leaving, and when Orlando wanted to depart, I told him Lea had asked me to stay a while longer. After Lea and I saw Orlando and the last guests to the door, we began kissing passionately and disrobing each other. She had ample, enthralling breasts and a light mulatta-tinted skin. We made it to the bathroom as Lea slipped off her briefs. I couldn't wait any longer. I pushed her up against the shower wall, lifting her long legs as she wrapped them around me, and thrust deep inside her. It was the most explosive encounter of my life. After that we went to her bedroom for more subdued love-making, talking and embracing until sunrise.

Lea hosted the party in part because she was leaving for Cuba in a few days. She had made a number of prior trips to Cuba because of its renowned medical facilities and her work in the field of health. But this trip was for personal reasons. In a visit to Havana several months before, Cuban doctors had detected a discoloring in her uterus and urged her to have it removed because it might be cancerous. Coincidentally, Nora Astorga, her best friend and the Nicaraguan ambassador to the United Nations, had died earlier in the year of breast cancer at the age of 39.

Lea and I spent several delightful days together before she left for

Havana. I talked with her about the impending medical procedure, noting that I had read recent medical articles indicating that doctors (particularly males) were excessively disposed to operating on and removing female reproductive organs. She understood, and said she had similar reservations she would discus with the doctors when she arrived in Havana. She expected to return to Managua in a couple of weeks, even if she did undergo a surgical procedure. I left for the Bay Area the day after Lea went to Cuba. We both looked forward to our next encounter.

Two weeks later, George H. W. Bush was inaugurated as the 41st president. It was unclear what his policy would be towards Nicaragua and Central America, given the setbacks of his predecessor. Based on the earlier Esquipulas accords, the Sandinistas took the initiative, convening a meeting in La Paz, El Salvador on February 13, 1989, of the five Central American presidents, Daniel Ortega, Vinicio Cerezo of Guatemala, Jose Napoleon Duarte of El Salvador, Oscar Arias of Costa Rica and Jose Azcano of Honduras. The United States was noticeably excluded. Daniel Ortega presented specific proposals to advance Esquipulas, offering to move the Nicaraguan presidential and national assembly elections up 10 months to February 1990 if the Contras would disarm and pursue a political path. The voting booths would be supervised by observers of the Organization of American States and the United Nations.

A month later, on March 15, I returned to Nicaragua to continue work with Orlando on the new book on the transformations in the socialist world, particularly the Soviet Union and China, and what they meant for revolutions in Latin America. Of course, I also wanted to see Lea. This time I went with my eight-year-old son Matthew. It was Easter vacation, and he flew from Washington, D.C., where he was now living with his mother, to meet me in Houston. There we caught a flight to Managua. Pat and I had come to an informal agreement that Matt would spend his vacations and summers with me. I eagerly looked forward to spending time with him in Nicaragua. He was about the same age as Orlando's son, whom we would stay with.

Surprisingly, I had heard nothing from Lea since I left her in January. Her home phone in Managua went unanswered and I had no way of reaching her in Cuba. When Matt and I arrived at Orlando's house, I asked about Lea, and Orlando said, "I don't know what she's up to. I haven't seen her since you left." The next day we drove over to her house. A young woman answered the door. She guided us into the patio by the pool where Lea lay on a reclining lawn chair. She greeted us warmly and I noticed she had lost weight. Lea said, "I just returned yesterday. I almost died in Cuba." Slowly her story unfolded. When she got to Havana, she told the doctors that she didn't believe the discoloration in her uterus was cancerous or even precancerous. The doctors more or less agreed, but insisted that it was best if she had her uterus removed because sooner or later something could go wrong. She resisted at first, but after several days of badgering, she consented to the surgery.

"A couple of days after the operation," she related, "I came down with an infection and a high fever. The doctors could do nothing to contain it." Her condition continued to worsen and her former husband, Julio Lopez, and 11-year-old son were summoned from Managua to her bedside. Hovering between life and death for days, she finally began to recover. The medical team found out that her infection was caused by a perforation of her intestines during the surgery. Years later, a US medical panel verified Lea's and my belief that surgery was not necessary. It stated: "There is no existing method of screening for ovarian cancer that is effective in reducing deaths.... In fact, a high percentage of women who undergo screening experience false-positive test results and consequently may be subjected to unnecessary harms, such as major surgery."

We spent the next few days between Lea's house and Orlando's, with Matt getting to know her son, Yali, who had a good set of Nintendo games. Then as Easter weekend approached and Managua shut down, Lea and I decided to take a trip by ourselves to the Pacific Coast. On Good Friday we drove to Casares, a picturesque fishing village. The couple of rustic hotels were full, so we went to a nearby bluff overlooking the ocean. There we camped out on a balmy, tropical night under a brilliant starlit sky. We made love, tenderly. The Cuban doctors had told her she shouldn't have carnal relations for two months. Of course we didn't think much of their prescriptions, given how they botched the surgery. We humorously surmised that the order for abstinence might have come from her previous lover who had been the Cuban ambassador to Nicaragua. He was sometimes referred to as the tenth member of the nine-member Sandinista National Directorate that determined government policies. As a representative of Fidel Castro, the ambassador was influential in deciding how to proceed in the war against the Contras and the United States.

The night was magnificent. Time stood still as the ocean waves crashed endlessly on the beach below. Nirvana, a state of absolute bliss and harmony enveloped us. Lea, the woman I had long been searching for, a fellow traveler in the revolutionary quest for utopia, lay with me, our bodies and spirits entangled.

39. Oceanic Crash: The End of Life as I Knew It

"We are little flames poorly sheltered by frail walls against the storm of dissolution and madness, in which we flicker and sometimes almost go out."
–Eric Maria Remarque, All Quiet on the Western Front

We arose at dawn and went down to Casares, having a typical but tasty breakfast at a rustic beach cafe of *frijoles, huevos revueltos* and tortillas with *cafe con leche*. It was March 25, 1989, Holy Saturday, when Christ, according to biblical legend, remained entombed, awaiting his glorious resurrection on Sunday. It was also Lea's fortieth birthday. Another serendipity; Orlando was about to publish a novel titled "Sabado de Gloria," Holy Saturday, about the travails of life over a 24-hour period in Nicaragua of people caught between the death of the old order and the advent of a new life.

We wanted to continue our escapade for another day, going to Huehuete, a remote beach less than a half hour south. But we were almost out of gas for her Toyota Land Cruiser, having barely enough to make it back to Diariamba, 30 kilometers away. Casares had no gas stations, but as we were about to turn back we found a fisherman who sold us several gallons from his boat, enough to continue our trip southward on an unpaved road. "This is our lucky day," I exclaimed to Lea.

We arrived at the Huehuete beach at high noon. About a kilometer long, it had dark sand and rocky flat areas that projected into the ocean. We found a spot on the beach with an opening between the rocks and cast our beach blankets on the sand. There were only a handful of people scattered around the beach.

Lea had a phobia about swimming in the ocean, fearing something monstrous would grab her from below. So I ventured out alone. I loved the ocean, its power and beauty had always mesmerized me. Unlike northern California where the waters are cold and forbidding, the Pacific Ocean off the coast of Nicaragua is warm and inviting for virtually the entire year. I never had the time to take up surf boarding, but I did go body surfing, swimming out and catching the waves to ride them in. As I walked on the sand towards the ocean, I stepped on a poisonous jelly fish, but pulled back before it stung me. Once again I thought, this is my lucky day. If I had been stung, I would be laid up for a day or two.

I swam into the waves, reaching the crest of the highest wave, then doing an about face, I rode the wave in towards the beach. The waves off the coast of Nicaragua are known to be some of the most powerful in the world and on this day the waves seemed to be particularly ferocious. I did this a number of times, sometimes going beyond the high waves where the ocean becomes calm on the surface. This can be dangerous because the strong undertow could carry you out to the open sea. But I had tempted fate this way a number of times and always managed to return.

After playing in the waves for about half an hour, I decided to go back to see Lea. I caught the highest wave, which I guessed to be about 12 to 13 feet high, hoping to ride it all the way to the beach. It was a ferocious wave, propelling me forward on its crest at a rapid velocity. Suddenly, as it neared the beach, it broke and tossed me downward, just as the undertow was drawing back. I crashed face down into a few inches of water, hitting the sand almost instantly. It felt like striking cement. The impact arched my back, twisting me sharply. I suddenly felt numb. The waves now receded, sucking me out into the deeper water. I had no control of my legs and even my arms were almost listless. I was completely at the mercy of the currents, being buffeted around, unable to reach the beach. I yelled for help, crying *"auxilio."* Lea noticed me, but given her fear of the sea, she could not make herself go out to help me. She tried to get someone on the beach to rescue me but they were also afraid, believing a shark had attacked me, and they might suffer a similar fate.

I became weaker, having difficulty keeping my head above water. I began to think this might be the end. Amazingly, I was calm as I began to take in water. There were no visions of my life flashing in front of me or pleas to a deity to save me. I thought of the book I was beginning to write with Orlando, hoping I had contributed enough ideas so he could finish it. Then, just as I was being sucked under for what I thought might be the last time, a slender teenager with indigenous features swam out, grabbed me and pulled me onto the beach.

Four or five people gathered around and Lea took charge. I could not move my lower limbs and the right side of my face where I struck the ocean floor was numb and paralyzed. Lea went to get her Land Cruiser and drove it onto the beach. Somehow she found a large carton that was about the shape of a stretcher and lifted me on to it into the back of the Cruiser with the help of the teenager. We headed towards Diriamba, the nearest town on the way back to Managua. There we found an ambulance donated by the Abraham Lincoln Brigade, an organization of US volunteers who had fought in the Spanish Civil War. The driving time from the beach to Managua is about two and a half hours, but to me it seemed like an eternity. I did not pass out, but everything seemed surreal, I was in a state of shock and intense pain.

Lea knew the Nicaraguan hospitals and the best doctors in Managua because she had been the Minister of Health. We went to Hospital Central and she called Dr. Vanzetti, a surgeon who dealt with back injuries. A German doctor who fought in the underground with the Sandinistas, he had taken Vanzetti as his nom de guerre from the Italian immigrant Bartolomeo Vanzetti, a fish monger and an anarchist who was executed in 1927 for crimes he did not commit in Bridgewater, Massachusetts.

The x-rays taken of my back were of little use, given the shortage of quality medical supplies in Nicaragua due to the war and trade blockade. But Dr. Vanzetti had seen similar accidents in the past and decided it was imperative to operate and remove fragments of the fractured vertebrae that were pressing on my spinal cord. He then performed a laminectomy, and I would subsequently find out that this procedure limited the damage to my spinal cord and probably saved my life.

I awoke on Easter Sunday, heavily sedated. I had risen from the dead, but little more. It was not a glorious day. My son, Orlando and Syta came to see me. Lea remained faithfully at my side and brought in ice and electric fans as the air conditioning system in the hospital was not working. I could not discern if my fever and delirium were attributable to the tropical air or my body. Over the next few days I got no better. My blood pressure dropped dangerously low on several occasions and I had hallucinations. Orlando, Syta and Carlos Fernando Chamorro came in at times to relieve Lea. They were afraid I might take a turn for the worse and would have to summon a doctor at any moment. Good x-rays when I got to California later on revealed I had embolisms in my lungs that came from blood clots in my legs that almost killed me.

Upon hearing of my accident in Washington, D.C., Pat Flynn

sprang into action. Her first task was to get Matthew safely home and by Wednesday she had arranged a flight back for him with my friend Peter Marchetti, a Jesuit priest in Managua. Matt came to see me before he left. Teary-eyed, he said he didn't want to leave, he wanted to stay with me. Months later he told me, "Dad, I thought that if I left, you would die and I would never see you again."

After Matt returned to Washington, Pat went to work on my situation. She called my insurance carrier in Berkeley and the claims manager said there was nothing he could do. Pat told the carrier that if he did not get me out and I died in Nicaragua, she would sue the company with the best lawyers in San Francisco. Apparently the company believed her. One week after my accident, on Saturday, March 29, a medivac plane flew into Managua with two nurses and two pilots, one of whom was a medical doctor.

Arriving at the airport in an ambulance with Lea and Carlos Fernando, I was carried to the runway on a stretcher as the plane landed. It was a sunny day and I'll never forget seeing Carlos Fernando waving the plane around as it taxied to where I waited. Once aboard it quickly took off and flew to El Salvador to make a technical stop at the international airport. It was the same airport where the Maryknoll nuns had landed nine years before and were murdered on the road into the capital. This time the Salvadoran guerrillas had launched a major offensive and the airport was closed to commercial traffic. We were allowed to land as a medical emergency, but then we sat there for hours waiting for clearance to depart. It was unbearable, the weather was hot and humid and my fever was going through the roof. I thought I would die there. It would have been ironic if after years of supporting the revolutionary movements, I became a "collateral causality" of a guerrilla offensive. Strangely I remember nothing about the pilots and nurses who attended me.

Finally we took off and made it to the Baylor City Medical Center in Dallas, Texas at night. I was rushed to the emergency ward and the doctors proceeded to take a number of x-rays, stretching my painful body across the hard x-ray table. They then took me to a private room at about 1 AM, and a few minutes later a woman with a cross around her neck seemed to float into the room. I wasn't sure if I was dreaming or having a hallucination or both. She said "Roger, do you remember me? I am your Aunt Agnes." Then it came back to me, she was my mother's sister who served as a Catholic nun in Dallas. I had last seen her just over a quarter of a century before, in late November 1963 when I had hitchhiked with a college classmate to Dallas in the aftermath of John F. Kennedy's assassination. My mother had been following my flight homeward, thanks to Pat, and she called Agnes when the plane landed in Dallas. We had a good talk; it was one of the few moments in the aftermath of my accident when I felt a certain calmness. Years later we would meet at my place in Annapolis, California. We talked about our encounter in Dallas and in the midst of the Redwood trees that hovered above us on the deck of my house, she said that she had moved away from traditional Catholicism, becoming a spiritualist, believing that these ancient trees were part of the eternal existence of life.

At dawn I was spirited out of my room to get ready for the last leg of my journey to California. A stern-looking doctor insisted on talking to me before I left. He said the x-rays revealed I had a complete severance of my spinal cord and I would never walk again. To this day, I don't know what good he hoped to do by telling me that. It only depressed me more and in fact, his prognosis proved not to be quite as dire as predicted.

40. The Long Road Back and My Left Foot

My Left Foot is a 1989 movie about Christy Brown, who was born with cerebral palsy. He learned to paint and write with his only controllable limb—his left foot.

I arrived at the Oakland International Airport as dawn broke and was sent in an ambulance to the intensive care unit at Alta Bates Hospital in Berkeley. The hospital seemed like a good omen, both of my children had been born there. But my situation had worsened due to the flight and the embolisms in my lungs. For the next week I hovered between consciousness and unconsciousness, having continual hallucinations. In the middle of one night I imagined I was ejaculating, thinking this meant I was on the road to full recovery. A doctor walked into the room and told me, "You are crazy, you should start focusing on letting the nurses roll you over on your side to prevent bed sores from developing on your butt."

Sometime in early April I was transferred to the Herrick Hospital in Berkeley to continue my convalescence and to begin the long process of physical rehabilitation. I was a shell of my former self, weighing 125 pounds and having no muscle fiber. No one knew what, if any physical mobility I might recover in my lower extremities. Many friends came to visit me. I am forever indebted to them for helping me survive this traumatic period in my life. Sandy Close, the head of Pacific News Service was incredibly supportive, alerting the broader community to my plight and launching an appeal for funds that brought in over $20,000. At the time of my accident I was an adjunct instructor at the department of Peace and Conflict Studies at the University of California, Berkeley, and it was unclear if I would ever resume this salaried position.

Linda, my partner whom I had been living with prior to my accident, came to visit me almost daily, often bringing my daughter, Allie. She knew about Lea but said nothing. I think it was a case of "(Lea) out of sight, out of mind." Linda was overwhelmed by my accident, lapsing into a state of virtual immobility. A previous boyfriend of hers had recently died in a knife fight outside a bar. Then her former husband and the father of her two older daughters committed suicide. She thought the men in her life were jinxed and that I would disappear at any moment.

In mid-April I fixated on the 24-inch TV that hung from the wall in the corner of my bedroom as the Tiananmen Square riots irrupted. For the next seven weeks I followed the twists and turns of the upheaval in China. Long a critic of China's authoritarian government, I was elated to see the Chinese students with the support of workers call for democracy, the right to speak and assemble, and an end to corruption. During the initial weeks, the communist party leadership split with General Secretary Zhao Ziyang favoring discussions with the students while the old party leader Deng Xiaoping hung in the background. Even some sectors of the army and police were sympathetic to the rebellious students.

Protests erupted in other major cities and the conservatives in the party, fearing chaos and the party's loss of control, turned to Deng to impose an iron hand. On the night of June 3, the army laid siege to Beijing and moved towards the square with armed vehicles, meeting opposition from workers and residents along the way. Tanks were set ablaze by the resistance, but by 6 AM the army had taken control of the square. Hundreds, if not thousands, were killed, the exact figures will never be known. Isolated resistance continued and on June 5 I watched video footage of the iconic "tank man," the lone figure in a white shirt who defiantly stopped the advance of a column of tanks. He climbed aboard the lead tank to talk to the soldiers inside and then returned to his position in front of the tank. He was eventually pulled aside by a group of people. His identity and ultimate fate are unknown.

On May 12, I celebrated my daughter's first birthday. It was a sad day, even though the sun shone brightly outside my hospital window. We had balloons and a birthday cake as I laid half propped up in bed. Allie, looking on in her mother's arms, tried to blow out the singular candle. I did not know what if any role I would be able to play in the long life that lay ahead of her. To this day I have two pictures next to each other in the corner of my bedroom. One is with Allie in the hospital on her birthday and the other taken three months earlier, with her riding on my shoulders and laughing as I walked down a street in Berkeley next to my office.

Sometime after my accident I began to have involuntary spasms in my legs, a normal occurrence in paralysis due to spinal cord injuries. Then I began to realize that I could control the spasms in the toes of my left foot. Gradually I began to get movement in the foot and ankle. My friend Glenn commented that I was the only person in the world who through sheer determination could take a spasm in his toe and turn it into a movement up my leg. Then at the end of May, the night nurse gleefully told me she saw I was having erections while I slept. Perhaps my earlier hallucination of having an ejaculation and coming back to a normal life was true. I began doing upper body exercises, and was soon able to transfer into a wheel chair. Sometime in early June I went out with my friends on my first wheel chair trip to an Italian restaurant a block away. It was tedious and painful, but it was a start. It looked like I would be discharged in a couple of weeks.

Linda continued to see me, making it clear to the nurses that she was the one in charge, chasing them out of the shower room as she helped bathe me. I realized the day was fast approaching when I had to make decisions about my relationships. My amorous life was a mess. I was still married to Pat, I lived with Linda, and I was in love with Lea. While Pat had rescued me from Nicaragua, neither of us wanted to get back together. Linda made it clear that she was willing to take care of me, whatever my disabilities. But I did not want to be taken care of, I was determined to resume my old, independent life, following my passions wherever they took me.

A few days after my 45th birthday on June 18, I was taken to Glenn and Marilyn's house in an ambulance. I was still a basket case, all my meals were prepared by others and I needed help to get to the bathroom. But I had made my decision, I would be Lea's companion. As fate would have it, she had begun working with the Pan American Health Organization, and was scheduled to spend much of the summer in a training program in Washington, D.C. A week after my discharge from the hospital, I flew out to Washington to join her. Linda came to the house to see me off. It was a heartrending scene. She kept a stiff upper lip as I was wheeled out to the waiting van. She started to walk away, but then came back and planted a big kiss on my lips. I was devastated, but had the driver continue lifting me into the van in my wheel chair. Absent from the scene was my daughter who was at her grandmother's house. In my decision to be with the woman I loved, I had not taken into consideration what effect it would have on my life long relationship with Allie.

I was virtually moribund when Lea met me at Dulles airport and spirited my body into a residential hotel not far from Rock Creek Park. There I spent the next 8 weeks in rehabilitation with her. Besides my left foot I had one other appendage that functioned heroically. Lea would get up early in the morning and take off for the Pan American Health Organization in Washington for meetings and seminars. I would spend the day in the room, watching CNN, moving ponderously from the bed to the wheelchair, to the kitchen or bathroom and then back to the bed. Lea would arrive at around 5 PM, on what was usually a warm humid day, take off her clothes and place her body astride me, coming on to me slowly. We'd make love for what seemed like hours. I was knocking on heaven's door and having some of the best sex of my life. Every muscle and nerve I had would spring into action. Lea was the greatest physical therapist I ever had.

After a few weeks we went out for dinner in the evenings. It was summer in Washington, hot and humid as usual. Those who saw us in the streets must have had wildly different views as to why an attractive Italian-Mulatto-Mestizo woman was pushing me around in a wheelchair. Was she a call girl, a physical therapist, or a cosmopolitan wife with an ill-fated husband?

I also saw a good deal of my eight-year-old son Matt, who resided with Pat in Washington, where she worked for National Public Radio as a producer. In one of my earlier meetings with Pat she had told me she was filing divorce papers that turned out to be similar to the documents I had filed over a year-and-a-half before. They were signed on a Sunday in late August when we met at Dupont Circle. It was anticlimactic for both of us. In our nine years of marriage we had experienced a gamut of emotions and were ready to move on. Shortly after that Lea flew off to Nicaragua and I went back to Oakland where I took up residence with Glenn and Marilyn. My maternal aunt, a Maryknoll nun, Sr. Nathan Maria, came to visit me from Japan. We conversed extensively about my accident and I declared, "I am determined to walk again, the next time you visit me I'll be on my feet, one way or another."

To attain this goal I needed to get into an intensive rehabilitation program. Sexual therapy with Lea could take me only so far. I applied to the Santa Clara hospital where they had an excellent program, but they rejected me, saying they would have no space until the next spring. I talked to Lea, who said I should come to Nicaragua where they had rehabilitation facilities due to the ongoing war. In October I arrived in Managua. I was in her living room watching the World Series between the San Francisco Giants and the Oakland Athletics when the signal was cut off, and Tomas Borge, the Minister of Interior, appeared on the TV to announce there had been an earthquake in northern California.

The rehabilitation facilities in Managua were paltry. Fortunately a Cuban doctor who knew Lea came to visit me at her house, and suggested I might want to go to Cuba where they had advanced facilities, including electrical stimulation, which I had already been exploring as an option to recuperate some of my muscle movement. Lea, given her former position as Minister of Health, and her friendship with high-ranking Cuban medical and political figures, was able to arrange for me to go to Cuba. My writings on revolution in Latin America meant that I was a known figure in Havana who over the years had worked with revolutionary movements. Years later, a Cuban professor who was a member of the Communist Party at the University of Havana told me: "When I was a student we were enthralled by your book, *Democracia y Revolucion.* Because it was a small paperback, we could carry it around in our pockets and read it while waiting in lines for the buses or monthly food rations." His comments touched off thoughts of Mao's Red Book, although I hoped my contribution was more benign and less dogmatic.

41. Historic Utopia Torn Asunder

At moments in the trek of humanity, a chasm opens up, and we are rendered immobile as our beliefs provide no succor or salvation.
　　　　　　　—Ralph Walbridge, Berkeley Poet

The year of my traumatic accident coincided with the collapse of the world's first utopia that captivated the imagination of millions around the globe. The brutal repression in Tiananmen Square in June 1989 and the fall of the Berlin Wall in November marked the beginning of the end of an epoch that were launched with the revolutions of 1848 and the publication of the *Communist Manifesto*. For almost a century and a half the quest for a socialist utopia drove revolutionaries, fascinated philosophers, writers, poets and journalists, and shook the ruling classes with the specter of communism triumphant. The utopian vision stirred up the passions of the dispossessed of the earth, especially workers and peasants, as they engaged in violent confrontations in the streets, the factories and the fields to overthrow their exploiters and rulers. Heroic men and women sacrificed their lives, faced imprisonment and were forced into exile.

It is easy to forget that this explosive revolutionary force at times appeared irrepressible and irresistible. The Bolshevik Revolution and the victory of the Red Army in Eastern Europe, Mao's Long March, the liberation struggle of the Vietnamese, first against the French and then the Americans, the triumph of the Cuban guerrillas, and the spread of revolutionary fires throughout the Americas—the advances of these movements and armies led many to believe that the capitalist west was in terminal decline.

But at the beginning of the last decade of the 20th century it was the communist utopia, and not the west, that lay in ruins. Although there were many differences among the communist nations, their governing regimes had two overriding and deeply flawed characteristics: an economic system in which the means of economic activity were overwhelmingly under state control, and a political system in which the leaders of the Communist Party enjoyed a monopoly of power.

Communist rule in the Soviet Union and Eastern Europe contradicted the democratic and participatory impulses that were at the heart of the original utopia that emerged in the mid-19th century and was briefly manifested by the Paris Commune in 1871. The popular classes believed socialism meant they would choose their leaders and participate in running the economy, especially the industrial plants and the fields. But the Communist regimes betrayed the democratic dream over the course of much of the 20th century, allowing the Western capitalist nations to appropriate the democratic banner and to wed it to capitalism.

Virtually all forms of dissent and calls for a democratic society were met by systematic repression. The Prague Spring of 1968 and the invasion of Soviet tanks proved particularly decisive in repressing a popular movement that was calling for a democratic opening within a socialist framework. Until Mikhail Gorbachev and Glasnost, the Communist regimes never relaxed their rule or moved their nations in genuinely democratic directions.

Latin America was the only region of the world where socialism and communism had a somewhat different trajectory. The Cuban Revolution, while adopting the political institutions of the communist system in the early 1960s, enjoyed widespread popular support. The barrio committees for the defense of the revolution, the associations of artists and intellectuals, and the membership of the Communist party had a voice and role in determining the direction of their lives and the destiny of the revolution. But with the failure of the 10 million ton sugar harvest in 1970, the volunteerism and participatory spirit of the revolution largely ended and a certain greyness settled over the country for decades to come.

The Popular Unity government of Salvador Allende (1970-73) represented a new utopian flame that captured the world's imagination because of its commitment to democracy. But it was snuffed out all too quickly by Henry Kissinger, Richard Nixon and their collaborators in the Chilean bourgeoisie. With the advent of the Sandinista revolution, I transferred my quest for utopia from Chile to Nicaragua. When the

Communist regimes began to unravel in 1989, I could still keep the faith that Nicaragua was offering the world a new utopian alternative. The Sandinista army had dealt devastating blows to the Contras and in an effort to seize the political high ground, the presidential elections had been moved forward to February, 1990, in hopes that a victory for Daniel Ortega would compel the opposition to accept the democratic legitimacy of the Sandinista government.

The run up to the elections found me in Cuba, engaged in physical rehabilitation. On February 25, the day of balloting, I flew to Managua, expecting to celebrate a victory with my friends who had fought so hard for the Sandinista revolution for the past decade. Even the opposition led by Violeta Barrios de Chamorro expected defeat. Violeta, as she was commonly called, had chosen sides between her sons, joining Pedro Joaquin, a member of the counterrevolutionary directorate against Carlos Fernando, my close friend and the editor of *Barricada*, the Sandinista daily newspaper. A large international contingent of election observers, including a delegation led by former president Jimmy Carter and his wife Rosalynn of the Carter Center, were present to monitor the electoral process.

We were shocked when the results rolled in. Violeta defeated Daniel Ortega with 54 percent of the vote. As dawn broke on the following day, Ortega appeared at the Olaf Palme Convention Center to address the press and thousands of Sandinista supporters: "I believe that in this historic moment, the principal contribution we Sandinistas, we Nicaraguan revolutionaries, can make to the Nicaraguan people is the guarantee of a pure and clean electoral process, that is in accord with our consciences." Many in the audience became teary-eyed and wept openly as Daniel added: "Would that the sun rising this 26th of February illuminate the path toward the consolidation of democracy, of a mixed economy, of a free Nicaragua independent and democratic, in peace, not interfered with by any foreign power, in which all Nicaraguans would be able to demonstrate to the world that we can make these dreams and hopes come true." Daniel's words captured our dysphoria: we had struggled long and hard for utopia in the middle of the Central American isthmus, but it was not to be.

The Sandinista revolution had been broken by a decade of US hostility and funding for a surrogate army that caused 50,000 deaths and decimated the country's economy. Later in the day, as I was sitting in my wheelchair in front of Orlando's house, a woman vendor selling tamales passed by sobbing. I asked her what was wrong, and she said, "Daniel will no longer be my president." After exchanging a few more words, I queried her about who she had voted for. She replied, "Violeta, because

I want my son in the Sandinista army to come home alive." She understood better than any political analyst that if the Sandinistas remained in power, the US would continue to inflict destruction on Nicaragua in one form or another. A country of less than 3 million people could no longer resist the onslaught of the world's leading imperial power. The Nicaraguan people suffered a casualty rate higher than the United States did in the Civil War, World War II and the Vietnam War. The biblical story of David versus Goliath comes to mind but in this case Goliath even had the sling.

Moreover, the United States manipulated the electoral process with funds and political operatives from the National Endowment for Democracy, the US Agency for Development, the CIA and the US embassy. In mid-1989 US officials compelled the 21 querulous political organizations of the opposition to come together in the UNO, the National Union of the Opposition, and imposed Violeta Barrios de Chamorro as the singular candidate. A steady flow of dollars rained down on the country as the United States funded a myriad of pro-UNO fronts with seemingly innocuous names like the Institute for Electoral Promotion and Training and the Center for Youth Formation. The US role in financing the opposition in the elections was decisive. In the end, 20 dollars were spent for every vote captured by Violeta. George H.W. Bush spent $4 for each of the votes he procured in the US presidential elections of 1988.

I was devastated by the defeat. Almost 17 years after the brutal military coup by Augusto Pinochet against President Salvador Allende I once again found my dreams and hopes for a better world smashed. With the entire socialist world in disarray there was no country where I could turn to in order to renew my dreams. But my plight was nowhere near as desperate as that of the many Nicaraguans around me who had committed their entire lives to the Sandinista revolution. It is estimated that about 7,000 people worked in the Sandinista Front and the government, not including the army. Many of them had not bothered to get educational degrees or trade skills while they were swept up in the revolutionary cause. Now they found themselves unemployed and unemployable.

But fortunately, unlike Chile—where the personal upheaval was immediate and traumatic as many found themselves in the underground, in jail and tortured, in exile, or even dead—a peaceful transfer of power took place in Nicaragua. The Sandinistas forged a pact with the incoming government of Violeta Chamorro in which it was agreed that the Sandinista army would remain intact with Humberto Ortega at its head. There would be no bloody wave of repression. Many of the Sandinistas, including Orlando Nunez, even envisioned the survival of a vibrant Sandinista movement at the grassroots. The government of Violeta Chamorro was a shell, as the parties and organizations in the UNO quarreled among themselves over the spoils of office. They had no organic social and civic organizations like the Sandinista trade unions, the small farmers association, or the Sandinista party, all of which had a mass base. Moreover, the new government was bound by the Sandinista constitution of 1987 that established a supreme court and a judiciary that could not be tossed out of office overnight.

My immediate friends moved into the opposition, determined to take on the new political order. Orlando Nunez turned the government offices of CIERA, the Center for Investigations and Studies of Agrarian Reform, over to the incoming administration, and moved across town to set up CIPRES, the Center for Rural and Social Promotion, Research and Development, on lands purchased with aid from the Dutch government. Virtually all the international funding that went to CIERA now went to CIPRES as the donors were intent on supporting progressive land policies, not an organization staffed by US lackeys. CIERA folded within a year after Orlando walked out of its doors.

Carlos Fernando Chamorro continued as editor of the Sandinista newspaper, *Barricada*. It had a hardcore readership and enjoyed wide respect because of the quality of its journalism. It was not a political propaganda piece like the Cuban daily, *Granma*. After the election of 1990, *Barricada* enjoyed more autonomy than ever, and became a strident critic of the economic and social policies of the government. But then, in 1994, *Barricada* and Carlos Fernando became caught up in an internal power struggle within the Sandinista party as Daniel Ortega sought to dominate the party and control the pages of *Barricada*. In Managua at the time, I tried to get Carlos Fernando and Orlando, who remained loyal to Daniel, to meet and talk about resolving the conflict. My efforts went nowhere, of course, as Carlos Fernando and the entire editorial staff were fired. *Barricada* became a propaganda organ for Daniel and the party. Its readership dried up, and in 1998 it ceased publication. Carlos Fernando went on to become Nicaragua's most prominent independent journalist, writing a weekly news report and hosting a Sunday investigative news program akin to "60 Minutes."

Lea had skills and resources that enabled her to readily transition to a new life. She had almost finished her doctoral thesis in public health from the University of Lausanne, Switzerland, and in 1989, at the time of my accident, the Pan American Health Organization (PAHO) was actively recruiting her to work in Nicaragua with an eye to heading up the PAHO office in San Jose, Costa Rica. Several days after the election,

Tomas Borge, the Minister of the Interior, knocked on the door of her home early in the morning as we were getting up. A suitor of Lea's (he was renowned for pursuing other women as well), he was not bearing flowers or presents this time. He came to discuss turning back to Lea the estate on the outskirts of Managua that she had ceded to the Sandinistas in the early 1980s to use as a training camp for the Salvadoran guerrillas. Now it was being dismantled and Borge wanted her to have the deed to the land. She readily agreed.

I went with her several times to visit her newly recovered property. In spite of shooting ranges, three meter high training walls, and thousands of spent munitions, it still had most of its buildings intact, including a bedroom where we set up camp. Lea had little use for the estate, although I, given my farming roots, began to imagine how it could be tilled and turned into a successful enterprise. Of course my fanciful thoughts were not acted upon. A couple of years later she would lose control of the estate as one of her half-brothers disputed its ownership, and then local squatters moved on to it. Lea stoically said, "This is the way it is meant to be. The land should belong to those who till it."

42. The Abyss

"There is scarcely any passion without struggle."
–Albert Camus, The Myth of Sisyphus and Other Essays

For two years after my accident I bounced around the hemisphere in quest of physical and medical rehabilitation programs that would enable me to walk again. One of the treatments I pursued was electrical stimulation. It involved placing electrodes on distinct leg muscles that were connected to a small computerized battery-powered unit strapped around the waist that transmitted electrical pulses at programmed intervals to provoke coordinated leg movements. In the United States, Rancho Los Amigos Hospital in Downey, next to Los Angeles, was experimenting with this technology in conjunction with Medtronics, a private firm with offices in Los Angeles.

Surprisingly, the medical research center at Julio Diaz Hospital on the outskirts of Havana was pursuing a similar research program. Starting in late 1989 and for the next two years I made about a half dozen trips to Los Angeles and Havana, getting cutting-edge treatment at both sites. In an effort to promote "technological exchange," I pilfered an electrical stimulation unit from Downey and took it to Cuba. I had even learned to program the minicomputer in the box. I disassembled it with Dr. Raul Hernandez who worked at Julio Diaz.

Lea provided me with her unmitigated love as I began my medical adventures. She had her house remodeled to accommodate me in a wheelchair and we would go out in her 4-wheel-drive Toyota in the warm Managua evenings. During the day she would have a driver take me to physical therapy and medical appointments. But the relationship could not solidify because of geographic realities. Neither of us was destined to live in Nicaragua. Her work with PAHO took her increasingly to Costa Rica. I would go to Cuba for treatment, and about half of the year, to the Bay Area to be with my son and daughter and to maintain the nonprofit organization, the Center for the Study of the Americas, of which I was the director. I was also a visiting scholar and part-time lecturer in the Peace and Conflict Studies Department at the University of California, Berkeley.

Despite my best efforts to advance in this brave new world, I became angry and depressed about my physical condition. It was psychologically wrenching for me to know deep down that I would probably never walk again. I took a lot of medications for my pain and other bodily functions. I was impatient with myself, with Lea, and was distant from her 13-year-old son Yali who lived with us part-time. A mutual friend of ours related to me privately that Lea had told her: "Roger's not the same anymore." She was right; I was a pain in the ass to be around.

And then the unimaginable happened: Lea's first true love from France, Javier, who she had met in her early 20s while studying at the University of Lausanne, Switzerland, appeared on the scene. Lea had forsaken him to return to Nicaragua to join the Sandinista movement in the 70s, and married a fellow militant, Julio Lopez. Javier did pursue her to Nicaragua, but Lea's life was the revolution, with all its political passions. Now, over a decade later in 1990, he reappeared in Managua as a successful French journalist in pursuit of Lea once again.

Given our mutual comings and goings around the hemisphere, there was no immediate need for me or Lea to confront the new amorous situation. Lea finally took the initiative, saying she wanted to break up with me. I realized that it was not just Javier, but my terrible disposition as an angry, frustrated disabled man that she found difficult to deal with. I was devastated, but agreed to accept the situation. Lea's emotions, however, proved fugacious. Whenever I appeared in Managua, on my way to or from Cuba, or to work with Orlando on our new book, she would often appear at my doorstep and we would make intense and passionate love. On one occasion we spent almost an entire day in bed, breaking only for food and drink, and then resuming our love making. It was as if she were addicted to me. I, of course, was also infatuated with her warm, erotic body, and did not want to lose her to eternity. I remember the Beatles' White Album and Dylan's New Morning as the music that often played in the background. Lea was still the best lover I had experienced in years.

But after a while the situation became wrenching for me. I didn't know what to expect next. Sometimes, when I came to Managua, she would appear, other times she would not. Once she invited me to come to Costa Rica where she was spending more of her time. She drove me crazy. Finally I had Orlando, who was a friend of both of us, intervene. He went to her and told her the simple truth: that I was becoming an emotional mess and she shouldn't see me anymore. The romance with Lea came to an end. Even my relationship with my daughter was shattered because of the rancor of the breakup with her mother.

I stood at an abyss. My life was a disaster. My politics, my struggles, my romance, my utopias had all come to a crashing dead end. Even my relationship with my daughter was in shambles because of the bitter breakup with her mother. I was physically incapacitated and rode around in a wheelchair most of the time, able to walk perhaps a hundred paces with crutches a couple of times a day. But I did not regret where life had taken me. My years of dreaming and imagining had carried me far beyond the limited horizons of a Wisconsin farm and I had witnessed and participated in dramatic turning points in the 20th century's struggle for socialism.

45. From Zapatismo to the Battle of Seattle

A gallant knight,
In sunshine and in shadow,
Had journeyed long,
Singing a song,
In search of Eldorado.

But he grew old-
This knight so bold-
And o'er his heart a shadow
Fell as he found
No spot of ground
That looked like Eldorado.

And, as his strength
Failed him at length,
He met a pilgrim "Shadow,"
Said he, "Where can it be-
This land of Eldorado?"
Eldorado!"

—Edgar Allan Poe, Eldorado

All my adult life I have been searching for my version of El Dorado, utopian socialism. From the Cuban revolution onward I studied and experienced the revolutionary struggles of Latin America that marked the end of the old order and the opening up of new utopias based on egalitarian, democratic and socialist principles. But by the beginning of the 1990s the experiments in Chile and Nicaragua had failed and Cuba was in crisis, with its people experiencing even hunger. Neoliberalism reigned as the supreme economic doctrine, and the end of history was proclaimed, meaning that capitalist democracies were the final form of political and economic organization for the nation states of the world. "There is no alternative," or TINA, proclaimed Margaret Thatcher, prime minster of Great Britain. Except for a few die hard, usually sectarian parties, the left stood dumbfounded and demoralized.

A quarter century later, I see that the failures and difficulties we faced with the collapse of state socialism did not mark the end of history. Utopia is an unending quest, a fluid pursuit for a new society that is forever changing and evolving. The human species is constantly in motion, always pursuing new dreams. The quest for utopia may be Sisyphean, but I was determined to embark on a new odyssey, driving my body and mind to their utmost limits.

Just as the left was experiencing its darkest moments, the Zapatista National Liberation Army (EZLN) burst upon the scene on January 1, 1994 in the state of Chiapas, Mexico. Called by many the first postmodern movement, including correspondents of The New York Times, it used the internet to reach out to the world, proclaiming war on corporate-dominated globalization and its economic doctrine, neoliberalism. The Zapatista chief spokesperson, Subcomandante Marcos declared, "This isn't just about our demands and rights, it's about the whole neoliberal project."

I departed for Chiapas 10 weeks later from San Francisco with a Global Exchange delegation and linked up with another delegation member, Jesse Clarke. We became fast friends as he helped me get on and off buses, go through military checkpoints and even visit and maneuver around the magnificent Palenque Mayan ruins. (This encounter would lead to collaboration on future projects. Jesse and I would go on to coedit an anthology on September 11 and the US war.)

As we found out on our visits to Zapatista-run communities and in conversations with EZLN representatives, the uprising was not merely a revolt of indigenous peoples who wanted to retake their lands and expel the rich who exploited them. It was a rebellion that consciously sought to move beyond the politics of modernity, be they of past national liberation movements, or of the repressive modernization policies of the Mexican government. What distinguished the EZLN from its predecessors is that it did not seek power in Mexico City, nor did it call for state socialism. Its objective was to spark a broad-based movement of civil society in Chiapas and the rest of Mexico that would transform the country from the bottom up.

The new local-global politics of the Zapatistas marked a radical departure from capitalist electoral politics and from traditional left internationalism. The Zapatista discourse and praxis challenged not only the neoliberal world order, but also conventional political wisdom across the spectrum. In Mexico and globally, a broad-based international movement sprang up around the demands for democracy, social justice and an end to neoliberalism.

Interested in understanding the history of the modernization project that shaped the rise of the EZLN, I gathered information from the archives at the state capital, San Cristobal de las Casas, and wrote an article for New Left Review, "Roots of the Postmodern Rebellion in Chiapas." My interviews and research in Chiapas also reshaped some of the ideas of the book I was coauthoring with Boris Kagarlitsky and Orlando Nunez, *Globalization and Its Discontents*. As the book went to press I submitted a subtitle, *The Rise of Postmodern Socialisms*.

My foray into postmodern Marxism left many of my intellectual comrades aghast. Kagarlitsky, who wrote only the chapter on Russia for the book, lambasted me in the pages of *Monthly Review* magazine, while the other coauthor, my long-time friend Orlando Nunez, conducted an intensive study of postmodernism starting with Jacques Derrida. He reported to me, "Postmodernism is a useless deviation from Marxism. It offers us nothing."

In 1997 I visited the offices of *Monthly Review* in Manhattan for one of the weekly gatherings of the staff and visitors. Over the years I had enjoyed tossing around thoughts and experiences at these meetings about what was happening in the far corners of the world. This time my visit did not go so well. Harry Magdoff, the long-time coeditor of the magazine and a mentor of mine, peered up from his reading glasses after glancing at the Kagarlitsky critique and said, "Roger, how could you do this to us?" It was the last time I would see him. He died on January 1, 2006 at the age of 92.

Fortunately, after leaving *Monthly Review* on that dreary late fall day, I found solace at the offices of NACLA on the Upper West Side of Manhattan. There I worked with Fred Rosen, the editor of NACLA's *Report on the Americas*, putting the finishing touches on an essay on socialism he had asked me to write for the 30th anniversary volume of NACLA. Titled "Socialism is Dead, Long Live Socialism," I declared in the first sentence: "Twentieth century is moribund," and went on to argue that the new social movements in Latin America were constructing alternative economies and communities that were laying the foundation for postmodern socialisms.

In the 1990s I burned the candle at both ends, with my writings and in my personal life. More driven than ever, I was determined to prove to the world that nothing had changed with my accident as I traveled to five continents in search of utopia using the lens of postmodern socialism. I refused to follow in the footsteps of Herman Hesse's Goldmund who, as he got older, retreated from the Renaissance world to the monastery to live out his life with his old friend Narcissus.

One of my more audacious explorations led me to the new China under the tutelage of Franz Schurmann, the codirector of Pacific News Service. I combined study with a personal milestone. My 50th birthday found me sitting on the Great Wall of China with my 13-year-old son Matt. I'll never forget the young solider of the People's Army who carried me up and down the broken-down parts of the wall on his back, as Matt pushed my wheel chair behind.

We spent about two weeks in Beijing, and although I confess to being a total amateur in Chinese studies, I found little to contradict my initial belief that China was in transition from state communism to state capitalism. The Chinese people, like the countries of Eastern Europe and Russia I had visited two years before, did not want to hear about socialism or the old order. The difference was that the societies of the old Soviet bloc experienced the new horrors of neoliberalism while a strong state in China produced economic growth and new opportunities for much of the Chinese population, albeit with a great deal of corruption at the state and party levels.

In this period, my amorous relationships covered the gamut, from a university professor in Los Angeles, to an 18-year-old aspiring artist in Nicaragua, and a dentist in Chile. Unlike Goldmund, I did not find women ignoring me as I got older. Indeed, the passage of the Americans with Disabilities Act in the United States opened up a global debate on the rights and needs of the physically challenged, and it seemed to be in vogue in the 1990s to have an affair with a disabled person.

One of my more preposterous and fascinating relationships was with Laura, a follower of Meher Baba, an Indian spiritual master who proclaimed he was the avatar, a God in human form. After several months of intense lovemaking and even meeting her father as an honored guest, one evening she looked me in the eye and asked, "Is there no possibility you can believe in a greater spirit or in reincarnation?" I looked straight back and said: "No, I know you really believe you have spiritual experiences, but I do not." She then announced that she could not have a mate who did not partake in her beliefs. I responded, "I'd have difficulty respecting someone who places more importance on an imagined life than on real relationships in this world." Luckily she didn't make a counterattack on my own reliance on imagined utopias as a guiding star in my life's course.

The last years of the millennium witnessed a surge in the anti-globalization movement in the Americas. Just over a month after the breakup with Laura, I headed for Brazil to cover the 1998 presidential elections and to talk with representatives of the MST—the Landless Workers' Movement—the largest social movement in the hemisphere. The MST was part of a Latin American insurgency of social movements that included the coca growers of Bolivia, the indigenous peoples of Ecuador, the Mapuche of Chile and the Zapatista of Mexico.

A postmodern politics had taken hold throughout Latin America as movements drew on their roots and constructed their own particular forms of social and political struggle. These struggles began locally. They often first sought to address direct threats to survival, such as land expropriations, violent coca eradication, or water privatization. They took on worldwide dimensions because, in fact, the source of these threats was a global neoliberal model mediated by transnational actors, such as the IMF and the World Bank.

Anti-neoliberal movements also arose in the United States. In 1999, tens of thousands of demonstrators gathered in the city of Seattle to protest the meetings of the World Trade Organization (WTO). They held workshops and forums, staged marches, occupied the streets of downtown Seattle and blockaded the entrances to the WTO gatherings. Environmentalists of all stripes were present in Seattle, as well as farm organizations like the National Farmers Union. Marching with them were trade unions from such divergent organizations as the Teamsters, the American Federation of Teachers and the International Workers of the World. The demonstrations had a distinctive international flair as a hefty number of trade union representatives came from Latin America, Europe, Asia and Africa. The Zapatistas, the MST and indigenous organizations also appeared in Seattle.

On November 30, the day the WTO formally convened its meetings at the Washington State Convention and Trade Center, I parked my wheelchair along with other protesters in front of the gates and entranceways to the Center, effectively blocking access for WTO delegates. I was delighted when Amy Goodman came up to interview me, but said something simplistic about free-trade agreements that never appeared in the footage she edited for her TV program, Democracy Now!

I soon found myself joining with thousands of militant marchers in the streets of downtown Seattle. "Turtles and Teamsters," we were called, reflecting the diverse array of WTO protesters that came together in Seattle. About noon, as the winter sun cast its brisk rays over the city, I saw black-garbed figures break off from the demonstration and begin smashing the windows of corporate buildings. Called the Black Bloc, they were young anarchists who were making their first major appearance on the US political scene. The word in the street was that many of them came from nearby Portland, Oregon. The police soon appeared to lob tear gas indiscriminately into the entire crowd. Most of the demonstrators fled, but I could not keep up as I spun the wheels of my manual chair. Two policemen grabbed me and hoisted me in the chair onto a bus with about 30 other demonstrators. We were headed for the county jail but when we arrived, the jailers realized they could not accommodate me in their already filled cells and released me.

During the waning months of the old millennium I took separate trips with my son and daughter. Matt had weathered well the breakup of his parents in the mid-1980s. He stayed with his mom during the school months, and the rest of the time with me, usually in Northern California. As Matt relates to me, "Dad I always looked forward to my time with you, it was like being on vacation."

Alas, with Allie, our relationship was more troubled because of the chasm that opened when I broke up with her mother. My visits with Allie were usually difficult to arrange, so I went to court to regularize my visitation rights. But there was a certain reluctance on Allie's part to come to visit with me on the designated dates. I attributed this to her mother who questioned my values and did not want her daughter to be influenced by me.

In August, 1999, when Allie was 11, we flew to New York and stayed with friends. During the day we walked the streets of Manhattan, going to Central Park, museums, the World Trade Center, and took the ferry to Ellis Island. Yet, there was a certain distance between us; she was not a happy camper.

Years later we were at my home, where I have a picture of Allie standing on top of the World Trade Center that was reduced to ashes on September 11, 2001. I asked her, "What went wrong? Why was our trip and relationship in general so difficult?"

She responded, "Dad, I hardly knew you during my early years, you were not around." Indeed, reflecting on those years, I realize that I was dedicated to my rehabilitation after my accident in Nicaragua, spending time in hospitals, going to Los Angeles and Cuba to seek out cutting-edge technologies in dealing with spinal cord injuries. As Allie recounted,

"When you started coming around more often, I felt you were a stranger, someone I didn't know."

As 1999 drew to a close, I flew into Cairo, Egypt with Matt, now 18 years old. It was an insane adventure we will never forget. On the 31st, we went to the Giza pyramids and rented two camels. I managed to get onto the camel and he took off. After about a quarter kilometer of bouncing around I managed to rein him in as the frantic owner of the camels came running up and pulled me off. After that we joined the festivities and the spectacular concert taking place at the base of the pyramids, with strobe lights giving off an aura, as if we were in another world.

A few days, later we took a train south to Luxor and the ancient ruins of the Valley of the Kings. Next, we traveled over to the Sinai peninsula and stopped off at Dahab (gold), a town fronting the waters of the Gulf. We stayed in the Bedouin village area, renting a tent room for $2 and went next door to an open-air restaurant with delicious local cuisine. Then our waiter asked if we wanted to retire to the sofa for dessert and a water pipe to smoke a blend of local herbs and marijuana. As the sun set over the waters, I was in a state of bliss, in harmony with the cosmos.

We then proceeded to cross over to Gaza, and up to Jerusalem where we stayed at a hotel run by an Israeli settler. We went out to see the traditional sights and experience a bit of life in the city. It was appalling, everywhere we saw discrimination against the Palestinians, who were treated as little better than dogs. We flew out of Tel Aviv airport a couple of days ahead of our scheduled departure, the first time in my life that I aborted a trip.

46. The Millennial Quest for Utopian Socialism

After the turn of the millennium I traveled mainly to Latin America where a remarkable history began to unfold, which provided hope for a world torn asunder by wars and imperial interventions, particularly in the Arab and Islamic regions. For the first time since the Sandinista revolution in Nicaragua, Left governments came to power in Venezuela, Bolivia and Ecuador, raising the banner of socialism. The decline of the US empire, the eruption of antiliberal social movements, and the growing integration of the region on its own terms created a space for the rejuvenation of socialism after the dramatic setbacks of the last century. Cuba is part of this transformative process as its leadership moves to update the country's economy while the Cuban people experience new freedoms.

In January 2001 the first World Social Forum (WSF) met in Puerto Alegre, Brazil under the slogan "Another World is Possible." Bringing together a vast array of social movements, civil society organizations, political activists and academics, the WSF, over the next decade, facilitated wide-ranging debates about tactics, strategies and visions for a counter-hegemonic and utopian world.

The most dramatic and historic address took place at the fifth annual gathering of the WSF on January 30, 2005, when Venezuelan President Hugo Chavez declared: "It is necessary to transcend capitalism ... through socialism, true socialism with equality and justice." As part of the roaring crowd of 15,000 at the Gigantinho stadium in Porto Alegre, Brazil, I heard Chavez go on to say: "We have to reinvent socialism. It can't be the kind of socialism that we saw in the Soviet Union, but it will emerge as we develop new systems that are built on cooperation, not competition." This marked the inception of "21st century socialism."

This call for a new socialism dovetailed with the precepts of post-modern socialism, which called for a socialism of many different forms and faces. Aside from the four leftist countries mentioned above, socialism is making an appearance in other countries through a variety of social actors. In Chile, the 2011 student rebellion ignited Chilean social movements, which are now rethinking the country's socialist legacy. Chile's neoliberal order and the maldistribution of income are being questioned as never before. In Brazil, the MST, the landless rural workers' movement, the largest social organization in the hemisphere, continues to espouse socialism in its platform and in the daily practices of its land reform settlements. It does not look to a paternalistic state as it seeks to maximize the participation of its own members in the running of their own cooperatives and communities.

Utopia pervades all these struggles, sometimes employing new concepts. The new constitutions of Bolivia and Ecuador call for people to live in harmony with "*Pachamama*," Mother Earth, and for *buen vivir*, or good living—a holistic vision of the world where people strive for harmony. It is more than a hollow dream; it influences contemporary policies in opposition to capitalist development. For example, food sovereignty as conceived of in the Andean countries is adapted to *buen vivir*. It breaks with the traditional concept of development, asserting that food production should not be driven simply by the marketplace, especially the international market. Food sovereignty means that people have access to nutritious and sanitary foods that are produced at the community level by local producers in accordance with local needs and cultures, be they Andean or non-Andean.

The promotion of food sovereignty and local production are part of the effort to construct solidarity economies, be they in Brazil with the MST or in Bolivia with the indigenous communities. Indeed, the expansion of solidarity economies in socialist-oriented and capitalist countries alike is the key to the construction of socialist societies from the bottom up and breaking with the state socialism of the 20th century. Worker-run cooperatives, municipal and community-owned enterprises, fair trade campaigns designed to assist small commodity exporters and cooperatives, microcredit banks and community-based funds that make loans to small producers (often in the informal sector)—all these activities and many others are generating alternative economies that are taking hold in Latin America as well as other parts of the world. The transition from capitalism to socialism will occur much as the transition from feudalism to capitalism: it will be a gradual process, in which alternative activities, political and social, as well as economic, take hold at the local level and undermine the existent order.

This is a period of turbulence and transitions. It is not the time of armed revolution as was the century past. Utopian socialism in 21st century Latin America is part of a complex of change sweeping the region. Today, different explorations or counter-hegemonic processes are at work. As Arturo Escobar—a Colombian-American anthropologist known for his contribution to post development theory—writes in *Latin America at a Crossroads*:

"Some argue that these processes might lead to a re-invention of socialism; for others, what is at stake is the dismantling of the neoliberal policies of the past three decades—the end of 'the long neoliberal night,' as the period is known in progressive circles in the region—or the formation of a South American (and anti-American) bloc. Others point at the potential for *un nuevo comienzo* (a new beginning) which might bring about a reinvention of democracy and development or, more radically still, the end of the predominance of liberal society of the past 200 years founded on private property and representative democracy."

In sum, Latin America is a cauldron of political and social ferment. There are no discernible laws of history driving this upheaval, but utopian socialism is a central component of the brew that is being stirred up by the social movements and the popular forces. The 21st century radical left is admittedly eclectic and embraces and even celebrates a trial-and-error approach to socialism lacking in ideological clarity, which it views as a corrective to dogmatism. Rather than a lineal historic clash between capitalism and socialism that classic Marxism envisioned, we are now witnessing a plethora of struggles and confrontations that zigzag across the pages of history.

There is no single socialist horizon, rather a multiplicity of groups and movements are now imagining new utopias. "One world with room for many worlds," proclaim the Zapatistas. In the short term, 21st century socialism could flounder or experience setbacks in any of the countries where the socialist banner has been raised—Venezuela, Ecuador or Bolivia. But it will not disappear. Socialism runs deep in the historic waters of the hemisphere and the need for alternatives to a turbulent global capitalist order is ever increasing.

In the northern hemisphere, utopia is also being kindled in the bowels of the world's leading financial center. A utopian movement irrupted in September 2011 when Occupy Wall Street took over Zuccotti Park next to the New York Stock Exchange under the slogan, "We are the 99 percent." The Occupy movement spread like wildfire across the country to over 600 cities and communities. Some of the Occupy encampments became egalitarian, democratic, utopian communities. They held general assemblies, organized the preparation of food, had cleanup details, medical posts, childcare centers with teachers, and tent libraries. I identified with the Occupy movement in Oakland that took over the plaza in front of City Hall. The name Oakland Commune was adopted, harking back to the 1871 Paris Commune in France that Karl Marx wrote about. Raided by the police several times, the commune worked with trade unions, including the International Longshore and Warehouse Union, to call a general strike on November 2 that shut down the Port of Oakland and most of the downtown district.

"Occupy everything, demand nothing" was a slogan one often heard in the early days of the Occupy movement. On the surface it seems quite simplistic, but when you realize that the real meaning of "demand nothing" is that the movement did not want to take power or rule the country directly. The words, "Occupy everything," is a strategy and plan of action that is bent on changing the world. It is not simply a physical occupation; it aims to occupy hearts and minds, to change culture and society.

By the end of 2011 most of the Occupy encampments were broken up, usually by police repression. But like the historic movement of 1968, it changed the world. The Occupy movement shifted the political debate in the US by drawing attention to the gross maldistribution of income and the role of the banking and financial institutions in manipulating the political system. It is also important to note that the Occupy movement was part of a global movement, preceded by the occupation of Tahrir Square in Cairo, and the rise of the *Indignados* in Spain and southern Europe.

47. Mars and Utopian Existentialism

"One small step for a man, one giant leap for humanity."
–Neil Armstrong upon landing on the moon, July 1969

A cosmology buff, my aspiration is to live until the roving satellites on Mars discover cellular life, or even more dramatically, that the search for extraterrestrial intelligence, SETI, detects radio signals and intelligent life on one of the 40 billion earth-like planets that exist in our Milky Way galaxy.

Kim Stanley Robinson, in his science fiction novel *2312* envisions human settlements throughout the solar system, even on some of the largest asteroids which are hollowed out and terraformed. New economies take root, deriving in part from their origins as scientific stations. As Robinson writes: "In this early model, life in space was not a market economy; once you were in space, your housing and food were provided in an allotment system.... Capitalism was in effect regulated to the margin, and the necessities of life were a shared commons."

Today, on our planet in the epoch of globalization, it is mammoth transnational corporations that dominate global and nation state politics. They have created a dystopia, driven by hyper-speculation, the concentration of wealth, perpetual conflict for markets, and the destruction of the environment.

I have come to realize that the most effective utopia quests are existential. Thomas More's *On Utopia* is fixed and essentialist. To be existential means utopia is derivative of reality; as history flows forward, utopia is also changing and adapting to the existent world.

There will not be one kind of utopian community and one kind of life. There will be many types of communities with divergent political institutions. Some communities will be more attractive than others, and some will wither away. Some people may be part of different communities in the course of their lives and play different roles in each. Utopia is a framework for personal utopias, a place where people are free to join together voluntarily to pursue and attempt to realize their vision of the good life, where no other group or set of institutions can impose their beliefs on others.

Ultimately, utopia comes down to what we see as the potentiality of the human species, whether it will always experience wars, economic exploitation and inflict suffering on others, or whether our cultures and values evolve so we can live in cooperation and harmony on this splendorous, fecund planet with innumerable species, many of which we are now pushing to extinction.

The answer to this question has preoccupied me throughout my odyssey. What I have learned is that in spite of dictators, torture, repression and exploitation, utopia is an integral, inspirational part of human history that is always evolving as it never assumes a final shape. Each generation draws upon this heritage, creating its own legacy. There will probably always be conflict and strife. But even in the darkest of times utopia is being constructed. It is at once a tangential and an infinite process. We are all part of it.

48. Epilogue: Utopia and the Grim Reaper

In recent years, I find in my life that the *leitmotif* of Herman Hesse's Goldmund is being replaced by Ingmar Bergman's knight in the film *The Seventh Seal*. Returning from the Crusades, the knight encounters the Grim Reaper on a beach. Trying to evade death's embrace, the knight challenges the Grim Reaper to a game of chess, hoping to win more time and "knowledge" about the questions that have daunted him—about life, death and the existence of God.

Agreeing, the Grim Reaper lets the knight know he ultimately cannot escape, saying, "I've already walked by your side for quite some time." Indeed, as I reflect on my Goldmund years, I see that death was always near me in different guises. I became fascinated with heroic death when I lived in the Andes in the mid-1960s where youthful guerrillas in Peru and Che Guevara in Bolivia died heroically, fighting for a better world. Then in Chile in September 1973 the Grim Reaper appeared in the form of General Augusto Pinochet. My friends were murdered and I barely evaded his tanks and troops in the streets of Santiago.

Shaken but undeterred by these events, half a decade later I became a fellow traveler of the Central American guerrilla movements and then collaborated with the Sandinista government. These were the times of the killing fields, as peasants, workers, guerrillas, missionary workers, priests and leftist political leaders were murdered by dictators and US-backed civilian puppets in the name of anti-communism and democracy.

Like Berman's knight, the Grim Reaper directly confronted me on a beach. I was seemingly at the apex of my life, having experienced nirvana the night before, an amorous utopian moment, on a brilliant star-lit night with my lover on a Nicaraguan bluff overlooking the Pacific Ocean. The next day, the Grim Reaper appeared as I rode a powerful ocean wave that pitched me face down into the retreating undertow, snapping my back and sucking me back into the swelling ocean. But a fisher boy dared to swim out and grab me, pulling my water-logged body onto the beach.

For 15 years after that I kept the reaper at bay, living life to the fullest. Then in March 2004, the Grim Reaper mounted a more determined assault, once again in Nicaragua. This time I had terrible intestinal pains and thought I had a case of food poisoning. My longtime friend Carlos Fernando Chamorro drove me to a hospital and after two days of tests, a young doctor who had been trained in Cuba ascertained that I had an incurable blood cancer, multiple myeloma.

Now I played chess with the Grim Reaper in earnest. Cancer is more difficult to manage than most bodily injuries and in today's world, the understanding of cancer is constantly evolving. A number of clinical trials were taking place across the country and I hopped from one trial to another for the next six6 years. By 2010, the chemo-like drugs had taken their toll. My last treatment had me flying to the Mayo Clinic in Scottsdale, Arizona once a month to see a doctor for 20 minutes in order to pick up my designated drug.

On winter solstice of 2010 I elected to undergo a stem cell transplant at the University of California at San Francisco medical center. I expected to be out in mid-January but the treatment didn't go as planned. I wound up spending four months in hospitals and convalescent centers, experiencing some dark days in a state of delirium. I had trouble conversing with friends, often unable to utter a complete sentence.

I recovered, however, beating back the Grim Reaper who often appeared in my primordial dreams. For over two and a half years I was in remission. Since the multiple myeloma reappeared, I have used new treatments that should give me another two to three years; and then there is a good possibility that a cure will be found based on tweaking DNA genes in the blood and bone marrow. Who knows, I may live forever as a bionic man with an infusion of chemical and gene-altering treatments.

That is, of course, the ultimate utopian dream—that we can live forever, finding heaven on earth, keeping the Grim Reaper at bay for as long as we wish. And with longevity, we can deepen the yearning of our ancient ancestors to understand the stars and the heavens, perhaps even discovering other worlds in the cosmos with their own alien utopias.

Now, I find my heavenly and earthly utopian quests are converging. I take great solace when I look at the brilliant stars shining through the large bedroom skylight at my country house near the Pacific Ocean, recalling the words of the late cosmologist Carl Sagan, "We are all stardust."

Reflecting on the odyssey of the human species, he said: "We began as wanderers, and we are wanderers still. We have lingered long enough on the shores of the cosmic ocean. We are ready at last to set sail for the stars." As a participant in this cosmic journey, I believe I will be around for eternity, along with my loves and with my once and future utopias.

A few weeks after Roger finished the final draft of this manuscript the Grim Reaper made the final move and Roger died on March 5, 2015.

www.ingramcontent.com/pod-product-compliance
Lightning Source LLC
Chambersburg PA
CBHW060042100426
42742CB00014B/2665